Developing Leadership Character

This book focuses on the element of leadership that has largely been neglected in the literature: Character. Although character is often thought to be a subjective construct, this book argues otherwise. It demonstrates the concrete behaviors associated with different character dimensions in order to illustrate how these behaviors can be developed, and character strengthened.

Based on research involving over 300 senior leaders from different industries, sectors, and countries, Crossan, Seijts, and Gandz developed a model for leadership character that focuses on eleven dimensions. The book begins by setting the context for the focus on character in business, asking what character is and whether it can be learned, developed, molded, or changed. Next, the book focuses on each dimension of leadership character in turn, exploring its elements and the ways in which it can be applied in a business setting. The book concludes with a summary of the key insights, an exploration of the interactions between the character dimensions, and a call to the reader to reflect on how to develop one's own and others' leadership character.

Bridging theory and management practice, *Developing Leadership Character* will interest students and practitioners alike. Readers will benefit not only from a new, robust theoretical framework for leadership character, but will also learn how character can be developed further.

Mary Crossan is a Distinguished University Professor and a Professor of Strategic Leadership at Ivey Business School, Canada. She has published several books, best-selling case studies, and articles in top academic journals including the *Strategic Management Journal*, the *Academy of Management Review*, and *Leadership Quarterly*.

Gerard Seijts is a Professor of Organizational Behavior and Executive Director of the Ian O. Ihnatowycz Institute for Leadership at Ivey Business School, Canada. He teaches in several leadership programs, and has published in leading journals including the *Academy of Management Journal*, the *Journal of Applied Psychology*, and the *Journal of Organizational*

Behavior. He is the author of *Good Leaders Learn*, also published by Routledge.

Jeffrey Gandz is Professor Emeritus of Strategic Leadership at Ivey Business School, Canada. He has authored or co-authored seven books, many articles in academic journals and practitioner magazines, and over 100 case studies that are used in business schools around the world.

It is always a difficult task to decide which of multiple co-authors of a specific book or article will be listed first, as the senior author. In the case of this book it is impossible to do so. We have all been engaged in developing the core frameworks, writing parts of the text, editing each others' writing, working through multiple drafts, and so forth. We are true collaborators, friends, and scholars in a common cause ... the understanding of leadership character.

Character and Leadership go hand in hand when establishing a successful team. Individuals willing to not only make tough decisions, but *act* on them, are important to establishing a culture of success. Leaders shine brightest when they have the competence and commitment to achieve a goal, not for personal accolades, but for the benefit of the team. This is a must-read for anyone who wishes to escape the norm and dare to lead.
— Ron Francis, General Manager, Carolina Hurricanes Hockey Club, Canada

Leadership effectiveness is more than what a leader knows. It depends on who a leader is, a discipline that continues to come of age, driving critical thinking and behavior. Hats off to Crossan, Seijts, and Gandz; *Developing Leadership Character* reveals how underlying personal values and our ability to evolve them constitute leadership character and why this is central to our effectiveness.
— Steve Mader, Vice Chairman and Managing Director, USA

The foundation of good leadership in life and work is character. *Developing Leadership Character* is a conversational, research-based read that will help you understand the various dimensions of character and how to develop it in yourself and your organization. This thought-provoking book is filled with stories of real-life people and leadership experiences that will truly hit home – and help make you a better person and leader.
— Mary Barra, Chief Executive Officer, General Motors Company, USA

Developing Leadership Character

Mary Crossan, Gerard Seijts, and Jeffrey Gandz

Routledge
Taylor & Francis Group

NEW YORK AND LONDON

First published 2016
by Routledge
711 Third Avenue, New York, NY 10017

and by Routledge
2 Park Square, Milton Park, Abingdon, Oxon, OX14 4RN

Routledge is an imprint of the Taylor & Francis Group, an informa business

© 2016 Taylor & Francis

Library of Congress Cataloging in Publication Data
Crossan, Mary M.
  Developing leadership character / Mary Crossan, Gerard Seijts,
  Jeffrey Gandz. – 1 Edition.
    pages   cm
  1. Leadership. I. Seijts, Gerard H.   II. Gandz, Jeffrey.   III. Title.
  HD57.7.C7647 2016
  658.4′092–dc23   2015024406

ISBN: 978-1-138-82562-8 (hbk)
ISBN: 978-1-138-82567-3 (pbk)
ISBN: 978-1-315-73980-9 (ebk)

Typeset in New Times Roman
by Out of House Publishing

Mary Crossan
To my family and the amazing people in my life who inspire me every day.

Gerard Seijts
To my mom, who created many fond memories for her family.

Jeffrey Gandz
To Elizabeth and the many characters I've met in leadership roles.

Contents

Preface

Good leadership is a function of competencies, character, and the commitment to doing the hard work of leadership. Of these three, character has traditionally received the least attention – both in research as well as in our day-to-day practices and conversations. Yet, when we think about both the famous and infamous leaders of recent times, whether in the spheres of business, politics, sports, or others, it's impossible not to think of their characters. Understanding what provides strength of leader character and what undermines it is the essence of this book.

Consider the following: Nelson Mandela's extraordinary combination of courage, humility, and humanity as he led South Africa out of the apartheid era; Bernie Madoff's criminal duplicity, callousness, and lack of integrity that devised and executed the largest Ponzi scheme ever in the history of the United States; Bill and Melinda Gates and their remarkable personal philanthropic activities and leadership of a renaissance in social awareness and action; Silvio Berlusconi's synthesis of political acumen with apparently out-of-control sexual proclivities and reluctance to pay taxes; Narayana Murthy's humility, courage, and collaboration in building a world-class organization – Infosys, India's second largest information technology service company; Margaret Thatcher's drive and perseverance that gained her the leadership of the Conservative party and election as prime minister, and her steadfastness in using that role to reshape and reenergize the United Kingdom's moribund economy at the expense of hundreds of thousands of employees in mining, manufacturing, and other blue-collar industries that were shuttered during her time in power, leading to harsh criticism that she was lacking in humanity; or Conrad Black's ambition and drive to create an international newspaper empire stretching from the United Kingdom, Australia, Israel, the United States, and Canada, coupled with his arrogance, conceit, narcissism, and lack of remorse that led to his conviction as a felon for fraud and obstruction of justice in the United States and a sentence to serve penitentiary time rather than plead guilty to some lesser charges and pay a fine. Indeed, it is not an exaggeration to say that when we think of those who made their marks as leaders, be they famous or notorious, whether their deeds led to good or bad outcomes, we do in fact think of their characters.

In our work with senior executives in the public, private, and not-for-profit sectors, we found, unsurprisingly, that character matters – a lot. For example, executives and directors had little difficulty talking about how they thought character had played a role in the lead-up to the financial crisis. But we also found that there was no consistent understanding of what character really meant. Character is a term that is often loosely defined and for many people is a rather ambiguous construct that is hard to grasp. As a result, it is seldom used in recruiting, selecting, promoting, or developing current and future leaders. Why is that? What explains the significant disconnect between the perceived importance of leader character and its actual use in organizations? Why don't we emphasize leader character in business school curricula to the same extent as competencies?

We can think of at least three explanations. First, character is a "loaded" word and, as we quickly found out during our conversations with leaders, it has different meanings for different people. There was also disagreement as to how character can best be assessed, as well as what can be done to develop character in current and future leaders. Second, a language or vocabulary with which to address leader character in the workplace is lacking. Leaders told us that what they need is a contemporary, practice-focused vocabulary with which to address character in performance management discussions, leadership development interventions, and corporate governance issues. Third, leaders told us they need tools if they are to move from thinking and talking about character development to actually doing something about it.

In *Developing Leadership Character* we present the voice of the leader as well as our ongoing research on leader character. Leaders from the public, private, and not-for-profit sectors have been actively engaged in developing our approach to leader character. We have built a solid foundation from which to bridge research and management practice; and we offer our insights and advice to leaders as well as individuals who have the ambition to lead or make a difference. We view character as a differentiator in leadership success, perhaps more so than competencies – it is what truly differentiates one leader over the next.

Our hope is that *Developing Leadership Character* is just the start of a lifelong journey to a new understanding of leadership. We hold the belief that character supports both the position and disposition to lead. For example, people in many arenas of society – business, education, government, medicine, law, sports, arts and culture, religion, and so forth – must exert acts of leadership without holding a formal leadership position. For this to happen, character provides an important resource to draw on. The book is therefore written for three audiences. First, a fundamental purpose of the book is to help current and future leaders to better understand and appreciate the role of character in individual and organizational success; to articulate the various dimensions of leadership character; to offer ways in which character can be further developed; and to come up with ideas to embed character in organizations. The book and subsequent reflection on the materials presented (e.g. suggested readings, videos, and exercises) will help build a solid foundation of developing the character dimensions vital to success in any leadership career. Second, we fully expect that *Developing Leadership Character* will be used in educational settings. For example, curricula across disciplines – business, education, political science, medicine, and so forth – should pay as much attention to character as they do to competencies. Students should be encouraged and assisted to consider dimensions of leader character as part of the decision-making process in the public, private, and not-for-profit sector. This book provides a start.

And third, leadership and organizational development specialists may find ways to add more value to their organizations through implementing processes and programs through which to more fully exploit the potential of leadership talent – in particular, leader character. For example, we have been fortunate throughout our research to have worked with engaged audiences in business and government who enthusiastically weaved leader character into their leadership profiles. These profiles act as beacons – they signal what it takes to be successful as a leader in the organization and what various stakeholders should expect of employees and leaders in the organization.

Acknowledgments

We would like to acknowledge the leaders from the public, private, and not-for-profit sectors who participated in our research on leader character and contributed to our intellectual stimulation over the past six years. A special thank you goes out to Ian O. Ihnatowycz, President and CEO, First Generation Capital Inc., Bill Troost, President and CEO, Peel Plastic Products, and Walter Zuppinger, Chairman and CEO, Domco Foodservices Group of Canada Limited, for their ongoing interest in and financial support of our work that led to *Developing Leadership Character*. We thank Alyson Byrne, Daina Mazutis, and Mark Reno for their ongoing research support and Lucas Monzani for his help in putting together the supporting materials referenced throughout the book. A warm thank you also goes to Julie Carswell from Sigma Assessment Systems Inc. Julie was instrumental in the development of the Leadership Character Insight Assessment. We are grateful to the membership of the Leadership Council of the Ian O. Ihnatowycz Institute for Leadership and our Ivey colleagues for their insights, and we appreciate the administrative support provided by Debbie Zoccano, Stephanie Brooks, and Cam Buchan throughout the writing of the book. We are indebted to Jeffrey Cruikshank for his superb editorial support in getting the book written. Thank you, Jeffrey! We are grateful to the Social Sciences and Humanities Research Council for the funding that has supported much of our research.

1 Leadership and Character

Consider the following list of leaders, whose names we have drawn from a fairly diverse set of backgrounds:

- Nelson Mandela (the late South African leader),
- Bill Gates (co-founder of Microsoft, philanthropist, investor, and inventor),
- Kenneth Lay and Jeffrey Skilling (former Enron executives),
- Silvio Berlusconi (Italian business and political leader),
- Oprah Winfrey (American media proprietor, talk show host, actress, producer, and philanthropist),
- Lance Armstrong (former competitive cyclist),
- Bernie Madoff (former stockbroker, investment advisor, financier, and chairman of Bernard L. Madoff Investment Securities),
- Halla Tomasdottir (co-founder of Audur Capital financial services, Iceland), and
- Richard Fuld (last CEO of Lehman Brothers).

What do these former and current leaders, from their very disparate walks of life, have in common? We think of them first and foremost in terms of their character – or in some cases, their lack of character. And then there are the countless unsung heroes in our daily lives who make a difference through their leadership and character – showing the inclination and ability to lead without necessarily having a leadership position.

This begs a question: What is "leader character" and how can it be developed? This is the critical question that we seek to answer in this chapter, and throughout this book. We believe that, given the tools, you can indeed develop character.

The Backdrop: Disaster

Our interest in this subject can be traced back to the global financial crisis that unfolded between 2007 and 2009. In retrospect, that crisis can be understood as a cyclical recession overlaid with an extraordinary banking crisis. The result? The longest, deepest global recession since the 1930s. With the benefit of a half-decade of hindsight, we know that catastrophe was avoided – at least on the global scale. But millions of small catastrophes were not avoided. Individuals lost their jobs, homes, savings, and retirement nest eggs. Whole nations – notably Iceland, Greece, Italy, and Ireland – were compelled to adopt austerity budgets in order to protect their standing in the global economic community, and the people in those countries suffered accordingly. Less dramatically, the frustratingly slow rebound of the developed world left literally millions of people unemployed, and without much hope of employment, for years – a hidden cost of the great meltdown that will be with us far into the future.

Getting to the 3C Framework

In the summer of 2009, as the first fragile signs of economic recovery began to be seen, a small interdisciplinary group of faculty at the Ivey Business School – a group that included this book's authors – began asking questions about the "why" of the fiasco. Fairly quickly, we focused in on the question of leadership – actions taken and not taken, by the financial companies at the epicenter of the meltdown, regulators and politicians, and in the broader economy. We summarized our initial hypotheses in a relatively brief working paper.

Next, we organized a series of more than a dozen focus-group discussions, in all major Canadian cities, New York, London, and Hong Kong. The participants – who were all either CEOs or other C-suite executives, from both large and small organizations and both the public and private sectors – were asked to read the paper in advance, and prepare to discuss it at their session.

As it turned out, those discussions were lively and far-ranging. Some dug deeply into organizational culture, executive compensation, and other motivating influences in the financial sector. Others came to focus primarily on the issue of leader character. This was a somewhat surprising development, from our point of view. It was an issue that we had long been interested in, but we weren't certain that practically minded, real-world practitioners would grab hold of it. But in many cases, they did.

In the wake of these large meetings and a series of smaller focus groups – which ultimately comprised some 300 global business leaders – we continued to sharpen our ideas. We drew upon the fruits of those discussions, and we also attempted to capture and absorb what was by now a steady torrent of materials being generated by participants in and expert observers of the financial meltdown: books, articles, speeches, talk show appearances, and so on. We took note when Dominic Barton – head of McKinsey's global consulting practice – raised the character issue in a commencement address at Ivey. "When we think about leadership," Barton told our graduating class, "we focus too much on what leaders do ... and we don't spend enough time on who leaders are – the character of leaders."[1] Similarly, we took note when Mark Carney, then Governor of the Bank of Canada, who now has a similar role at the Bank of England, observed that "to restore trust in banks and in the broader financial system, global financial institutions need to rediscover their values ... Employees need a sense of broader purpose, grounded in strong connections to their clients and their communities."[2]

Yes, these practitioners tended to use a variety of terms as they put forward their analyses and prescriptions, but we thought we heard a pretty consistent theme: "when it comes to leadership, character matters."

In 2010, our core working group (which included, in addition to the three authors of this book, our colleagues Carol Stephenson and Daina Mazutis) published a monograph summarizing our interim findings. Entitled *Leadership on Trial: A Manifesto for Leadership Development*, the monograph attempted to both "set the record straight" on key aspects of the financial crisis and help shape a research agenda going forward. Like most manifestos, ours concluded with a call to action, suggesting specific steps that we thought could and should be taken by five key constituent groups:

- Current and next-generation leaders of private and public sector organizations
- Boards of directors
- Management educators, and
- Leadership- and organizational-development specialists.

As we had hoped, the publication generated a continuing and productive dialogue both in the academic and business communities. To our surprise, it also sold pretty well: one of the most credible forms of validation!

This book builds upon the core findings of that monograph – and significantly extends them. Very briefly stated, the financial crisis that wreaked such havoc between 2007 and the present grew out of three kinds of leadership failures:

- Failures of competence,
- Failures of commitment, and
- Failures of character.

We detailed those failures in the monograph. While so doing, we realized that this litany of failures practically begged to be stood on its head – to arrive at a prescription for good leadership. So not surprisingly, as we see it, good leadership can be said to rest on three foundations, as summarized in Figure 1.1 below.

We concluded that competencies reflect what a person can do. Commitment describes the degree of effort that someone will put into

Figure 1.1 The Effective Leader

doing those things, which is based on things like their level of aspiration, their degree of engagement, and the extent to which they are willing to sacrifice to reach a goal. Character influences the choices people make about what to do, as well as whether they will acquire the requisite competencies, and make the commitment to do so in any given situation. (We will return to the bullets listed under character – values, virtues, and traits – shortly.) We concluded further that if any of these three foundations are deficient, the shortfall will undermine the two others, and – ultimately – lead to performance problems for leaders, organizations, and related stakeholders.

A Focus on Character

Based on the research described above, and also based on positive reactions to that work from a broad range of constituencies, we were encouraged to carry that work a step further – and in a particular direction.

Business schools and businesses alike have tended to focus their developmental efforts on competencies, whether on the individual or organizational level. Commitment, too, seemed to get an appropriate amount of focus – both on the hiring end and in the developmental process that unfolds over the course of a career.

Increasingly, we felt compelled to focus on the left-hand side of Figure 1.1, above: the character component. As noted, we weren't alone in that focus, and concern. A clear majority of the people we talked to seemed to agree that character was critically important to good leadership. Many identified character weaknesses or defects as being at the epicenter of the build-up in financial-system leverage over the preceding decade, and the subsequent meltdown. Conversely, the participants also identified leader character as a key factor that distinguished the companies that survived, or even prospered, during the meltdown from those that failed or were badly damaged.

When talking about character, those participants focused on issues of both leadership and governance. Among them were: overconfidence (bordering on arrogance) that led to reckless or excessive risk-taking behaviors; lack of transparency, and in some cases, lack of integrity; sheer inattention to critical issues; lack of accountability for the huge risks associated with astronomical individual rewards; intemperate and injudicious decision-making; a lack of respect for individuals that actually got in the way of effective team functioning; hyper-competitiveness among leaders of major financial institutions; and irresponsibility toward shareholders and the societies within which these organizations operated. Taken together, these and other character elements were identified as root or contributory causes of the excessive build-up of leverage in financial markets and the subsequent meltdown.

At the same time, those we have interviewed over the years almost always wondered why such issues were seldom addressed prior to the crisis. They noted the absence of ongoing meaningful discussions about character in their own organizations, even in critical issues such as talent recruitment, selection, development, and retention and succession management.

We think there are a number of reasons for this inconsistency. These include, for example:

- Many decades and many millions of dollars have been spent by private- and public-sector organizations developing competency profiles and ways of measuring competencies. No such emphasis has been placed on character.
- Competencies are manifested in behaviors, and we can actually measure them, however imperfectly. Character, on the other hand, addresses a capability in individuals that may not yet have been tested, and the evidence for which is frequently vague. Up until now, we have not had a way of framing and measuring character which could be seen as comparable to such measures on the competency spectrum.
- "Character" is a loaded word. We tend to avoid talking about character in the workplace, because it seems such a subjective construct. To compound this problem, character has generally been seen as a "moral" or "ethical" issue, which somehow feels extraneous to a business perspective.
- To date, the language of character has been complicated and inaccessible to those unversed in philosophy, ethics, and advanced psychological terminology. It is often viewed as a "soft" and certainly a non-quantifiable construct in a world that looks for hard data.

It's a seemingly daunting list. But we remained intrigued, and undeterred. What if we could come up with a framework that could translate the arcane terminology surrounding character into contemporary managerial language?[3] What if we could create a typology of character dimensions that pertain to the business context, and describe the good and bad behaviors associated with these character dimensions in the appropriate business contexts? What if we could avoid the quicksand of orthodoxy (whether philosophical, ethical, psychological, or managerial) through balance, transparency, careful wording, and clear definitions?

This has been a focus of our ongoing research.

Digging Deeper

But this accounting, detailed as it was, raised as many questions as it answered. Gradually, we distilled that myriad of smaller questions into three overarching questions:

- What is character? It's a term that we use quite often in everyday conversations: He's a bad character; a person of good character; or a character reference. But what do we really mean by leader character?
- Why is it so difficult to talk about someone's character? Why do we find it difficult to assess someone's character with the same degree of comfort we seem to have in assessing their competencies and commitment?
- Can character be learned, developed, shaped, and molded, or is it something that must be present from birth – or at least from childhood or adolescence? Can it change? What, if anything, can leaders do to help develop good character among their followers and a culture of good character in their organizations?

Let's begin with the first and most important question: What is character? One way of answering that question is to state what character does – in other words, its impacts. Character is foundational to effective decision-making and functioning. It shapes a number of things, including: what we notice in the context in which we operate; how we engage the world around us; what we reinforce through our rewards and punishments; who we engage in conversation and how we conduct those conversations; what we value; how we interpret feedback; what we choose to act on; how we deal with conflict, disappointment, and setbacks; the goals we set for ourselves; how we communicate; and so forth. For example, aspiring leaders must commit to stretch assignments to develop their competencies, take in and act on constructive feedback, learn to take ownership for personal mistakes made, develop a cross-enterprise view of the business, and be willing to collaborate well with others on enterprise- or industry-wide projects.

Now let's move from what character does to what character is. As suggested in Figure 1.1, above, we define "character" as an amalgam of virtues, traits, and values. At this point, let's define each of these terms a little more carefully, and work them a little harder.

Virtues are central to our analysis, and to the prescriptions that grow out of that analysis. Virtues are patterns of situationally appropriate behaviors – for example, courage and accountability – that are generally considered to be emblematic of good leaders. They are, in effect, clusters of traits and values that add up to good behavioral habits that are practiced consistently.

The opposite of virtues are vices: unworthy behaviors such as cowardice, arrogance, recklessness, or foolhardiness. In excess, many virtues become vices. Excessive courage may lead to recklessness. Excessive integrity – a concept that many of our audiences initially have trouble imagining – can lead to a dysfunctional self-righteousness.

Of course, the notion of virtues as behaviors is far from a new concept. "We are what we repeatedly do," Aristotle wrote. "Excellence, then, is not an act, but a habit." Aristotle identified and defined twelve virtues: courage, temperance, generosity, magnificence, magnanimity, right ambition, good temper, friendliness, truthfulness, wit, justice, and practical wisdom. That last virtue, in particular, was deemed necessary by Aristotle to live the "good life" and thereby achieve happiness and well-being.

Aristotle's catalog of virtues is hard to improve upon, at least from the standpoint of an individual interacting with the world. Try to add to it, or subtract from it. Not for nothing is he considered one of the most profound thinkers in human history.

We define traits as personality dimensions – patterns of thought, behavior, and emotion – that are relatively stable in individuals across situations and over time.[4] These might include things like extroversion, resiliency, creativity, and so on. Some traits shape virtues, while others do not. In our work, we focus on the former category. If one of your traits is, for example, conscientiousness, that trait very likely helps to shape some of the virtues that combine to create your character.

We tend to think of a trait as something that is acquired. It seems clear, though, that some personality traits also can be inherited. For example, studies have shown that identical twins share more traits than non-identical twins – clearly indicating that nature as well as nurture plays a role in trait development. By logical extension, some aspects of character are influenced by heredity.

Values are deep-seated beliefs that influence or guide behaviors. Again, they overlap with – but are distinguishable from – virtues. They are usually associated with words like "should" and "ought" as in, "Leaders ought to treat everyone with dignity and respect."

Values tend to be individual beliefs, rather than organizational beliefs. Values can change with life stages, and also according to the extent to which a particular value has already been achieved. The artist who achieves international renown may come down out of the garret. The newly minted professional with burdensome student loans may opt for a high starting salary; decades later, he may place a higher value on living near his grandchildren, or having better access to recreational outlets.

Certainly, values are affected by context. In Western democracies, we value Lockean and Jeffersonian ideals: life, liberty, and the pursuit of happiness, for example. But other cultures place a higher value on order, harmony, non-violence, and equality. On a more granular level, our values may be influenced by religion, our home life, fraternal organizations we join, experiences gained in obtaining an education, the companies we work for, our friends, and so on.

We may espouse – and even hold – certain values, but fail to manifest them under pressure. For example, when loyalty conflicts with honesty, when fairness conflicts with pragmatism, or when social responsibility conflicts with our obligations to shareholders, we become conflicted. And when we act in ways that we know are inconsistent with our values, we experience guilt, anger, and embarrassment. We may rationalize our actions (or inactions), blame others, or try to minimize the significance of what has happened, but on some level we know we are coming up short. We are betraying our values in pursuit of some other goals, and that betrayal rarely feels good.

Again, in our work, we are most interested in those values that help shape virtues – and by extension, help shape the character of a leader.

From Virtues to Dimensions

Our continuing research led us to try to recast these somewhat abstract discussions in a way that would make them more practical and actionable for the business practitioner. We have been greatly aided in this effort by the previous work of Christopher Peterson and Martin Seligman, who bridged philosophy and psychology with a focus on individual well-being.[5] This is part of a larger trend in modern psychology. Rather than focusing on what makes people come up short, or even fail, psychologists have emphasized positive aspects of organizational life – things like hope, optimism, and character. We try to take that work a step further, bridging theory with practice in the context of leadership.

We have addressed one of the three overarching questions posed above: What is character? But we still have to wrestle with the remaining two questions:

- Can character be assessed?
- Can character be learned, developed, shaped, and molded?

We decided that a good first step toward answering the first of these two questions would be to recast Aristotle's "virtues" into what we chose to call "dimensions of leader character." This involved both updating language, and also shifting from a focus on the individual in isolation to the individual in an organizational context. We identified eleven such character dimensions, with an illustrative set of elements that describe each dimension.[6]

Let us stress again that the wording of these dimensions and their associated elements has been heavily influenced by the language used by the executive- and board-level participants in our *Leadership on*

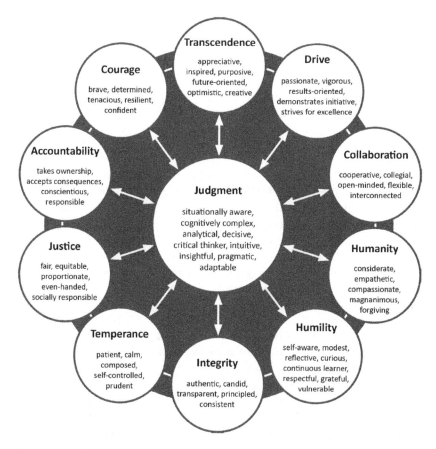

Figure 1.2 Character Dimensions and Associated Elements

Trial research. It has also been shaped by subsequent qualitative and quantitative work with leaders, managers, and students, as well as by endless debate within our own research team. And again, our goal was to ensure that we had identified the dimensions that were relevant to the successful leadership of organizations, and that we described those dimensions (and associated elements) in clear and accessible terms. If we seek to come up with metrics for assessing someone's character, there is no room for terminological fuzziness. That work is summarized in Figure 1.2, above.

Following are some key takeaways from this chart about the nature of character:

• Each dimension is composed of several defining character elements. Each of these elements has an impact on the strength of the particular character dimension.

- The dimensions are interdependent. They work together to determine the overall strength of our character.
- Judgment plays a central role in character, controlling when and how we choose to behave.

A word more on that central dimension: judgment. Each of the other dimensions of character represents reservoirs of varying depth – in other words, people may have lots of courage or a little, or great integrity or not so much. How an individual's character influences their actual behavior in a particular context depends on their judgment. It serves to moderate and mediate the way that the other dimensions determine individuals' behaviors in different situations. In effect, it acts as a sort of air traffic controller, determining when courage should be shown and when it is better suppressed; when collaboration is appropriate and when a leader should go it alone; when it's appropriate to demonstrate humility and when to demonstrate great confidence; when to be temperate and when to be bold; and so on. Conversely, judgment without the other dimensions moderating it is inherently superficial.

Returning to an idea introduced earlier: Can you have too much of a good thing, as well as too little? Yes, absolutely. Aristotle argued that virtues become vices not only in their absence, but also in their excess. This seems to have particular relevance in the organizational context, where dimensions of the few are multiplied by the many, especially in terms of inefficiency or compromised decision-making.

We will come back to this theme – excess and deficits – in Chapter 2. Then, in Chapters 4 through 14, we will look in depth at one character dimension and its associated elements per chapter, to really pin down what we mean and why that dimension is important – and how it is inseparable from all the other dimensions.

Can Character be Assessed?

With that background, we can now address the second of our overarching questions: can character be assessed? Can we actually bring all these dimensions and elements to bear on the business setting? Can someone's character – say, your character – be assessed in a way that can lead to subsequent action and improvement?

The answer is "yes." Over the past few years, we have developed a tool that we call the "Leadership Character Insight Assessment 360," or LCIA-360 for short.[7] As the name implies, it draws on the well-established 360-degree review model, whereby organizational leaders, colleagues, and direct/indirect reports rate your performance along a number of dimensions, but it brings that technology to bear specifically on the topic of leadership.[8]

We will describe the LCIA-360 in greater detail in Chapter 2, and explain how it helps the individual set a baseline for character development. While assessing character and receiving feedback on your character may seem challenging, we have been able to identify a set of behaviors that help people unpack the dimensions of character in a way that makes character accessible. We remind people that, much like your signature, character is a habit that is developed over time. If you sign your name and then switch hands to sign again, you discover the difficulty and challenge of signing your name. But your signature is simply a habit developed over time, and you can think about character in the same way. Drawing on the ideas in this book, you will be able to identify character strengths and deficiencies and begin to chart a course for developing the habits to strengthen your character.

Can Character be Developed?

This brings us to our third and final overarching question: Can character be developed, shaped, and molded?[9]

Again, the answer is "yes."[10] A growing body of evidence – including the findings of the research that we've been involved in – supports the contention that your character is developed over your lifetime, and you can enhance the development of character through deliberate practice. Every situation presents a different experience and opportunity to exercise, apply, and develop character.

Note that character development starts from within. Warren Bennis, an expert on the subject of leadership development, addressed the role of individual responsibility in becoming a leader:

> The leader never lies to himself, especially about himself, knows his flaws as well as his assets, and deals with them directly. You are your own raw material. When you know what you consist of and what you want to make of it, then you can invent yourself.[11]

So an understanding of the "raw material" is critical, underscoring the importance of tools like the LCIA-360. So is personal dedication to the task of character-building: the determination to improve oneself.

Equally, we believe, character development is greatly aided by supportive leaders within a supportive organization. Simply talking about character – making it a legitimate and valued topic of conversation – stimulates discussion and facilitates individual reflection. Arkadi Kuhlmann, the current CEO of ZenBanx, conducts postmortems on organizational events like a die-hard hockey fan analyzing the performance of his or her favorite team. "People will argue for hours about why a goal was scored, or not scored, and how an individual played, and so on," Kuhlmann recently observed. "But in business, and even in family situations, we just won't do those kinds of postmortems."[12] Tools like the LCIA-360 can aid and assist the process of character self-awareness, but senior leaders must embrace it as a valuable and valued activity – and this is done best when they do it by example.

When organizations develop leadership profiles, and when they address leader character in those profiles, they emphasize its importance, especially in the context of developmental coaching. Dimensions of leader character need to be addressed explicitly in the organization's coaching and mentoring. They need to be reinforced through training and development. They need to be actively invoked in the all-important processes of recruitment, selection, and succession management.

Mission statements and explicit values statements certainly have their place. But all too often, they are little more than posters on a wall. One inherent challenge here is that the values in a value statement are often "cherry-picked" to align with the organizational cultures and strategy. It's like a values buffet: The organization's leaders simply stress what it's convenient to stress. Character is foundational, and isn't dependent on corporate culture and strategy. There is no buffet line for character. Unless their content is built into the work that people are doing – in a meaningful way – they are rightfully ignored. Similarly, unless leaders "own" those statements, they have almost no impact. It's a simple organizational truth: Anything that senior management takes seriously is taken seriously; everything else is marginalized. So senior leaders need to take the lead, and keep at it.

Once Again: Character Matters

When it comes to leadership, it's sometimes useful to envision a "triple helix": a braid of three elements woven tightly together. Those elements, as discussed earlier, are competencies, commitment, and character.

The problem, up to now, is that character – in our estimation, the most important of the three braided elements – has been largely invisible. We are determined to work against that invisibility. Why? Because it is important to your personal effectiveness as a leader to have the capacity to exercise all dimensions of character. Our conversations with executives in the public, private, and not-for-profit sector told us that leaders had no language or essential vocabulary for leader character and what it meant in the workplace. Hence, deep levels of conversation around character and character development are restricted. We are determined to help senior executives to get the language right.

No, character is not the air we breathe. But take it out of the leadership equation, and you get characters like some of those listed at the outset of this chapter: Lay and Skilling, Berlusconi, Armstrong, and so on.

Our experience, over the past half-decade, is that a renewed focus on character sparks the best in people, and fuels them in their personal journeys to become better leaders. Embracing the invisible – but very real! – strand of character helps people to bring out the best in themselves, and to support others toward the same end. It helps ensure that organizations will perform at the highest level – and in so doing, help (rather than harm) society.

That is the journey that we describe in this book.

Notes

1 Speech delivered at the 2014 MBA Convocation, Western University, Ivey Business School, June 6.
2 From "Rebuilding Trust in Global Banking," the 2013 Thomas d'Aquino Lecture on Leadership, delivered on 02.25.13 by Mark Carney at Ivey; http://www.bankofcanada.ca/2013/02/rebuilding-trust-global-banking/.
3 In the interest of broad accessibility, this book primarily will take the general manager's perspective and use language familiar to business practitioners. For a more academic approach to many of the concepts in this and following sections, see Crossan, M., Mazutis, D., and Seijts, G., "In search of virtue: the role of virtues, values, and character strengths in ethical decision making," *Journal of Business Ethics*, Vol. 113, No. 4, April 9, 2013, 567–581.
4 This definitional material is drawn in large part from Crossan, M., Gandz, J., and Seijts, G., "Developing leadership character," *Ivey Business Journal*, January/February 2012, reprint #9B12TA07.
5 See, for example, Christopher Peterson and Martin Seligman's *Character Strengths and Virtues* (American Psychological Association/Oxford University Press, 2004).
6 The observant reader will remember that Aristotle identified twelve virtues, as opposed to our eleven "dimensions." The lists are more different than that discrepancy might indicate. Eight of our dimensions are not on Aristotle's list, and nine of his virtues are not on ours. That said, some of the differences arise out of an updating of language. Others reflect our determination to speak to the business community.
7 We co-created the LCIA with Sigma Assessment Systems, Inc. in London, Ontario; http://www.sigmaassessmentsystems.com/.
8 Clearly, the traditional "360" touches on some of these same dimensions, but the LCIA-360 dives deep.
9 In this book, we focus mainly on character development in the business context. We have also focused on the same challenge in the academic context. See, for example, Crossan, M., Mazutis, D., Seijts, G., and Gandz, J., "Developing leadership character in business programs," *Academy of Management Learning & Education*, 2012, Vol. 12, No. 2, 285–305.
10 Aristotle, Plato, and other ancient Greek philosophers believed that character was something that could be habituated – that is, acquired through the consistent application of the virtues over the course of one's lifetime. See, for example, Crossan, M., Mazutis, D., Seijts, G., and Gandz, J., "Developing leadership character in business programs," *Academy of Management Learning & Education*, 2012, Vol. 12, No. 2, 285–305.
11 Bennis, Warren, *On Becoming a Leader*. (New York, NY: Random House Business Books, 1989).
12 This quote is taken from *Good Leaders Learn: Lessons from Lifetimes of Leadership* (Routledge, 2014) by Gerard Seijts.

2   Leading with Character

In Chapter 1, we focused a spotlight on the global financial crisis that unfolded between 2007 and 2009, the aftershocks of which are still with us today. We suggested failures of leadership were responsible for much of that debacle. Loosened regulatory restraints led to an unholy collusion between banks and ratings agencies, which led in turn to massive amounts of sub-prime loans being packaged into collateralized debt obligations (CDOs) and then into derivatives.

The riches proved too powerful to resist. Once-sleepy banks found ways to generate unprecedented returns, and they quickly became hooked on those high returns.

This sorry scenario begs the question: Did anyone resist? And if so, why and how?

The answer, of course, is "yes." All down the chain of fiasco, isolated voices could be heard expressing skepticism – and in some cases, those voices prevailed, and set the course of their respective institutions, and those institutions largely escaped the catastrophe. Let's look at just one of those individuals – Ed Clark, CEO of Toronto-based TD Bank until he retired in 2014 – and the good decisions that he and his colleagues made.

TD Bank is a venerable old Toronto institution ("TD" is institutional shorthand for "Toronto-Dominion"), with roots dating back to 1855. It operates in four primary markets: Canadian personal and commercial banking, U.S. personal and commercial banking, wealth management, and wholesale banking. It ranks second (behind Royal Bank of Canada) on the list of Canada's top five banks, in terms of market cap and net income. It has the largest U.S. presence of any Canadian bank, largely because between 2004 and 2010, it spent billions upgrading its network of U.S. retail banks, which span the U.S. east coast from Maine to Florida.[1]

Clark – a graduate of the University of Toronto and Harvard, where he earned a PhD – spent his early working years in the federal public service, rising rapidly through the ranks to a senior level. After a change of government he left the public service for a second career in banking, spending time with corporate, wholesale, and retail banks. He joined TD Bank in 2000, when it acquired Canada Trust's parent CT Financial Services, Inc., of which Clark was president and CEO. He helped integrate the two firms, and was named president of TD Bank two years later. This was in some ways an unlikely success story, given that Canada Trust was fundamentally a retail banking operation – well known for strong customer service, but not exactly in the fast lane of early twenty-first-century banking.

Clark was impressed with how volatile banks' earnings were. Indeed, TD Bank had recently lost huge amounts of money through bad loans to telecommunications companies in North America that it had written off or restructured. He determined to avoid such high risk business and, rather, concentrate on the much less volatile retail banking business.

He was not, however, against taking risk. He orchestrated the U.S. expansion that began in 2004 (which resulted in TD Bank having more branches in the U.S. than in Canada). But, significantly, Clark declined to get into the banking gold rush that was then underway, especially in the U.S. "When we went into the United States, we refused to do subprime lending," he told Bloomberg News. "We said, 'I don't care what the spreads are, we are not going to do that.'"[2] TD Bank actually sold off its then-profitable structured products business, did not get involved in securitizing mortgages and a lot of the "sophisticated" credit-management products such as credit-default swaps and their derivatives. As he often said in presentations and speeches to his executives and more broadly to the general public: "We don't get into things we don't understand" and "We wouldn't sell things to the public that I wouldn't sell to my mother."

Of course, this meant that Clark had a certain amount of proselytizing to do among his own ranks, some of whom looked hungrily at the fortunes being made south of the border. "If something seems too good to be true, it probably is, and we won't do it or sell it," he was fond of saying. "We'll walk away from opportunities."[3]

In the 2004–2007 build-up of massive credit, TD Bank was often referred to as "under-performing," "conservative," and "staid." But Clark held his ground as the froth in the credit markets grew and grew. He was helped in this by Canadian banking regulations and the structure of the mortgage market in Canada which was backstopped by government insurance but, even among Canadian banks, TD Bank was the least exposed to credit risk.

Then came the financial disaster of 2008–2009. TD Bank was not immune to the liquidity crisis that hit all large banks and saw its shares fall along with others. But, by 2011, the benefits to Canada of the relatively conservative approach taken by Canadian banks – including TD Bank – was clear.[4] Wealth levels in the U.S. had dropped by 8 percent, on average, since 2007. In Canada, they were up 3 percent, on average.

In October 2011, Clark was honored at the Ivey Business Leader Award Dinner as a distinguished business practitioner.[5] In his prepared remarks that evening – entitled "Preserving the things that matter in a world of constrained resources" – Clark spoke at length about widening gaps between rich and poor, and about how a lack of courage, vision, and discipline had contributed to the world's economic woes in recent years. He surprised many in the audience by expressing sympathy for both the Tea Party and the Occupy movement, then flourishing in the U.S. Members of both groups, he suggested, felt that they had played by the rules, and not reaped the expected benefits: "They don't like how the world is turning out."[6]

Toward the end of his speech, Clark described the kinds of leaders that Canada – and the world – would need, in order to address mounting economic, social, and political problems:

> Leaders: Who understand the issues. Who choose the pragmatic over the dogmatic. Leaders who build a consensus around the problem and solution – and paint a vision of a better Canada.
>
> Who celebrate fairness, make tough choices – who are empathetic and convincing.
>
> Who recognize the practical implementation of old principles may be very different from what we have done in the past.
>
> Leaders who recognize that, in the end, economic growth matters and dividing smaller and smaller pies won't work and that international competition is increasing, not decreasing.

Again, Clark was prescribing for the political realm, but that prescription tracks closely with many of the virtues defined by Aristotle, millennia ago – and also with many of the dimensions of business leadership that we advocate in this book, and which we explore in this and subsequent chapters.

It is no coincidence that as of 2013, TD Bank was rated the eleventh-safest bank in the world (a position confirmed by *Global Finance* in late 2014) and one of only four privately owned banks in the world with an Aa1 rating.[7]

The Dimensions in Depth

At the center of the Ed Clark/TD Bank story is the attribute of judgment (but we also see the influence of many of the other character dimensions). You will recall from Chapter 1 that judgment is the central dimension of our constellation of leader character attributes (see Figure 2.1, below).

Let's consider these eleven dimensions in greater depth. As we go, we will explain the elements that are illustrative of each of these dimensions (e.g. the dimension of courage comprises the elements of bravery, determination, tenaciousness, resilience, and confidence). We will also resume the discussion, begun in Chapter 1, of whether you can have "too much of a good thing."

Let's start in the upper right-hand corner. **Drive** is essential in leaders so that they will establish stretch goals and the plans to achieve them. Leaders with drive demonstrate a passion to achieve results, the vigor to motivate

Figure 2.1 Character Dimensions and Associated Elements

others, and a natural curiosity that must be satisfied, and they demonstrate initiative and a desire to excel.

We believe that this drive comes from within for good leaders. Good leaders drive for results because they are intrinsically rewarding; they are not being driven by external forces such as incentive plans or the will of others. In its extreme, drive may be shown in hyper-competitiveness, overconfidence, and arrogance – characteristics that can impede collaboration and lead to destructive excesses and eventual under-performance. When you are recruiting or developing leaders, you want people with drive – not people who are driven.

Collaboration is essential for leaders to form effective teams, to cooperate with others, and to work collegially. They have to be open-minded and flexible so that they can work with those in their own organizations as well as in external groups. However, collaboration for its own sake may result in endless deferral of decisions until consensus is reached, while lone-wolf decision-making squanders the opportunities to benefit from a diversity of views, better-quality ideas, and the smoother implementation of decisions.

Humanity, which we describe as consideration for others, empathy, compassion, magnanimity and the capacity for forgiveness, is essential to developing followership. Without it, a person can be an effective boss, but never a good leader. We do not view humanity as a soft or weak dimension of leadership character but, rather, as a fundamental strength that is often at the core of fostering quality and candid conversations. However, we recognize that being tenderhearted may induce paralysis in decision-making, especially in situations in which some people may be disadvantaged, such as discipline or downsizing. We also recognize that being cold-hearted, callous, or indifferent destroys human relationships, and usually results in leaders being rejected by their followers.

Humility has long been regarded as an essential quality for leaders; without humility, it's impossible to learn from one's mistakes or those of others. This dimension embraces a degree of self-awareness, the capacity for reflection, and a sense of gratitude toward those who have helped one learn or achieve success. However, as with the other dimensions, it is important to guard against excessive humility, such as might lead to self-abnegation. This is actually a failure to recognize personal strengths and it can undermine the self-confidence that leaders must have.

Integrity is essentially about wholeness, completeness, and soundness of leadership character. It is most readily apparent in principles such as honesty, authenticity, transparency, candor, and consistency, but it is also used to describe high moral standards. It's knowing who you truly are and being true to yourself. It's both saying what you think and doing what you say. Arguably one can never have enough integrity and, indeed, people often describe integrity as a "binary" variable. However, there are times when people with high integrity display rigidity of thinking and even dogmatism and self-righteousness that make them less effective as leaders. Making decisions in complex and ambiguous circumstances often requires the reconciliation of opposing principles and the exercise of a degree of pragmatism.

Temperance allows leaders to be calm when others around them panic, to think things through, and to act in the best long-term interests of the organization. It helps them avoid overreacting to short-term success or failure, and to assess both the risks and the rewards of alternative courses of action. However, leaders must guard against temperance that is so strong that it contributes to undesirable temerity. For example, boards actually want leaders to take risks, provided that the leaders understand these risks and know how to manage them.

Justice is a dimension that is central to followers' decisions to accept an individual's leadership. This dimension incorporates fairness and even-handedness in both procedures and outcomes, such as the allocation of work and dispensation of rewards. It includes a sense of proportionality with respect to praise or censure and – in a broader sense – recognition of the requirement of a leader to contribute to the growth and development of the societies within which they operate. Leaders who act unjustly soon find themselves violating societal expectations, which may lead to over-regulation and excessive controls that will likely undermine long-term performance.

Accountability includes a sense of ownership, being conscientious in the discharge of leadership mandates, and acceptance of the consequences of one's actions. However, taking the whole world on one's shoulders is an excess that can result in burn-out, or paralyze people from taking action. On the other hand, ducking legitimate responsibility results in negligent and reckless conduct that will lose leaders the respect of their peers, those whom they report to, and those who work for them.

Courage is a requisite character dimension for leaders. It includes preparedness to take risks, to challenge the status quo, to test uncharted waters, to speak out against perceived wrongdoing, and to be prepared to admit to concepts such as "I don't know" or "I screwed up." Sometimes it requires courage to adopt a lower-risk strategy and foregoing the immediate returns of a higher-risk route. It may include a degree of resilience as leaders fail in their first efforts to accomplish something. The absence of courage results in compliance with authority, a moral muteness that allows wrongdoing to go unchallenged and unreported, and average or even mediocre returns. An excess of courage, one that is not tempered by other character dimensions, may lead to foolhardiness and excessive risk-taking.

Transcendence is the dimension that allows leaders to see the big picture and take the long view. It is focused on future possibilities and means doing what's right for their organizations in the long run, rather than pursuing the expedient or momentarily satisfying route, climbing above petty rivalries or personal feelings. It often requires creativity. Transcendent leaders are also optimistic: they focus on the future and inspire others to do the same. Transcendence is not a detached other-worldliness, which may detract from focus on the here and now. Nor is it the pursuit of perfection to the point where the organization fails to achieve acceptable results in the shorter term.

And finally, we arrive at **judgment**, which – as we noted in the context of the Ed Clark/TD Bank story – has a central place in people's character. Each of the other dimensions of character represents reservoirs of varying depth: People may have lots of courage or a little, or great integrity or not so much. Whether and how a person's character influences his or her actual behaviors in a particular context depends, to a great extent, on judgment. Judgment serves to moderate and mediate the way that the other dimensions determine individuals' behaviors in different situations. As noted in Chapter 1, judgment acts like an air traffic controller, determining when courage should be shown and when it is better suppressed; when to be temperate and when to be bold; and so on.

While the dimensions and elements of character are non-negotiable, their development and expression are deeply personal and unique to each person, much like a fingerprint. For example, Nelson Mandela's 27 years in prison shaped his character in ways that are unique to him. Others in his situation might have allowed such an experience to erode their character; he, apparently, used it to strengthen his character. For example, his understanding of the element of forgiveness as essential to the character dimension of humanity must have been severely tested by his scarring experience of seemingly endless incarceration – and yet, he managed to emerge with the view that "forgiveness liberates the soul."

We should also stress that this is not about having an "average" or "optimal" amount of a particular dimension, but rather, deepening each dimension as much as possible – recognizing that what prevents the exercise of excess in one dimension is strength in the others. In other words, courage avoids becoming recklessness because of temperance, humility, justice, accountability, and so on.

We will explore each of these eleven dimensions in greater depth – illustrated by real-world examples, good and bad – in Chapters 4 through 14. But first, let's take a look at a second example of values in action. Do these elements of leader character have any relevance in the real world? Can institutions embrace them?

Back to the Real World: Leader Character at Parker Hannifin

Having looked in depth at leader character on the individual level, and having begun to explore the integration of individual behavior with organization context, let's look at a real-world example of a company that has tackled the issue of leader character with determination – and has achieved some success.

Our example involves Parker Hannifin Corporation (PH), the world's leading diversified manufacturer of motion and control technologies and systems,[8] providing precision-engineered solutions for mobile, industrial and aerospace markets.[9] Founded in Cleveland, Ohio in 1918, PH has grown to a $13B USD global company with more than 865,000 products, distributed through 13,000 outlets in 1,100 markets, employing approximately 58,000 people in 139 divisions and 341 manufacturing plants in 49 countries around the world.

From the beginning, PH has attributed much of its success to its values-based culture and employee engagement. The organization prides itself on its history of fair dealings, valued customer relationships, and ongoing adherence to core values of integrity, honesty, respect, and ethical behavior. Since 2001, empowered employees have represented the foundation of PH's "Win Strategy" to become the number one motion and control company in the world. In 2011, the company introduced the "Winovation" new product development approach, which is specifically designed to ensure that only those technologies that can make a significant contribution to solving some of the world's largest social and environmental issues make it through the process. For these and other reasons, employees at PH have a great sense of pride for the company they work for, and are "hardwired" to think about the legacy they want to leave behind.

A Focus on Virtues

In April of 2012, in light of its growing operations and internationalization, the board of directors approved a new approach to winning through ethical behavior that would be built around seven classical virtues: compassion, courage, trust, justice, wisdom, temperance, and hope.[10]

PH's leaders felt that the company's strong values-based employee culture was a key component of its competitive advantage. As PH pursued an ambitious global growth and acquisition strategy, the board and top management was concerned about preserving and protecting the company's culture, and – by extension – its reputation. Rather than retrenching around more formal compliance-based tools and tactics which were seen to have a negative focus, PH opted instead to take the more positive strength-based approach to crafting culture rooted in the virtues.

Although one could already characterize the culture at PH as reflective of these virtues, senior leaders saw value in trying to crystallize what made PH so distinctive, to safeguard this source of competitive advantage for the future, especially as ever-greater numbers of its employees worked and lived far from the company's Midwestern "home."[11]

The Process

Beginning with a series of senior manager, employee, and stakeholder consultations, Peter Rea – PH's vice president of ethics and integrity – first secured buy-in on the virtues-based approach before presenting his plan to the board. Vital to laying this foundation was setting the business case for a focus on virtues.

In fact, for those leaders who go looking for it, there is abundant evidence to support such a business case. For example: With more than 70 percent of all organizational costs tied to human capital, companies need to pay close attention to the level of employee engagement in the workplace. Recent studies have indicated that "as many as two-thirds of today's workers are either actively looking for new jobs or merely going through the motions at their current jobs. While they still show up for work each day, in the ways that count, many have quit."[12] A focus on virtues is then one way in which employees can align their own personal values with those of the organization to increase trust and pride, both of which have been linked to positive outcomes such as increased productivity, customer satisfaction, profitability and reduced turnover, absenteeism, and employee theft.

The objective at PH, as Rea saw it, was to raise employee awareness of the virtues, draw their attention to how these virtues help PH win in the marketplace, and commit to future actions based on these virtues – an awareness/attention/action model – in order to empower employees and solidify employee engagement.

Given the many different existing virtue typologies, PH chose a relatively narrow set of virtues – again, compassion, courage, trust, justice, wisdom, temperance, and hope – that it deemed to be specifically applicable to its business. These virtues were drawn primarily from the writings of Aristotle, although attention was also paid to labeling, so that the virtues would seem more directly relevant to a workplace setting (e.g. using compassion instead of love; trust rather than faith). In developing the program, Rea consulted with a broad variety of academics in business, positive psychology, education, and the military, even visiting three of the United States service academies (Army, Air Force, and Navy) to better understand how these organizations drive their cultures around virtues.

Rea and his colleagues defined the seven PH virtues in terms of actions:

- **Trust**: We look out for the interests of others as if their interests were our own.
- **Compassion**: We demonstrate care and concern for our customers, colleagues, and partners.
- **Courage**: We live by our convictions not our circumstances even when the burden is great.
- **Justice**: We are fair, objective, and impartial when serving all stakeholders.
- **Wisdom**: We practice resiliency in the face of adversity and humility in times of prosperity.
- **Temperance**: We practice self-control, restraint, and self-discipline.
- **Hope**: We are grateful for opportunities to be part of a purpose greater than ourselves.

The virtues collectively were given a simple but compelling name: "Winning with Integrity." They were then carefully linked to PH's traditional leadership philosophy. For example, PH summarized "Winning with Integrity" by stating that "character defined by virtue transcends every culture and language, and provides a common platform for guiding our behaviors, actions, and decisions, including execution of the Win Strategy. Together, we can preserve Parker's reputation and protect our financial strength."[13] Significantly, they were described not as yet another new program – which might have been dismissed as the ethical "flavor of the month" – but rather, as a distillation of what the company's employees already understood, and already embraced.

Rea began engaging small groups of employees in discussions and workshops around the virtues, which allowed for an open and transparent exploration of the meaning of the virtues in practice. For example, employees would be asked not only "what is courage?" but also "why is courage important to Parker Hannifin?" and "how can we foster more courage in our organization?" Through a process of personal reflection and peer feedback, employees had a chance to uncover which virtues of the seven were most relevant to them, and how they already had brought these character strengths successfully to practice.

The rollout of "Winning with Integrity" also included the development of a cultural instrument tool based on the virtues, as well as an education website that included exercises whereby employees could explore what it meant to engage the virtues at work. As of this writing, pilot talent review processes and various coaching models that select for and reinforce the virtues are being developed. Although Winning with Integrity is still a work in progress, PH employees have proven themselves open to the virtues-based focus of this initiative, evidently finding both personal and professional meaning in the application of a character-based approach to business.

The Impact of Character Dimensions on Leader Behavior

The Parker Hannifin story underscores the fact that organizations can, indeed, embrace values – and that a values-driven strategy can be a key competitive weapon. But it also underscores the fact that values don't reside in corporate structures; they reside in people. Yes, Peter Rea and his colleagues effectively leveraged a strong institutional culture – but that culture almost certainly grew out of the behaviors of key individuals over PH's long history.

We have arrived at a critical point in our argument. As illustrated in Figure 2.1, above, dimensions are defined by their component elements. Those elements, in turn, are anchored in behaviors. In other words, it's helpful – but not enough – to understand that integrity comprises the elements of authenticity, candor, transparency, principle, and consistency. What we need to understand next is how these elements translate into appropriate leader behaviors.

This explains why organizations often fail to get what they claim they are seeking when it comes to dimensions like integrity and accountability, which are very often cast by those organizations as core values. Integrity isn't just something you have or don't have; instead, it needs to be developed, and then expressed. But that expression – that behavior – may well involve drawing on more than one element. In other words, you can be principled but, without candor, you are unlikely to express your principles. You're unlikely to behave in the way your organization hopes you will – and ultimately, as the Ed Clark/TD Bank example amply illustrates, behaviors are what it's all about.

One caution, before we move forward: The linear format of a book means that we once again have to examine these dimensions one at a time. But of course, they too need to be linked to each other. Remember that, as one of our colleagues likes to say, "If you have integrity without humanity, you are likely to be an authentic a.hole."

Table 2.1, presented in the following two pages, lays out behaviors that are associated with our eleven leader character dimensions. Of course, this is our own list of appropriate behaviors that grow out of leader character dimensions – although again, it is derived from our work with senior corporate leaders over several years. Depending on your specific circumstances, your own organization's list might have additional specific behaviors related to those circumstances.

Again, making an explicit link between dimensions and behaviors is what transforms an otherwise abstract discussion into a managerially useful framework. We venture to guess that as you read the bulleted points in Table 2.1, you are either saying, "Yes; this is what goes on in my organization," or, quite possibly, you are saying, "Yes; this is what I wish were going on in my organization!"

If it's the latter, read on.

The Impact of Character on an Organization

Now let's look at how leader character – its presence or absence – comes to bear on an organization. In other words, if the organization's leaders have successfully cultivated the dimensions described earlier, and have translated them into the sorts of behaviors listed in Table 2.1, what will that organization look like? And conversely, what will it look like if no such cultivation and translation have taken place? Take a look at Table 2.2, below, which summarizes both circumstances.

With this chart in front of us, it may again be instructive to reflect on the Ed Clark/TD Bank example cited earlier. Take "temperance," for example. It's far too simplistic to say that any individual embodies only the elements listed in either the "absent" or "present" column. And yet, wasn't TD Bank under Clark's leadership characterized by effective risk management and reasoned decision-making? Didn't it forgo short-term gains as a result of taking the long view?

As a sidelight, Clark's remarks expressing sympathy for the Tea Party and Occupy movements can be interpreted through the lens of "justice." Fairness fosters trust, Clark told his audiences during that difficult period of societal transition, which continues today. Inequity erodes trust.

Table 2.1 How Leader Character Dimensions Translate into Behaviors

	WHEN THE DIMENSION IS PRESENT LEADERS...
Courage	- Put themselves in "the line of fire" to support ideas that may be unpopular but the right move - Will vocally support the right thing to do, even in the face of strong opposition
Drive	- Pursue projects with dogged determination - Show unrelenting energy in the pursuit of objectives - Strive for excellence in everything they tackle
Collaboration	- Understand how to work with different people and personalities in a productive way - Leverage others' ideas, opinions, and contributions to build better solutions - Stay open-minded in the face of opposition - Invite constructive dissent
Integrity	- Walk the talk - Are honest and transparent in their business dealings and hold others to the same standard - Bring the organization's values to life in their own behavior - Don't ask others to do things that are morally questionable
Temperance	- Are calm, cool, and collected even in difficult situations - Demonstrate restraint - Have an appreciation for the risks associated with decisions and actions - Know when to stop talking and listen
Accountability	- Don't shirk responsibility - Own their mistakes - Don't deny reality - Don't skirt the difficult questions
Justice	- Reward good performance and confront poor performance - Remain objective when hearing others out - Are respectful of others' differences – don't treat people in a "one size fits all" way - Will vocally support others who have been wronged

Table 2.1 (cont.)

Humility	- Talk about accomplishments as "we" versus "I" - Are aware of their weaknesses and delegate accordingly - Acknowledge and appreciate the contributions of others - Don't feel compelled to talk about their accomplishments - Are not bullies
Humanity	- Genuinely care about their people - Are available and generous with their time and resources - Can move past a bad experience with someone and maintain a productive relationship - Invest in the development of others
Transcendence	- Can recognize good ideas that are ahead of their time - Truly appreciate excellence in the work of others - Show a strong sense of purpose that inspires others - Bring a fresh, creative, elevated perspective to problems - Help others see things in new ways
Judgment	- Consistently make good business decisions - Add insight, direction, and clarity to problem-solving discussions - Don't make assumptions or jump to conclusions - Tailor solutions to the situation

Table 2.2 The Impact of Character – and Lack of Character – on Organizations

	Present	Absent
Courage	- Decisions are made in spite of uncertainty - There is opposition to bad decisions	- There is agreement with poor decisions - Satisficing rather than maximizing is the norm - Moral muteness prevails
Drive	- Innovation thrives - There is sustained momentum around focused priorities and high productivity	- There is widespread lethargy and low productivity
Collaboration	- Effective teamwork enhances productivity - There is diversity in teams that contributes to innovation, understanding, and appreciation for others' ideas	- An "every man for himself" mentality breeds a hostile competitive climate that alienates potential allies - Lack of information-sharing leads to poor understanding of decisions, resulting in friction and conflict
Integrity	- There is trust, transparency, and effective communication	- People operate from a position of self-interest and mistrust which impairs their ability to make good business decisions
Temperance	- There is effective risk management governed by reasoned decision-making - Thoughtful consideration (versus impulsive overreaction) to events that impact the business	- Short-term gains dictate strategy - Desire for instant gratification trumps a more measured "what is best over the long term" approach
Accountability	- There is ownership of issues and commitment to decisions and their execution	- There is failure to deliver results and take responsibility for poor decisions and outcomes
Justice	- There is perception of fairness that fosters trust - People go above and beyond what is required	- Inequities exist that erode trust - Widespread favoritism and nepotism exist
Humility	- There is a willingness to identify and discuss mistakes - The organization supports continuous learning	- Interactions are ruled by arrogance and overconfidence - Problems and projects are approached with complacency
Humanity	- There is a deep understanding of what is important to stakeholders that fosters unique insights and competitive advantage	- There is a failure to acknowledge critical social implications of decisions and actions
Transcendence	- There is commitment to excellence - There is clarity on superordinate goals and a focus on big-picture thinking - Inspiration motivates innovation	- Strategy is dictated by narrow goals and objectives - There is failure to acknowledge, appreciate, or strive for excellence - People are not inspired to create and contribute
Judgment	- There is recognition of key issues relevant to situations - Decisions are predicated on excellent understanding, analysis, and insight	- There is a lack of comprehensive and balanced assessment of issues leads to poor decisions, confusion, and resistance to change.

The Role of the LCIA

Up to now, we have talked about the importance of leader character, the dimensions and elements that make up that character, and the impact of appropriate leader behaviors on organizations. But we haven't talked about how you get from here to there – in other words, how you as an individual can master those dimensions and associated behaviors. Is that possible?

The answer is an emphatic "yes." Character is developed over your lifetime and you can enhance the development of character through deliberate practice. Every situation presents a different experience and opportunity to exercise, apply, and develop character.

This process begins with self-understanding. In Chapter 1, we introduced a tool that we have developed over the past few years, which we call the "Leadership Character Insight Assessment," or LCIA for short.[14] If the question is, "Can someone's leader character be assessed in a way that can lead to subsequent action and improvement?" the answer, again, is an emphatic "yes."

First, we should stress that there is no objective external standard for leader character – no particular profile that you need to conform to. It is not like a high-jump competition, in which you know you have to clear a bar that has been set at a certain height. Rather, developing leader character is a lifelong journey, which is deeply personal and unique. The LCIA is a tool that can help you on that journey.

Of course, there are many other tools out there that purport to do something similar. For example, there are personality-inventory tools, such as the Myers-Briggs Type Indicator© – that attempt to categorize people within certain personality types. Typically, these tools wind up suggesting that you "put your strengths to work," and compensate for your weaknesses by leveraging the skills of others.

The LCIA takes a more personal approach. It helps people self-assess their leader character, and – in its "360" version – provides other perspectives that may be helpful. Both are important. There is an inner world that we feel/believe, which can be summarized as our intent. There is also an outer world that others experience: our actual behaviors. Much can be explained by the fact that we judge ourselves by our intention, but we judge others by their behaviors. There are often significant gaps between the two.

The LCIA-360 draws on the well-established 360-degree review model, whereby organizational leaders, colleagues, and direct/indirect reports rate your performance along a number of dimensions, but it brings that technology to bear specifically on the topic of leadership.[15] Simply stated, your "reviewers" are asked to rate you according to each of 61 sets of behaviors, which collectively comprise the dimensions and elements of Figure 2.1. If you get a "1," that means that the reviewer thinks that you are very unlikely to engage in a given behavior. If you get a "5," you are very likely to act in this way.

Table 2.3 Sample rated characteristics from the LCIA

Item	Dimension	Element
Controls strong emotions like anger or disappointment, especially in difficult situations	Temperance	Self-controlled
Takes advantage of any opportunity to learn from someone else	Humility	Continuous learner
Recognizes the need for and takes prompt action, without being asked to do so	Drive	Demonstrates initiative
Demonstrates the ability to generate original and innovative ideas, products, and approaches	Transcendence	Creative
Is sensitive and accommodating to the circumstances of others in order to allow them to perform at their best	Humanity	Compassionate
Actively seeks to resolve differences amicably	Collaboration	Collegial

Table 2.3 presents a half-dozen examples of the behaviors comprised by the LCIA-360, with the associated dimensions and illustrative elements (which the reviewer would not see) included.

The LCIA-360, like the more traditional 360 review, provides the subject of the review with four kinds of information:

- Some general commentary on the nature of leadership character, including the components and elements contained in Figure 2.1.
- Some observations about why character is essential for effective leadership and organizational performance.
- A character snapshot, which provides an overview of results along each character dimension, allowing for easy identification of specific strengths and weaknesses.
- A detailed character profile, which as its name implies provides detailed, charted results on each dimension and element, breaking responses into rating groups (i.e., leaders, colleagues, and direct/indirect reports), and also providing comments from reviewers and development advice and guides to additional resources.

Based on these bullet points alone, it is probably difficult to judge just how much impact an instrument like this can have. Almost nothing in our business careers prepares us for having, for example, our integrity assessed along five elements (consistent, principled, transparent, candid, authentic), and to have that assessment charted out in simple, graphic ways. At the risk of understatement, it can be gratifying, startling, or even shocking to learn how your colleagues and your direct reports rate you on an element like authenticity.

As you read our expanded descriptions of the eleven dimensions of leader character that begin in the chapters following the next one, remember that they can serve as helpful background in your effort to understand, and develop, your leader character.

In Summary: Six Key Points

As you review the stories and arguments contained in Chapters 4 through 14 – one for each of our eleven dimensions – there are a half-dozen key points to keep in mind about the nature of character:

- Although the definitions of what we call "dimensions" of leadership character can certainly vary from context to context, the concepts at the heart of those ideas can be considered universal. They have been supported across cultures, geographies, and time.
- Each dimension is composed of several defining character elements. These elements are intended to be illustrative of the dimension, and we are confident that others will add to these lists over time. Each of these elements has an impact on the strength of the character dimension.
- All dimensions and elements of character matter, and therefore it is important to understand both your strengths and developmental areas. In other words, it is important to your personal effectiveness as a leader to have the capacity to exercise all dimensions of character.
- The dimensions are interdependent. They work together to determine the overall strength of our character.
- Judgment plays a central role in character, controlling when and how we choose to behave. But the ability and the stimulus to make certain judgments reside in the other dimensions – for example, a person who lacks humanity will not make an excellent judgment call in a situation in which humanity has to be considered.
- Character is developed over a lifetime. It is a journey, rather than a destination. Every situation presents a different experience and opportunity to exercise, apply, and develop character.

Notes

1 See the TD Bank profile at www.wikinvest.com/stock/Toronto-Dominion_ Bank-(TE:TD).
2 From "TD Bank: A safe bet among financials?" *Minyanville*, 02.15.12, online at www.minyanville.com/businessmarkets/articles/bank-share-price-dividends-sub-prime/2/15/2012/id/39411.
3 The quote is from one of Clark's speeches. See "Toronto-Dominion Prepares for CEO transition," *New York Times*, 03.29.12, online at http://dealbook.nytimes.com/2012/03/29/toronto-dominion-prepares-for-c-e-o-transition/?_php=true&_type=blogs&_r=0.

4 Also helpful was the relative lack of a housing bubble in Canada, which limited the overall exposure of Canada's banks. See "Toronto-Dominion Prepares for CEO transition," *New York Times*, 03.29.12, online at http://dealbook. nytimes.com/2012/03/29/toronto-dominion-prepares-for-c-e-o-transition/?_ php=true&_type=blogs&_r=0.

5 In the spirit of full disclosure, we should note that both Western University and the Ivey School of Business have ongoing relationships with TD Bank, especially in the realm of executive education. These relationships have given us good insight into the decision-making processes at TD Bank during Clark's tenure.

6 For the full text of the speech, see the 10.19.11 article in *The Globe and Mail*, "Read Ed Clark's speech," online at http://www.theglobeandmail.com/ report-on-business/read-ed-clarks-speech/article558081/?page=2. Clark underscored his remarks about the Tea Party and Occupy in an interview with a reporter the same night. See the 10.20.11 article, "Canada must tackle tough issues, bank CEO says," thestar.com, online at http://www.thestar. com/business/2011/10/20/canada_must_tackle_tough_issues_bank_ceo_ says.html.

7 See the 10.01.13 article, "World's safest banks, 2013," in *Global Finance*, online at https://www.gfmag.com/magazine/october-2013-1/worlds-safest-banks-2013.

8 Core motion and control technologies include electromechanical, hydraulic and pneumatic, fluid and gas handling, filtration, sealing and shielding, climate control, process control, and aerospace.

9 This case study is taken from a working paper – "Leadership virtues and character: A perspective in process" – authored by Mary Crossan, Daina Mazutis, Mark Reno, and Peter Rea. The three academic members of this team were fortunate to have Parker Hannifin's Peter Rea join us as an informed and impassioned collaborator.

10 It's instructive to compare this list with Aristotle's list of twelve virtues, as introduced in Chapter 1: courage, temperance, generosity, magnificence, magnanimity, right ambition, good temper, friendliness, truthfulness, wit, justice, and practical wisdom. Perhaps the most distinctive PH variant is "hope."

11 We should stress that this case study focuses on an internal initiative. It is instructive to compare this internal approach to the company's outward-facing statement of its values. See "Our values," including the downloadable summary statement, on PH's website at www.parker.com/.

12 Bardwick, Judith M., *One Foot Out the Door: How to Combat the Psychological Recession That's Alienating Employees and Hurting American Business* (New York, NY: AMACOM Books, 2007).

13 Parker Hannifin Internal Documents, "Winning with Integrity."

14 We have developed a leader character diagnostic – the Leader Character Insight Assessment – in both self-administered and 360-degree formats, in partnership with Sigma Assessment Systems Inc. based in London, Ontario, Canada.

15 Clearly, the traditional "360" touches on some of these same dimensions, but the LCIA-360 dives deep.

3   Character and Context

Let's begin this chapter on the water – specifically on a sailboat, by means of a story told by Peter Aceto, CEO of ING Direct, Canada.[1]

Aceto is known as a principled and authentic leader, who insists on transparency in his bank's business dealings – a stance which helps makes ING Direct one of Canada's most admired enterprises.[2] He is active in all kinds of social media, and – as our students at Ivey Business School learned recently – he is also a good storyteller.

After describing his bank's guiding principles and mission statement, Aceto made what seemed like an abrupt change of direction in his talk. He started talking about sailboats. "Most people think that a sailboat works because the wind blows," he began.[3] "It catches the boat's sails, and the boat moves through the water. Pretty simple, right?"

Actually, Aceto continued, that's not entirely true. There's something missing in that interaction between wind and boat. "If the wind just blew at a boat's sails," he said,

> "the boat would go wherever the wind happened to be blowing that day. Or maybe the boat would capsize, and sink. But sailboats are designed with another really important feature, called the keel, which hangs from the bottom of the boat below the water line. The wind blows against the sails, and the opposing force is the keel's resistance, under the water. That's what keeps the boat from tipping over, and what allows the boat to thrust forward in the direction that the captain wants to go."

Then Aceto drew an analogy between a sailboat and the bank he leads. "Our keel at ING Direct," he explained, "the force that keeps us going in the direction we want to go, and stops us from capsizing, are our mission and our principles."

What Aceto was describing that day was a context for judgment. The keel, in his metaphor, is what counterbalances strong – even dangerous – forces. It is judgment coming to bear. "We have a thousand employees in our organization," he continued. "At any point in the day, there are probably thirty meetings going on in which people are making important decisions – and I'm not there. So how do I know these decisions are being made right? Because of the principles and values of the organization.

"We all speak the same language at ING Direct. We all share the same vision. And we always remind ourselves to stay on course when we start veering off of it."

Report from Social Science: Beware of Situational Pressures!

Aceto's parable speaks explicitly to a complex group process of calibration, interpretation, and triangulation: It's the shared values and principles of the organization that help us keep each other on course. But beneath that group process of setting norms – we would argue – is a parallel individual process. Each person attending those thirty meetings brings an individual perspective to the table: a perspective that is shaped in part by the organizational context, and in part by his or her own character. In other words, it's the interplay of context and character that determines behavior in organizations. The organization's keel is its values and vision; an individual's keel is his or her character.

In subsequent chapters, we will take a deep dive into the eleven dimensions of leader character described previously. First, though, let's look at context, and see how it comes to bear on character and behavior.

Clearly, life in today's business world involves a lot of buffeting – perhaps more than ever before. Think of the forces that come to bear on enterprises today: competitive (someone invents a better mousetrap than yours), political (does the company overtly or covertly back a supportive candidate in the upcoming election?), economic (the currency keeps fluctuating), regulatory (the waste-disposal process that was legal yesterday is illegal today), technological (is your data base safe?), market-based (the price of fuel just spiked!), and so on. Add to that the constant pressure from the owners of the company – whether public or private – and you develop a picture of people under pressure.[4]

And these are only the external pressures to which people in business are subjected. Add to that the internal pressures of a workplace – whom do we welcome here, what behaviors do we tolerate, how do we deal with bad news, how does peer pressure come to bear, and so on – and the result can be overwhelming. Cultures can be healthy, like the one at ING Direct described by Peter Aceto, or they can be terribly unhealthy. Context can facilitate good decisions, or it can steer individuals away from quality decision-making.

In February 2008, Philip G. Zimbardo – professor emeritus of psychology at Stanford University, and former president of the American Psychological Association – gave a challenging TED talk. Entitled "The Psychology of Evil," it was based on his book *The Lucifer Effect*.[5] His basic premise was that the line between good and evil is not fixed, but permeable, and that "good" people can easily be persuaded to do bad things – and, conversely, that "bad" people can be helped to recover. His ideas emerged in part from the celebrated Stanford Prison Experiment, which he designed and led, and which assigned to student volunteers the roles of "prisoners" and "guards" in a simulated prison environment. The students were screened for any prior history of mental illness, emotional distress, or criminal records, and only those with spotless backgrounds – totally "normal" kids – were included. The experiment was part of a larger research program that focused on how atrocities like the Holocaust could be conceived and perpetrated. Were the Nazis monsters, or were they ordinary people under extraordinary pressures, who were ultimately corrupted by power? And if the latter were the case, could it happen anywhere?

As "Prison Superintendent" Zimbardo later wrote of that experiment, which was conducted in August 1971:

> Our planned two-week investigation into the psychology of prison life had to be ended prematurely after only six days because of what the situation was doing to the college students who participated. In only a few days, our guards became sadistic and our prisoners became depressed and showed signs of extreme stress.[6]

In his TED talk, Zimbardo focused on his work with soldiers accused of abusing prisoners at the Abu Ghraib prison in Iraq in 2003 during the second Gulf War. When reports of that abuse first began to surface, Zimbardo recalled, the Bush administration's first response was that the system was not at fault, but rather, that a few "bad apples" within the military were responsible. This response frames a "who" question: Who is responsible? Zimbardo suggested that a "what" question would be more appropriate: What was there about the circumstances in which these Army reservists found themselves that persuaded them to cross the line? Was it a case of a bad barrel, rather than a few bad apples within that barrel? Or was it a systemic problem – a manifestation of bad barrel makers at work?

Complicating and working against the "bad apple" explanation, at least in the Abu Ghraib context, was that the military police who were swept up in the abuse were Army reservists, rather than military professionals. In other words, they were more like ordinary civilians – more like "normal" kids; more like us – than we might want to believe. So yes, what they brought to that prison was important, but so was the system that created that context: one that aggressively devalued the individual, rewarded group conformity, and bestowed significant power with minimal oversight. The abuses at Abu Ghraib went on for three months, meaning – as Zimbardo put it – that nobody was minding the store.

As a result, rules got broken, and lines got crossed. "That line between good and evil is permeable," Zimbardo said. "Any of us can move across it … I argue that we all have the capacity for love and evil – to be Mother Theresa, to be Hitler or Saddam Hussein. It's the situation that brings that out."

Do we have a keel below us? Can we count on it to direct our judgment, and counter ill winds? And if we don't have it yet, can we find a way to put it in place? Our answer to that last question is yes. It's less about people being inherently "good" or "evil," and more about reinforcing your capacity for making good decisions by exercising judgment.

We have focused here on Philip Zimbardo's findings, but those findings confirmed work done by other researchers – including, for example, Stanley Milgram. Milgram's seminal studies, which began in the early 1960s, showed that seemingly "good" people would – under instructions from an authority figure – administer what they thought were extreme electrical shocks to other study participants who answered questions incorrectly.[7] In a less dramatic but equally compelling set of experiments, psychologist Solomon Asch demonstrated that people are so determined to "fit into" a group that they are willing to go along with a majority consensus – even though they know, for sure, that that consensus is incorrect.[8] We humans have a powerful, even irresistible, urge to conform.

Aiming for the Virtuous Mean

Many, perhaps most, of us are vulnerable to situational pressures. We are quick to abuse power – and each other – quick to conform, and, yes, sometimes, slow to stand on principle. Zimbardo did offer some hope, when he pointed to heroism as the "antidote to evil." And, he argued, the same situation that seduces some individuals into evil-doing can inspire others to become heroes – not "professional heroes" like Gandhi or Superman, but everyday heroes. As a practical first step, he called for classes for young people – classes that would teach them to begin to think of themselves as "heroes in waiting."

We applaud both the concept of the "hero in waiting" and Zimbardo's prescriptions for nurturing those heroes. It is strongly resonant with our own thinking, which – as noted – focuses primarily on people in business who are subjected to extraordinary pressures, both internal and external. So what is to be done in that context? How can heroes in waiting be nurtured in the workplace? Our prescription is distilled in Figure 3.1, below.

This figure captures our sense of how an individual can and should act in a complex, "pressurized" context. By now, you will not be surprised to learn that we believe that you can and should come to the table with leader character – the bottom triangle in Figure 3.1. Leader character is the antidote to situational evil – or less dramatically, the counterbalance to the seductive pressures that our work lives can impose upon us. Saying that "bad apples aren't the whole story" doesn't let us off the hook: We still need to avoid being one of those bad apples, and we need to consider when and how to change an organizational context that is eroding, rather than fostering, character. When and how do we make the transition from a hero

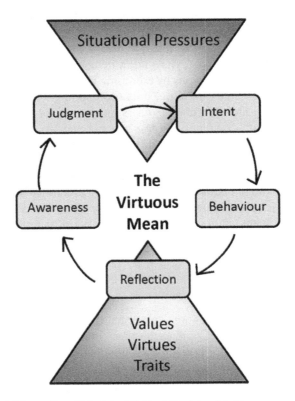

Figure 3.1 A Virtue-Based Model of Ethical Decision-Making

in waiting to a hero in action? When do we stop blaming the bad apple, or the bad barrel, and start taking responsibility as the barrel makers?

Yes, context affects individuals, for better or worse. But leader character affects context: It defines and makes possible the better barrel, if the leader accepts that challenge.

The material in the next eleven chapters focuses on that challenge, which – we argue – begins, ends, and often returns to reflection. Reflection shows up in a particular place in Figure 3.1 – mainly to keep that figure reasonably simple! – but you can imagine it showing up throughout the cycle depicted in the figure. We need to reflect not only in real time, under pressure in the marketplace, but also in more contemplative moments afterwards. Another word that might work here is mindfulness: We need to be mindful of what we're doing, and what we're becoming.

Moving clockwise "up" Figure 3.1 from the bottom, we arrive at awareness. A critical part of leadership character is being aware of our own blind spots, and working to overcome them. Equally, leader character is built upon our ability to assess a situation correctly, recognize the interests of the various stakeholders, and deal effectively with both their good and darker motives. Again, think of mindfulness: What are we noticing, and what are we choosing not to notice – and why?

In the language of psychology, we need to understand and counteract the cognitive biases that are at work in a given situation – the kinds of irrationalities that blur judgment and impede rational decision-making.[9]

Psychologists have identified literally dozens of such biases, which act upon us in subtle and sometimes pernicious ways. In one remarkable experiment, Paul Piff – a faculty member in the University of California (UC) at Irvine's Department of Psychology and Social Behavior – set up a rigged Monopoly game involving pairs of students.[10] The players were pitted against each other in a totally unfair contest – one in which one of the two players received far more money at the outset of the game, got more opportunities to move around the board, and earned more money whenever he or she passed Go.

The predestined winners and losers were chosen, in their presence, by a coin toss. They soon discovered how important that initial coin toss was: The disadvantaged players were inexorably ground down and defeated by the advantaged ones. No surprise there, of course: That's how the game was rigged to come out. But what was surprising were the different behaviors exhibited by the winners and losers (as recorded on hidden cameras). The winners moved their pieces around the board more noisily and aggressively, counted their money more ostentatiously, ate more pretzels from the single bowl on the table, and generally behaved more rudely toward their opponents.

Most surprising of all, at the end of the game, the winners tended to minimize the importance of their opening advantage – which in fact was all-important – and instead boasted about their Monopoly skills. In other words, the intoxicating effect of winning changed their behavior and clouded their judgment. Discouraging, right? We are manipulated by our contexts in ways that make us behave badly, we know we are being manipulated, and yet, we still go ahead and act badly.

In other experiments, Piff and his colleagues showed that drivers of expensive cars were five times less likely to stop for pedestrians in crosswalks (as required by California law) than were drivers of less expensive cars. This is even more discouraging: When we're behind the wheel of a fancy car, our empathy for the people around us is diminished. Rich people, Piff asserts, are less empathetic than poor people. But – and this is the crucial point – this has less to do with any innate qualities of meanness or generosity, and more to do with the context of decision-making.

But Piff also offered some reassurance: His research suggests that even small psychological interventions can change behavior for the better, and restore impulses of egalitarianism and empathy. In one experiment, he had their subjects watch a 46-second-long video about childhood poverty. An hour after watching the video, rich and poor subjects were equally likely to offer help to a stranger in distress whom they unexpectedly encountered in the lab. Again, we are exquisitely responsive to changes in context – and that responsiveness can make us "better" people or "worse" people, at least temporarily.

We are all susceptible to cognitive biases, which brings us back to the importance of reflection. When we are confronted with a circumstance that contradicts one of our biases, that discrepancy creates a tension that we are driven to resolve. Why? It appears that we are not comfortable living with the knowledge that the lens through which we see the world may be distorted. We want to find a new way of understanding things, which we achieve through critical reflection.

In other words, reflection leads to enhanced awareness, which in turn allows us to bring judgment to bear on the situational pressures that we face in the workplace (again, moving clockwise "up" Figure 3.1). Hopefully, we bring our hard-won judgment to bear on the workplace, where – again – we are sure to be subjected to a contextual buffeting.

Out the other side of that contextual buffeting, we emerge with intent, which either does or doesn't determine our behavior. In other words, gaps tend to open up, at this point in the cycle: We may intend to do the right thing, but still wind up behaving badly. Here again, the dimensions of leader character may prove helpful in closing gaps. Drive can give us the tenacity to stay on track. Courage can keep us focused on excellence.

We should underscore, at this point, that the cycle depicted in Figure 3.1 captures both Abu Ghraib and the antidote to Abu Ghraib. Yes, we can be worn down, even corrupted, by context. But the example that we set as "everyday heroes" (to draw again on Zimbardo's concept) can also help fix that context. This might be called the "contagion effect" of leader character. Think of Ed Clark's example, cited in Chapter 2. Think of the dramatic scene in the 1960 version of the movie *Spartacus*, in which the Roman general Crassus (played by Sir Laurence Olivier) demands that a group of rebellious slaves who have been defeated in battle – and who now sit sullenly on the ground, chained together – avoid crucifixion by turning over the one called Spartacus. The real Spartacus (Kirk Douglas) wearily climbs to his feet, and announces that he is Spartacus – and one by one, all of his fellow slaves do the same.[11] The cry rings across the dusty valley: "I am Spartacus!"

No, life is not the movies, but there are reasons why we humans respond to moments like this. Character can be contagious. Witnessing strength of character can activate within each of us latent character, by reminding us that character matters, and perhaps connecting us to a time and place where we exercised that same character dimension. Or – at the very least – a display of strength of character can reassure us that even in a world filled with challenge, leader character can prevail.

The end result of all this good and hard work is striving for the "virtuous mean," shown at the center of Figure 3.1. We borrow the term directly from Aristotle, who argued that, for example, the virtue of courage was the virtuous mean between the excesses of rashness, on the one hand, and cowardice on the other. Aristotle was careful to point out that the "mean" was in no way a mathematical concept. In other words, finding the midpoint between two extremes is not likely to be an ideal solution.

So the virtuous mean is, most narrowly, a state in which your dimensions of leader character are strong and in balance. Less narrowly, it is a state of both equilibrium and openness to change. When you strive for the virtuous mean, you retain the capacity to accumulate experiences that deepen character strengths, while not taking on board experiences that undercut those strengths. Your leader character buffers you against the negative performance of those around you.[12] And if you're fortunate enough to work at a place like ING Direct – as described by Peter Aceto – your leader character will be reinforced by the positive behavior of your peers.

The Solution Involves More Than Just "Diversity"

At this point, let's take what might seem to be a slight detour. We are arguing that character is the antidote to challenging contexts. Many observers have offered an alternative prescription: diversity. Diversity is a complicated concept which may have any number of facets: racial, gender-based, cognitive, economic, experience-based, cultural, or whatever. At the risk of oversimplification, the theory is that homogeneous organizations are more inclined to go off the rails than heterogeneous ones, because they may fall victim to "groupthink," and to the kinds of cognitive biases described above. Conversely, heterogeneous organizations – the theory goes – escape this trap.

And up to a point, that's right: A broader base of perspectives – for example, the presence of a devil's advocate, either inside oneself or in the midst of a group – certainly does help an organization avoid certain kinds of traps and dead ends. The problem is that the lens of diversity is a poor substitute, at best, for the lens of character.

Sometimes we discover diversity and character through the same act of reflection. D. J. DePree, the founder and longtime leader of the Herman Miller furniture company, used to tell a story about an episode in 1927 that changed his life.[13] He got word that one of the millwrights who worked for him had died, so he went to the widow's house to pay his respects. He wasn't much surprised to see that the furniture and woodwork in the house was of the highest quality; after all, the late millwright was an expert woodworker. What did surprise him was when the widow pulled out a sheaf of papers, which turned out to be poems – good poems – that her late husband had written. As DePree later recalled:

> This was quite impressive. You see, I had just known him as a mechanic who kept the machines going. It amazed me that the man could write poetry like this. Then a few days later I attended his funeral, and the minister read some of that poetry […] I'd been brought up by a

couple of people who were very tough on labor. They thought that was the way to handle it. But by the time I got back to the front porch of my house on Pine Street, I had come to a conclusion that we were all extraordinary.

DePree's son Max – who succeeded his father as head of Herman Miller – recounted that story in his extraordinary little book called *Leadership is an Art*. "Was he a poet who did millwright's work," DePree asked rhetorically, "or was he a millwright who wrote poetry?"[14]

The shop floor was far more diverse than D. J. DePree knew. But DePree's real revelation that day – the fruits of his reflection – was that the millwright had dimensions of character that had previously been hidden. He was compelled to change lenses – overcome his biases – and find a new way of seeing the world. For DePree, this began a lifelong search for character in the people around him – a search for people from whom he could learn.

Diversity is surface; character is substance. Imagine a workplace in which people looked past the surface and connected with the character below the surface. Imagine how much more effectively people connected by character could resist the pressures of the workplace, and how much the quality of their judgment and decision-making would improve.

Again, quoting Peter Aceto on his ING Direct colleagues: "We all share the same vision. And we always remind ourselves to stay on course when we start veering off of it."

Who am I Becoming?

So our sideways glance at diversity was not so much of a detour after all, because it led us back to a core focus of this chapter: reflection.

Reflection begins with a somewhat obvious question: "Who am I?" We argue that reflection needs to continue on to a second question: "As I live my busy life, with all its swirling and contradictory pressures, who am I becoming?"

When we willingly accept complacency in the workplace, when we participate in unnecessary gossip, when we do not stand up for what we know to be right, when we act – or fail to act – out of fear, when we boast about something to mask our lack of confidence: These are the times when we fail to reflect on who we are becoming. And in the process, we give in to context, and sell ourselves short.

Context can challenge and change character, for better or worse. In a recent opinion piece in *Bloomberg View*, internet columnist Michael Lewis talked about the resurgent wave of ambitious young people signing up with Wall Street:

> The question I've always had about this army of young people with seemingly endless career options who wind up in finance is: What happens next to them?

The intense pressure to conform, to not make waves, has got to be the most depressing part of all, for a genuinely ambitious young person. It's pretty clear that the government lacks the power to force serious change upon the financial sector. There's a big role for Silicon Valley-style scorched-earth entrepreneurship on Wall Street right now, and the people most likely to innovate are newcomers to the industry who have no real stake in the parts of it that need scorching.

As a new employee on Wall Street you might think this has nothing to do with you. You would be wrong. Your new environment's resistance to market forces, and to the possibility of doing things differently and more efficiently, will soon become your own. When you start your career you might think you are setting out to change the world, but the world is far more likely to change you.

So watch yourself, because no one else will.[15]

Watch yourself, because no one else will. It was a low-level private named Joe Darby who stopped the abuse at Abu Ghraib. Was it an easy choice? Almost certainly not. Did it have negative consequences? Absolutely! For the first six months after Darby returned to the U.S., he and his wife were accompanied by six armed soldiers everywhere they went – underscoring the seriousness with which the Army took the death threats the Darbys were receiving.[16] The Darbys were advised by the military that they were no longer safe in their hometown of Cumberland, Maryland, and they ultimately had to start their lives over in a new city. Would he do it again? "Definitely," Darby told an interviewer. "They broke the law, and they had to be punished."

Context can challenge character, but it can also reinforce it.

As you read the definitions and stories in the next eleven chapters, think about them as components of leadership character that you have to balance within yourself – the virtuous mean – and also as the person you are becoming, and whom you are proud to take out into the marketplace.

Notes

1 ING Direct is one of the world's largest banking, financial services, and insurance conglomerates.
2 See the complimentary write-up of Aceto in "The bank executive they call 'the social media CEO'," in the 01.30.13 edition of *Forbes*, online at http://www.forbes.com/sites/carminegallo/2013/01/30/a-bank-executive-they-call-the-social-media-ceo/.
3 From a talk that Aceto gave at the Ivey Business School. See the full clip at https://www.youtube.com/watch?v=3C2N4vUqAV8.
4 In their interesting article on "Runaway Capitalism," Christopher Meyer and Julia Kirby compare the twin pressures of competition and return on equity to the peacock's tail: an evolutionary aberration that threatens the owner of that tail. See the January-February 2012 issue of the *Harvard Business Review*.

5 For more on Zimbardo, see his website: www.zimbardo.com. To watch a video of his TED talk, see http://www.ted.com/talks/philip_zimbardo_on_the_psychology_of_evil?language=en. As noted, the talk was based on his compelling book, *The Lucifer Effect* (Random House, 2008).

6 The simulation study is described in "Stanford Prison Experiment," on Zimbardo's website (http://www.prisonexp.org/) devoted to that study.

7 See, for example, *About Education*'s "The Milgram Obedience Experiment," online at http://psychology.about.com/od/historyofpsychology/a/milgram.htm.

8 There is a good 08.28.13 write-up by Nicole Plumridge of Asch's conformity experiments on psychminds.com, online at http://psychminds.com/solomon-aschs-experiment-conformity/.

9 For a more complete list – from which the material in this section is derived – see the relevant section in *Strategic Analysis and Action*, by Crossan, M., Fry, J., Killing, P., and Rouse, M., (Prentice-Hall, 2009).

10 See Piff's description of the experiment, and his interpretation of its significance, in a video of his October 2013 TED talk, online at https://www.ted.com/talks/paul_piff_does_money_make_you_mean#t-27421.

11 It's worth a revisit: https://www.youtube.com/watch?v=FKCmyiljKo0.

12 See the article by Crossan, M., Mazutis, D., and Seijts, G., "In Search of Virtue," *Journal of Business Ethics*, April 2013, online at http://link.springer.com/article/10.1007%2Fs10551-013-1680-8#page-1.

13 DePree was a giant in twentieth-century furniture design. See his *New York Times* obituary at http://www.nytimes.com/1990/12/13/obituaries/d-j-depree-who-broke-ground-in-furniture-design-is-dead-at-99.html.

14 This story is a short chapter in Max DePree's book, *Leadership is an Art* (Crown Business, 2004), and is also recounted by D. J. DePree in a 1986 interview (https://www.youtube.com/watch?v=jsTUDHGlvzg).

15 See more of Michael Lewis's "Occupational Hazards of Working on Wall Street" (2014) at http://www.bloombergview.com/articles/2014-09-24/occupational-hazards-of-working-on-wall-street.

16 See the chilling *60 Minutes* interview with Darby at http://www.cbsnews.com/news/exposing-the-truth-of-abu-ghraib/.

4 Drive

You will recall from Chapter 1 that our sustained exploration of leader character over the past decade or so – work that was advanced in large part through the contributions of leaders from the public, private, and not-for-profit sectors – led us to identify eleven dimensions of leader character. Each of those dimensions, in turn, is composed of several character elements that are illustrative of the particular dimension. Over the next eleven chapters, we will look at those eleven dimensions, and explore how the elements within them help shape each dimension. We will also explore how the dimensions interact with others to determine the quality of decision-making and action.

Our framework – which you've already encountered in Chapter 1 – is summarized in Figure 4.1, below.

Let's begin with drive: the highlighted box in the upper right-hand corner of Figure 4.1. What does drive consist of? How do the character elements of drive work together to support drive? How does drive complement the other ten dimensions? What happens when you have drive but you are unable to call upon the other dimensions?

If you have drive, you strive for excellence. You have a strong desire to succeed, you tackle problems with a sense of urgency, and you approach challenges with energy and passion.

Having drive is fundamentally different from "being driven." Drive arises from an internal, positive wellspring of energy that can be harnessed and put to good use. For example, specific personal needs fuel drive, providing purpose and direction.[1] But drive becomes dysfunctional when we allow other people or things to define our success. Being driven is the equivalent of allowing someone else, or something else, to drive us.

For example – returning for a moment to banking and the financial crisis discussed in earlier chapters – some individuals became addicted to money, power, and status. Seth Freedman worked as a stockbroker in London between 1999 and 2005. "The market felt like the most natural of environments in which to unleash my inner beast," he wrote in his book, *Binge Trading*. "Your personality begins to be molded around the macho image you portray during trading sessions."[2]

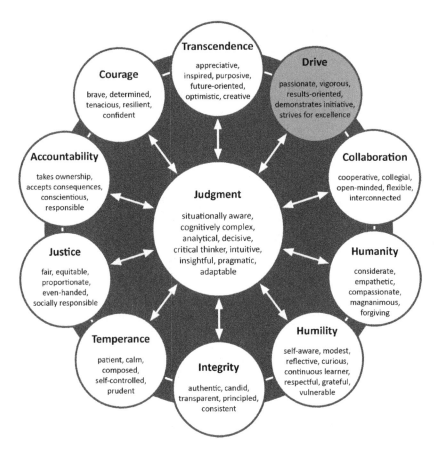

Figure 4.1 Character Dimensions and Associated Elements

There are many things – such as addictions; an insatiable or overweening need for praise, belonging, and affiliation; or hyper-competitiveness – that hijack us in such a way that we become driven. Seth Freedman ultimately left his industry, swapping expensive suits and ties for army boots and an M16; others never gain control over their impulses toward excess. As a result, they lose touch with reality, and begin to act with little or no regard toward the consequences of their actions for large numbers of the stakeholders that they might be expected to serve.

Being driven means that someone or something is pushing you toward the edge, or that your inner demons have gained control of you. Think, for example, of Michael Corleone's steady decline in *The Godfather* series, as he relentlessly pursued power to protect and enrich his family. Being driven can result in damage to personal relationships, and even health problems – anxiety, sleeplessness, depression, and so on. In short: Drive is good; being driven is (generally) bad.

One individual who has demonstrated drive in a business leadership position is Jack Ma Yun, executive chairman of Alibaba. The e-commerce giant is celebrated today as China's biggest company.[3] But it was no easy ride to the top. Back toward the end of the twentieth century, Ma – an English teacher from Hangzou who had tried and failed to start a Chinese version of the Yellow Pages, and subsequently was a government-employed tour guide – became convinced that the internet would "level the playing field," and enable small companies to compete successfully in a business-to-business marketplace.[4]

In 1999, along with seventeen like-minded colleagues, he founded web-based Alibaba to test that vision.[5] In subsequent years, Ma's overtures to potential backers in Silicon Valley were rejected more than 30 times, until he finally secured a billion-dollar investment from Yahoo in 2005.[6] "Once you meet an entrepreneur like Jack Ma," Yahoo's Jerry Yang said, "you just want to make sure you bet on him. It's not a hard decision."[7] Drive, no doubt, played a major role in Yang's assessment of Ma.

When Alibaba held its initial U.S. public offering in September 2014, it raised an astonishing $25 billion – the biggest IPO ever, anywhere. And for good reason: In 2013, two of the company's websites registered a combined $240 billion (with a "b") in sales: twice Amazon's volume, and three times that of eBay. More than 60 percent of the packages delivered in China today originate on one of Alibaba's websites.[8]

As Ma recently confessed to an audience in Hong Kong, he never thought he would be the head of one of the world's most dynamic companies – nor did he think it would be so difficult to earn that distinction. It was drive that helped Ma overcome his obstacles, and reach the top. It was also drive – that internal wellspring of positive energy – that helped Ma continue to expand his vision, year by year, even as his original dreams were being realized. Keeping in mind the concept of drive, consider these quotes from Ma:

- Today is cruel. Tomorrow is crueler. And the day after tomorrow is beautiful.[9]
- If you don't give up, you still have a chance.
- We will make it because we are young and we will never, never give up.
- If we go to work at 8 a.m. and go home at 5 p.m., this is not a high-tech company and Alibaba will never be successful. If we have that kind of 8-to-5 spirit, then we should just go and do something else.
- Alibaba is not just a job. It's a dream. It's a cause.
- In carrying out e-commerce, the most important thing is to keep doing what you are doing right now with passion, to keep it up.

Let's look at another example of drive, and consider what these examples – Jack Ma and Steve Jobs – teach us.

Drive and Being Driven: Steve Jobs

Apple Computer was launched on April Fool's day, 1976, with capital that had been raised by the company's two founders. Steve Wozniak had sold his HP 65 calculator, and Steve Jobs had unloaded his rundown VW bus, for a total of $1,300 – enough to enable them to begin assembling Apple I circuit boards in the Jobs family garage.[10]

In January 2015, Apple announced financial results for the first quarter of its fiscal year, which ended in December 2014. The company posted quarterly revenues of $74.6 billion, and quarterly net profits of $18 billion, with margins of just under 40 percent – all-time records for the company. The company had expected to sell some 65 million iPhones in the quarter; it actually wound up selling 74.5 million units. International sales accounted for 60 percent of the quarter's revenue. European sales were up 20 percent, and sales in China increased a whopping 70 percent.[11]

Much of the story of those intervening four decades revolved around the presence – and sometimes the absence – of a single compelling, charismatic figure: Steve Jobs. When he died in 2011, he was compared to Edison and Einstein. *Wired* magazine editorialized that heaven had received a "major upgrade" with Jobs's ascension to technological sainthood. At the heart of Jobs's contribution was his drive, which fueled his relentless insistence that his company retain control of all aspects of its products: software, hardware, and – eventually – its retail outlets. Vertical integration in the computer industry was (and is) a controversial stance: Many technophiles resent Apple's closed systems and the lack of competition that results. On the other hand, the ever-increasing line of Apple products – computers, phones, MP3 players, tablets, and watches – all work together seamlessly. They also share a highly polished industrial aesthetic, looking and feeling special. By single-mindedly emphasizing both form and function, and mostly ignoring his critics, Jobs effected revolutions in multiple industries.[12]

Jobs was also a ferocious competitor, who didn't hesitate to brutalize his employees to achieve his ends. He was lavish in his praise and harsh in his criticisms – sometimes capriciously – using every technique imaginable to push his people to higher heights. Why? Knowing in 2011 that he was dying of cancer, Jobs sat for extensive interviews with Walter Isaacson, his authorized biographer, and talked candidly about what made him tick:

> I don't think I run roughshod over people, but if something sucks, I tell people to their face. It's my job to be honest. I know what I'm talking about, and I usually turn out to be right. That's the culture I tried to create. We are brutally honest with each other, and anyone can tell me they think I am full of shit and I can tell them the same. And we've had some rip-roaring arguments, where we are yelling at each other, and it's some of the best times I've ever had ...

What drove me? I think most creative people want to express appreciation for being able to take advantage of the work that's been done by others before us… We try to use the talents we have to express our deep feelings, to show our appreciation of all the contributions that came before us, and to add something to that flow. That's what has driven me.[13]

So Steve Jobs emerges as someone who both had drive – in fact, astounding drive, and a thoroughgoing personal commitment to "excellence" at least as he chose to define it – and also was driven by the urge to contribute to the creative flow of humanity in an intensely competitive industry. He trod the line between inspiration and abuse, which certainly undercut his effectiveness at times. Many who worked for him over the years would say he stepped over that line repeatedly, and unnecessarily – but it is hard to argue with his bottom-line results.

Character Elements: What Goes into "Drive"?

Looking back to Figure 4.1, you can see that there are five character elements that illustrate, and combine to foster, drive. When you have drive, you are:

Passionate: You demonstrate both enthusiasm and conviction in your approach to work.

In our work with business leaders – and certainly with people several rungs down on the organizational ladder – this particular character element can be problematic. People sometimes confess to us that they don't feel passionate about what they're doing. So if they aren't passionate, are they not leadership material?

There are several responses. One is purely semantic: You are "passionate" about different things in different ways. You probably don't feel the same way about a great day at the office as you do about, for example, a fine wine, your life partner, or the best achievement in sports you ever had. And that's fine. Sometimes swapping in another word helps. In your professional life, do you think a lot about excellence? Do you know what it looks like, and when you've attained it? Do you know what excellence looks like in some other realm, and are you determined to "import" that standard into your current workplace? Are other people willing to buy into that definition of excellence? If you can answer "yes" to these kinds of questions, you easily pass the passion test.

A second response: Depending on where you are in your career, you may still be trying to find or grow into your passion. Over time we gravitate toward the things that inspire us, and distance ourselves from things that undercut our enthusiasm. We move away from leaders who can't create a context for passion.

This brings us to a third answer, which is less benign. People without passion or purpose are sometimes envious of those who possess these attributes – and they consciously or unconsciously set out to whittle away at individuals who express enthusiasm. If you are surrounded by people who are content to fail the passion test, you need to change something.

Vigorous: You bring a sustained level of energy and vitality to work. There is a physicality to leadership, in most cases, that requires an ongoing investment in one's physical health.

Yvonne Camus is a former H. J. Heinz executive vice president who participated in the 2000 Eco-Challenge Adventure Race in Borneo: a grueling 500-kilometer race through the jungle that had to be completed within twelve days.[14] Her four-person team was the first team of rookies to complete the race, despite the broken wrist suffered by Camus – among other mishaps and setbacks. One measure of the stress imposed by the Eco-Challenge: A competing team of U.S. Navy SEALS failed to finish the race.

One of the surprises for Camus in that experience was the negative impact that physical stress – sleep deprivation, extended physical exertion, reduced rations of food and water – had on her. Her ability to take in new information, and learn in real time, was impaired. "If your body and mind can't thrive," she explained in an interview, "the learning component shuts down, and you revert to the known processes that have been engrained in you. You have to set yourself up, physically and health-wise, to be capable of learning."[15]

And since leadership is based on continuous learning – as well as physical exertion – vigor is key.

Results-oriented: You pursue planned commitments and outcomes with a sense of urgency.

This is the essence of the Steve Jobs story. He constantly badgered his troops to do more, better, faster. He was especially disciplined in crisis situations. After being run out of the company in 1985, he was brought back by Apple's board of directors in 1997. In that fiscal year, the company lost $1.04 billion. Jobs – who now seemed determined to be a "real" CEO, rather than just a terrifying genius – laid off three thousand people, dramatically cut the company's product line back to four core products, and moved talented engineers out of anemic product areas and to refocus them on technologies of the future.

The result? In fiscal year 1998, the first full year after the staggering billion-dollar loss, the company made a profit of $309 million. And with the exception of 2001, when Apple lost $25 million, it has made money ever since.[16]

A more sympathetic biography of Steve Jobs describes the evolution of this iconic business leader from raw drive in his early years to quite polished and multi-faceted executive in the last few years prior to his untimely death.[17] It clearly presents the development of at least some of the dimensions of character as an evolutionary process – one that we will describe in subsequent chapters.

Willing to demonstrate initiative: You grasp the need for prompt action, and act without being asked to do so.

The former prime minister of Canada, Paul Martin, recently was asked when he first realized that he was a leader, and what particular gift he had that propelled him into a leadership position. He seemed puzzled by the question:

> I never woke up and said, "I must become a leader." … That is not the way I believe things occur. As you grow up, there are certain things you want to see happen. What has been a consistent theme throughout my life is that I wanted to get things done – and, essentially, the only way I could do it was to take the initiative, but it never crossed my mind that this was leadership. The question was more, "How do I accomplish what I want to do?"[18]

Martin went on to explain that whenever he wanted to get something done, the first thing he did was to gather together a like-minded group of people and push in that direction. "For example," he said, "when I was a kid, and I wanted to play baseball in the spring, I was always the guy who would call a bunch of friends and form a team." He joked that when it came to baseball, he wasn't very good – and that if he had waited for someone else to call him up to play, he would have waited a very long time.

One suspects that Martin could have pointed to any number of instances, from his childhood through his distinguished political career, in which he took the initiative: organized the team, and made things happen.

Inclined to strive for excellence: You hold yourself and others to high standards of performance.

This is one kind of challenge when you're on a winning team like Alibaba or Apple. It's a wholly different kind of challenge when your team loses, and loses, and loses again, year after year. That's the circumstance in which Ernie Banks – shortstop and first baseman for the Chicago Cubs from 1953 through 1971 – found himself.

The Cubbies were hapless throughout most of those years – a perennially terrible team – but "Mr. Cub" nevertheless held himself to the highest of standards.[19] He won the National League's Most Valuable Player Award two years in a row (1958 and 1959). He was a National League All-Star for eleven seasons, and played in a total of fourteen All-Star games. He hit 512 home runs, which tied him for ninth on the all-time list at the time of his retirement. In addition to his own high standards, he felt significant pressure to do his race proud. While some African-American activists urged Banks to parlay his celebrity into political influence, other prominent blacks – Nat King Cole, Lionel Hampton, Eartha Kitt, and Pearl Bailey among them – advised him to keep leading by example. "Their message to those of us in baseball," he later told an oral historian, "was to keep playing baseball. People are watching you, [so] just keep playing, keep hitting the ball."[20]

After his playing career ended, he coached, founded a charitable organization, became the first African-American head of a Ford Motor Company dealership, and made an unsuccessful run for public office in Chicago in the early '70s. "Someone asked [Mayor Richard J. Daley] where that baseball player was going to finish in the race for the 8th Ward," Banks later recalled. "He said somewhere out in left field. That is where I finished."[21]

The courage to win, the courage to risk losing, and the courage to strive for excellence in contexts where it's a scarce resource: These originate in drive.

These five character elements work together to support drive. Vigor and passion are linked, since passion yields energy and vitality. Simultaneously, vitality provides important fuel to develop passion. Demonstrating initiative takes energy, and is often a by-product of passion. Striving for excellence and result-orientation are also closely aligned, as those who strive for excellence do so in pursuit of something that in a business context – for example – would be tied to results.

Drive Complementing Other Dimensions

Throughout this book, we will make a point of looking at how each dimension complements or supports most or all of the others. Figure 4.1 could more accurately be drawn with arrows connecting most of our eleven leader character dimensions with each other. In the interest of graphic simplicity, we will leave it to you to overlay those additional arrows, as you read the observations that follow.

The physical and emotional vitality that are the essence of drive play a critical role in supporting all of the dimensions. For example, you can imagine the courage you may want to exhibit, but if you don't have the vigor to exercise it, courage will not be realized. The self-regulation of temperance can become very difficult to exercise if not coupled with the passion and striving for excellence that come from drive. And aspects of transcendence – creative, purposive, and future-oriented – can never be fully realized without drive.

Drive in the Absence of Other Dimensions

As we ask ourselves how a given dimension of leader character complements the other ten, we should also ask whether that dimension can stand alone. Again, we will ask this question in each of the following ten chapters.

Drive without other dimensions can lead to aimless and manic activity. At its worst, it can be undirected, unfocused energy that feeds on itself, and requires additional physical and emotional investment to sustain it.

If we have drive without integrity, we can often find ourselves moving down a path that does not align with our core values, and alienates people as a result of poor interpersonal relationships.

High drive combined with a lack of humanity can prevent us from behaving personably or with a lack of compassion. In an organizational sense, we may then be willing to pursue our goals at any cost, without considering the implications on our ability to act with empathy.

Individuals who have high levels of drive may give short shrift to collaboration. They may simply take over projects or deliverables because they want to "get things done ... now." But this is perilous. Without collaboration we are unable to build humanity, and often take on more than we can handle.

If individuals demonstrate high drive but lack a sense of justice, they may behave inequitably toward others in order to achieve individual or organizational goals. Followership may be sacrificed. Resentment – or worse – may result.

Like collaboration, temperance may be imperiled in individuals with high drive. They may take on more than a "fair" or healthy amount of work, and, as a result, may quickly lose patience with others and be unwilling to see other perspectives.

And finally, humility: In high-drive individuals, humility is critically important to understanding our leadership character and weaknesses or strengths in the other dimensions. Self-reflection and awareness help to keep our drive in check. Without humility, high-drive individuals may not see the error in their processes, to the point where it becomes mentally damaging, and could lead to excessive or very low courage.

A Closing Thought from Dr. Seuss

We began this chapter by distinguishing between "drive" (generally positive) and "being driven" (often not so positive). We want to end this chapter on a positive note, which is provided to us by children's book author Theodor Geisel, more commonly known as Dr. Seuss. Here's a quote from *Oh, The Places You'll Go!*, which nicely captures the essence of drive in balance:

You have brains in your head.
You have feet in your shoes.
You can steer yourself any direction you choose.
You're on your own. And you know what you know.
And YOU are the one who'll decide where to go.[22]

And here's a second quote from the same source, which adds a little extra spice:

> You won't lag behind, because you'll have the speed.
> You'll pass the whole gang and you'll soon take the lead.
> Wherever you fly, you'll be best of the best.
> Wherever you go, you will top all the rest.
> Except when you don't.
> Because, sometimes, you won't.

We are confident that all of our drive-endowed cast of characters in this chapter – from Jack Ma to Steve Jobs to Paul Martin to Ernie Banks to Yvonne Camus – could identify with both the optimism at the opening of that stanza and the cold splash of reality at its end.

Questions to Contemplate

1. Do you have drive (an internal wellspring of energy to achieve excellence), or are you driven by external forces?
2. Do you demonstrate passion, vigor, results-orientation, striving for excellence, and initiative in both your day-to-day behaviors as a leader, and in the longer-term decisions and actions you take?
3. Is your drive controlled and exercised with good judgment, so that it does not overwhelm other important dimensions of character, such as collaboration, humanity, humility, justice, and temperance?

Books and Articles to Read

The Only Way to Win: How Building Character Drives Higher Achievement and Greater Fulfillment in Business and Life Jim Loehr (Hyperion, 2012)

Better Under Pressure: How Great Leaders Bring Out the Best in Themselves and Others Justin Menkes (Harvard Business Press, 2011)

Leadership and the Art of Struggle: How Great Leaders Grow Through Challenge and Adversity Steven Snyder (Berrett-Koehler Publishers, 2013)

Steve Jobs Walter Isaacson (Simon & Schuster, 2011)

Becoming Steve Jobs: the evolution of a reckless upstart into a visionary leader Brent Schlender and Rick Tetzeli (Crown Business, 2015)

Drive: The Surprising Truth About What Motivates Us Daniel Pink (Penguin Group: New York, 2011)

"Primal Leadership: The Hidden Driver of Great Performance" Daniel Goleman, Richard Boyatzis, and Annie McKee (*Harvard Business Review*, December 2001)

Videos to Watch

"Drive: The Surprising Truth About What Motivates Us" RSA Animate ft. Daniel Pink (YouTube, 2010)

Carol Dweck: "Growth Mindsets and Motivation" The NCEA (YouTube, 2009)

"The power of believing that you can improve" TEDx Talk by Carol Dweck (YouTube, 2014)

"Success, failure and the drive to keep creating" TED Talk by Elizabeth Gilbert (YouTube, 2014)

Notes

1 See Locke, E. A. and Latham, G. P., *New developments in goal setting and task performance*, (New York, NY: Taylor and Francis Group, 2012).
2 Freedman, Seth, *Binge Trading* (Penguin, 2009).
3 See the 09.10.14 *New York Times* article by David Gelles on the Alibaba phenomenon, "Alibaba is bringing luxury, fast, to China's middle class," online at http://dealbook.nytimes.com/2014/09/10/alibaba-is-bringing-luxury-fast-to-chinas-middle-class/?_r=0.
4 The Yellow Pages story is from a 09.30.14 article by Parmy Olson on Jerry Yang in *Forbes*, online at http://www.forbes.com/sites/parmyolson/2014/09/30/how-je rry-yang-made-the-most-lucrative-bet-in-tech-history/.
5 The company's website is notably thin on history. See http://www.alibabagroup.com/en/about/history.
6 See Jasmine Siu's 02.03.15 write-up in *The Standard*'s of a recent Ma talk in Hong Kong, online at http://www.thestandard.com.hk/news_detail.asp?we_cat=11&art_id=153881&sid=43813659&con_type=1&d_str=20150203&fc=2.
7 From Parmy Olson's article, "Finding Alibaba," in the 10.20.14 issue of *Forbes,* online at http://www.forbes.com/sites/parmyolson/2014/09/30/how-jerry-y ang-made-the-most-lucrative-bet-in-tech-history/.
8 For more astounding Alibaba factoids, see Jillian D'Onfro's 04.16.14 *Business Insider* article, "22 astounding facts about Alibaba," online at http://www.businessinsider.com/alibaba-facts-size-growth-2014-4.
9 Quotes from Jillian D'Onfro's 05.25.14 *Business Insider* article, online at http://www.businessinsider.com/jack-ma-alibaba-founder-best-quotes-2014-5?op=1. The introductory copy for this article asserts that "Ma has succeeded because he is relentless," and that "relentlessness has formed his thinking." Despite its negative overtones, we can accept "relentlessness" as a rough synonym for "drive."
10 This story is largely based on the Ivey case series on Apple (9B12M027 and 9B12M028), written by Tom Watson under the supervision of Mary Crossan. A primary source for the series was Walter Isaacson's masterful biography, *Steve Jobs* (Simon & Schuster, 2011).
11 See "Apple announces record iPhone sales over holiday quarter," by Tim Higgins, 01.27.15, at www.bloomberg.com, online at http://www.bloomberg.com/news/articles/2015-01-27/apple-s-record-iphone-sales-top-estimates-for-holiday-quarter.

12 And here, we aren't even addressing his impact on the film industry through Pixar: another amazing story.
13 Isaacson, Walter, *Steve Jobs* (Simon & Schuster, 2011), pp. 569–770.
14 The race is explained in an 08.30.00 *Globe and Mail* article by Patricia Young, online at http://www.theglobeandmail.com/arts/heat-leeches-and-team-spirit/article1042052/.
15 See an interview with Camus online at https://www.youtube.com/watch?v=UV1OBvSnugg.
16 See a chart of Apple's profits at http://en.wikipedia.org/wiki/History_of_Apple_Inc. The company's margins have increased almost every year since 2001.
17 Schlender, Brent and Tetzeli, Rick, *Becoming Steve Jobs: the evolution of a reckless upstart into a visionary leader* (Crown Business, 2015).
18 From the Martin interview in Gerard Seijts's *Good Leaders Learn* (Routledge, 2014), p. 315.
19 See Geoff Loftus's "5 leadership lessons from Ernie Banks," in *Forbes,* 01.29.15, online at http://www.forbes.com/sites/geoffloftus/2015/01/29/5-leadership-lessons-from-ernie-banks/4/.
20 See the Chicago Historical Society's joint interview with Ernie Banks and Mae Jemison, in *Chicago History*, Volume 27, No. 3, available online as a PDF.
21 From an 08.13.13 ESPN article by Bruce Levine, "Ernie Banks tried to dissuade Obama," online at http://espn.go.com/chicago/mlb/story/_/id/9565325/ernie-banks-tried-talk-barack-obama-running-president. Based on his own abortive political career – described here with characteristic humor and good will – Banks tried to talk Barack Obama out of running for president of the U.S. in 2008.
22 Dr. Seuss, *Oh, The Places You'll Go!* (Random House, 1990).

5 Collaboration

In this chapter, we make the point that effective leaders must be capable of collaboration with others both inside and outside their organizations – some of whom share objectives, while others are pursuing goals that are different or even inimical to their own. Beyond this, leaders must be constantly striving to create collaborative networks and relationships that can be developed and mined to support sustainable creativity, innovation, and productivity to drive their organization's interests, as well as the common good.

Executives and managers who are unwilling or unable to collaborate with others – whether in formal teams, looser working groups or committees, trade associations, business government panels and commissions, or myriad other contexts – are of limited value in an increasingly interdependent world, in which networks of people and organizations form the basis of so much economic activity. A deep, visceral, and intellectual understanding of the nature of interconnectedness – and the development of a disposition to collaborate for mutual interest and the greater good – are critical to becoming and being an effective leader in a wide variety of contexts.

When collaboration is hard-wired into character, individuals ignore many of the temptations to not collaborate. Competition for personal career advancement, compensation systems that reward individual achievement rather than enterprise performance, the challenges of working together with people you may not like or even respect, or simply the additional time it takes to pursue collaborative solutions rather than going it alone – these are among the most common reasons that leaders cite as restricting effective teamwork or other collaborative efforts. But leaders with built-in collaborative values, beliefs, and traits seem to overcome these disincentives and push for collaborative solutions and action plans.

Interconnectedness

Albert Einstein wrote eloquently on many subjects, including what might be called "interconnectedness" – one of the core elements of collaboration:

A human being is a part of the whole, called by us, "Universe," a part limited in time and space. He experiences himself, his thoughts and feelings as something separated from the rest – a kind of optical delusion of his consciousness. This delusion is a kind of prison for us, restricting us to our personal desires and to affection for a few persons nearest to us. Our task must be to free ourselves from this prison by widening our circle of compassion to embrace all living creatures and the whole of nature in its beauty. Nobody is able to achieve this completely, but the striving for such achievement is in itself a part of the liberation and a foundation for inner security.[1]

The Dalai Lama – persecuted and living in exile since 1959 – certainly has had occasion to contemplate Einstein's "delusions of consciousness" and prisons of the mind, and has weighed in many times on the subject of interconnectedness. For example:

The reality today is that we are all interdependent and have to co-exist on this small planet. Therefore, the only sensible and intelligent way of resolving differences and clashes of interests, whether between individuals or nations, is through dialogue.[2]

Legendary investor and executive Warren Buffett offered another perspective on interconnectedness, when he observed that "someone is sitting in the shade today because someone planted a tree a long time ago."[3] But even if we agree with Buffett that we are interconnected – over time, and in real time in the workplace – that agreement doesn't automatically bring about collaboration. True collaboration takes conscious effort that, in our view, springs from an individual's character.

We invoke these quotes here to emphasize the *foundational* nature of collaboration, introduced above. It is more basic, and more powerful, than the transactional nature of much of what we call "teamwork." Teamwork binds us together by contract – formal or informal – whereas collaboration binds us together through a felt interdependency. Teamwork is then just one of the ways that interconnectedness is transformed into productive activity.

The difference between collaboration and teamwork manifests itself quite dramatically when we explore the difference between classical musicians working as a team in an orchestra context, and jazz musicians improvising in a club or at a recording session. The orchestra is a team, in effect – structured and coordinated in advance – whereas in jazz improvisation, the musicians must collaborate to co-create the music in real time.

The same turns out to be true when we look at the difference between a typical play and theater improvisation. A play, by definition, is scripted. Improvisation is unscripted. It builds on an approach called "yes and," which fosters collaboration that builds on the contribution of others.

In her book *Bossypants*, Tina Fey explained:

> The first rule of improvisation is AGREE. Always agree and SAY
> YES. When you're improvising, this means you are required to agree
> with whatever your partner has created. So if we're improvising and
> I say, "Freeze, I have a gun," and you say, "That's not a gun. It's
> your finger. You're pointing your finger at me," our improvised scene
> has ground to a halt. But if I say, "Freeze, I have a gun!" and you
> say, "The gun I gave you for Christmas! You bastard!" then we have
> started a scene because we have AGREED that my finger is in fact a
> Christmas gun.
>
> Now, obviously in real life you're not always going to agree with
> everything everyone says. But the Rule of Agreement reminds you to
> "respect what your partner has created" and to at least start from an
> open-minded place. Start with a YES and see where that takes you.[4]

When you are collaborative, you value and actively support the development
and maintenance of positive relationships among people. You encourage
open dialogue, and don't react defensively when you are challenged. You
are able to connect with others at a fundamental level, in a way that fosters
the productive sharing of ideas. And finally, you recognize that what
happens to someone, somewhere, can affect everyone, anywhere.

In this chapter, we explore some of the key elements of collaboration –
on the right-hand side in Figure 5.1, below – and look at how the dimension
of collaboration complements the other dimensions of leader character.

Character Elements: What Goes into "Collaboration"?

There are five character elements that contribute to the leadership character
dimension of collaboration. When you are collaborative, you are:

Cooperative: You get along with people and build strong working relationships. This may be more difficult than it sounds. Wharton Professor
Adam Grant points out that many of the structures in place at competitive
companies work against cooperation: forced-curve performance reviews,
most promotional systems (which tend to create many "losers" each time
they anoint one winner), and so on. The resulting prescription is obvious: Root out those structures and procedures, and invent new ones that
reward cooperators.

Disney Animation – the division of the Walt Disney Company responsible for creating the company's signature animated films – did just that
when it tackled the issue of teams and cooperation head-on in 2010.[5] Prior
to that time, the animation group had been organized in a traditional way,
with freestanding functional groups operating in a relatively "siloed" way.
Within those silos, managers ran their teams as hierarchies.

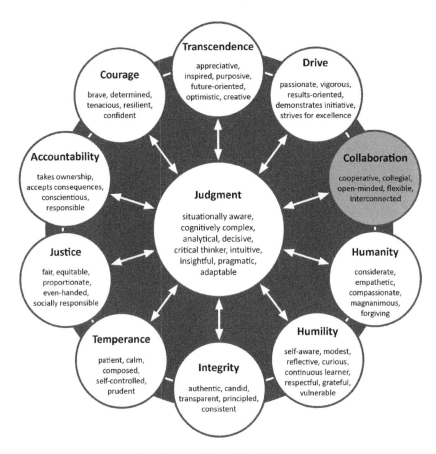

Figure 5.1 Character Dimensions and Associated Elements

Beginning in 2010, the deck was reshuffled substantially. Individuals were located in a matrix, and given some combination of "lead," "primary," and "secondary" responsibilities. These assignments were made with a deliberate eye toward breaking down the existing silos and fostering enhanced cooperation. At the same time, the company took care to avoid the traps often associated with matrix management – for example, the problem of employees having to meet conflicting demands from their several managers. (The three categories of responsibilities clearly delineated which manager had first, second, and third call on an individual who was in demand.) Meanwhile, it became clear that there was enormous benefit in giving employees latitude to focus on a particular challenge that had captured their imagination.

The push for increased cooperation was part plan and part luck. It wasn't clear at the outset, for example, how much impact an individual's personality could have on a given team; once this was discovered, managers invented a way to move an individual off a team without making that move look like a failure. The location of team members turned out to be important: Proximity spurred interactions, and formal meetings declined in number and length. This led, in turn, to reconfigurations of physical spaces, with casual meeting places built into technical areas for easy access and use. Managers gave up their offices in favor of centrally located workspaces, and were required to spend at least 20 percent of their time as functioning team members – that is, actually doing the work of the team. That requirement earned them the respect of their team members, and also kept managers in closer touch with what was happening on the shop floor. This accelerated the decision-making process, and cut down on the kinds of bureaucratic sludge that so often bogs down the workplace: memos, updates, status reports, and the like.

Collegial: You take a good-natured approach to working with others. You seek to resolve differences amicably, looking for "win-win" approaches to what may seem at first to be conflicts.

As the U.S. federal government has regularly ground to a halt in recent years – with partisan bickering gumming up the legislative works to an unprecedented degree – many observers have looked back wistfully to the days when Ronald Reagan was in the White House and Tip O'Neill – the longtime Democratic representative from Massachusetts – was Speaker of the House of Representatives.[6]

It is easy, in deep retrospect, to over-romanticize that era of relatively good feeling. In fact, the two veteran politicians didn't hesitate to savage each other, when circumstances called for it. O'Neill, for example, referred to Reagan as a "cheerleader for selfishness." For his part, Reagan enjoyed comparing O'Neill to a character in the Pac-Man video game: "a round thing that gobbles up money." They disagreed energetically – even bitterly – over issues like revisions to Social Security and the extension of the Clean Air Act in 1986.

And yet: They both hated stalemate more than they detested each other's politics. They got past the mutual name-calling to have drinks together at the White House at the end of the working day. Reagan helped raise the money for the O'Neill Library at the Speaker's beloved Boston College – and when Reagan was shot in an assassination attempt, O'Neill prayed at his bedside in the hospital.

Can you stand on principle and still be collegial? Can you disagree bitterly – to the extent of throwing verbal rocks at your adversary in public – and still do business? The answer seems to be, and needs to be, yes.

Open-minded: You examine many sides of an issue. You invite and seek evidence that challenges your personal perceptions, values, beliefs, and conclusions.

The consequences of being close-minded can be, literally, fatal. The *Columbia* space shuttle burned up during its re-entry into the earth's atmosphere on February 1, 2003, killing all seven astronauts on board.[7] Subsequent investigations determined that the mission management team – led by NASA official Linda Ham – was strikingly closed to seeking out and learning vital facts about the shuttle's ability to survive re-entry, even after it became clear that the spacecraft's protective heat shield had been damaged upon take-off.

Based on transcripts of the management team's meetings, it is clear that the mission management team was convinced that the 1.5-pound chunk of fuel-tank foam insulation that had crashed into *Columbia*'s left wing at 500 miles per hour "wouldn't do any damage." Engineers proposed to use spy-satellite imagery to determine the extent of the damage, but Ham cancelled that request. NASA originally decided not to even inform the *Columbia* astronauts that there was a potential problem, deciding on the ground that the foam strike and associated damage was a "non-issue." Only when reporters started asking about it did NASA decide to tell *Columbia*'s crew about the damage to the wing. The e-mail to the astronauts dismissed any concern about the foam strike as "not even worth mentioning."

Part of the problem, clearly, was hubris. "NASA's past success clouded their judgment as to just how serious this could be," said a manager at the Johnson Space Center after the destruction of *Columbia*. "They got overly confident."[8]

"We were all trying to do the right thing," a tearful Ham told an interviewer six months later. She argued, none too convincingly, that no one should be blamed for the disaster: "All along, we were basing our decisions on the best information that we had at the time." But there was better information to be had – and shared – and once the damage had been done to the shuttle, it was the Mission Management Team's obligation to seek out that information.

Flexible: You listen patiently and non-defensively when people question or challenge your position. You remain open to changing your personal opinions, and your conduct, when circumstances change.

Carol Stephenson – former dean of the Ivey Business School at Canada's Western University, and a former executive in the telecom sector – remembers an incident from when she was the CEO of Lucent Technologies Canada. At one point – along with the rest of the telecom sector – Lucent went into a deep slide. Stephenson was a seasoned executive, at that point, and she was pretty sure she knew what to do: Sit her relatively young workforce down, and talk about the tough realities of a business cycle – how deep the trough was likely to go, how long it was going to last, and how difficult it would be to get back to "business as usual." Her goal was to reassure them, as she recalls, and to relieve their anxiety:

> That presentation was the worst thing I could have done. What I forgot was to pay attention to the emotional cycles that people have to

go through. I hadn't allowed for the anger and grief to happen. I was into remedies and solutions, and so it was a terrible misjudgment on my part in terms of reading the situation and how people might be feeling.[9]

With the best of intentions, in other words, Stephenson's reversion to a tried-and-tested business textbook response – her lack of flexibility in response to a situation that was anything but business as usual – got her into trouble.

A contrasting example comes from the childhood of Lieutenant General Russel L. Honoré, who – after a distinguished military career that included leading the Department of Defense's response to the devastation of Hurricane Katrina – retired from the United States Army in 2008. Although a strong command presence – no one doubted who was in charge when General Honoré was in the room – he was also known for his patience, resiliency, and flexibility. When asked how he acquired these traits, he looked back across many decades:

> I think some of the resilience comes from the experience of growing up poor in Louisiana… From that experience, you learn to adapt to the situation – you adapt and overcome. I remember when I was young, we had two televisions – one had sound and one had a picture. Nobody said the picture and the sound had to come on the same one. You adapt. When the antennae got old, you got a little piece of aluminum foil and worked it just right.[10]

Honoré consciously distinguished between those decisions that were "on a clock" – in other words, which had an element of life-and-death immediacy – and those that could work themselves out over a longer time frame. No, don't over-study things – but don't rush things that don't need to be rushed. "Patience!" he counseled. "Change takes time, and it takes some people a little longer than others to adapt to change."

Interconnected: You sense and value deep connections with others, at all levels – both within your organization and in the broader society.

We began this chapter with this concept of interconnectedness, and how a rich and nuanced sense of how things fit together – locally, globally – is a vital contributor to collaboration. In that introductory context, we talked about improvisational actors and jazz musicians. To that universe of structured improvisation, built around talented and interconnected players who trust and complement each other, we can surely add team-based athletes. Hollywood presented a sugary and sanitized version of this in the 2005 drama *Coach Carter*, where the members of a basketball team – after watching the weakest member of the team being humiliated by a stern coach (played by a fierce-looking Samuel L. Jackson) – step forward to do the sprints and push-ups that their exhausted team member simply can't do. ""You said we're a team," says one of the athletes, explaining their action. "One person struggles, we all struggle. One person triumphs, we all triumph."[11]

That scene may have been polished to a high gloss, but the real world sometimes presents similar lessons. Mike Krzyzewski, legendary head basketball coach at Duke, uses the symbol of the fist to underscore the power of teamwork. The five fingers on the fist represent communication, trust, collective responsibility, caring, and pride. "All of us together are stronger than we would be separately," he explained to an interviewer. "Before you're facing anything else, you're fighting human nature to go beyond personal wants and needs. There's empowerment and maturity in a willingness to put all that aside and focus on those around you."[12]

George Cope – president and CEO of Bell Canada Enterprises Inc. and Bell Canada, – Canada's largest telecommunications company – draws a similar lesson from the career of hockey legend Wayne Gretzky, who won four Stanley Cup championships with the Edmonton Oilers between 1984 and 1988:

> I'm a sports junkie, and I find it interesting that the Edmonton Oilers won the Stanley Cup after Wayne Gretzky left, but Wayne Gretzky never won the Stanley Cup again after he left. That was a profound lesson for me. Gretzky is the best hockey player the world has ever seen, but he never won the cup without that team. There's no individual who's bigger than the team. It's always about the team.[13]

Cope is underscoring the fact that the end product – in this case, a Stanley Cup – requires the whole team to work together. A team will not reach its full collaborative potential if the participants, and especially its leaders, don't believe deeply that collaboration is essential for success.

Not surprisingly, these five character elements work together to support collaboration. Being interconnected requires being open-minded and flexible; otherwise, you are simply asserting your own point of view. Being interconnected fosters collegiality and cooperation since you more readily acknowledge and appreciate other perspectives. Being interconnected also allows us to remain receptive and open-minded when others challenge our thinking. Collegiality and being open-minded facilitates cooperation.

Collaboration Complementing Other Dimensions

Collaboration creates a conduit of connection to others that supports humanity. It is critical for humility, since the connection with others serves to provide important feedback and challenges individuals to address decisions and behaviors driven by self-interest. Collaboration can foster drive since it can bring with it a level of contagious energy. For example, this is how social movements emerge. It supports transcendence and courage because it brings others into the picture, which may spark possibility and help overcome obstacles. Demonstrating collegiality and open-mindedness fosters candor and transparency, which are part of integrity.

Being cooperative and demonstrating interconnectedness supports fairness. For example, a sense of interconnectedness facilitates interpersonal justice – in other words, the degree to which people are treated with politeness, dignity, and respect by third parties involved in executing procedures or determining outcomes. This, in turn, influences job-related variables including but not limited to job performance, organizational citizenship behaviors, retaliation behaviors, and loyalty.

Can Collaboration Stand Alone?

Collaboration without drive can lack rigor. Without justice, it may lead to friction between team members, thus squandering opportunities to benefit from a diversity of views and smoother implementation of ideas. Accountability ensures that there is closure and responsibility to collaboration.

Integrity helps to ensure that you don't lose sight of your perspective and principles in the course of being open-minded, thus avoiding the pitfall of groupthink. Groupthink is a process of concurrence-seeking whereby the desire for harmony in the group results in a poor decision-making outcome. People "censor" themselves to avoid conflict within the team, and they fail to volunteer alternative ideas in group discussions because they want to avoid disagreement. Recent examples of groupthink include the Penn State cover-up of the child sex scandal on the periphery of its football program, and Toyota's problems with faulty accelerators.

Collaboration Means Business

We've ranged far and wide in this chapter, in our discussion of collaboration in organizations. For our final example, let's go back to the business world, for a story that is still waiting for its ending to be written.[14]

Aecon Group Inc. is one of Canada's most important construction and infrastructure-development companies, with more than 12,000 employees in some 40 operating units. Its 2013 revenues were approximately $3 billion, with an after-tax profit of some $40 million. Aecon – with more than 125 years of experience in construction and related trades – prides itself on "building things that matter." Yes, the company had built iconic buildings such as Toronto's CN Tower. But when it recounted its accomplishments, it was likely to look past glitzy buildings and point at things like highways, airports, and improvements to the St. Lawrence Seaway – things that matter.

In recent years, Aecon had grown substantially through the acquisition of former competitors – many of them as proud and venerable as Aecon. The managers coming into Aecon from these companies were, for the most part, well entrenched in their practices and perspectives – which was a good thing, in that Aecon fully intended to draw on their experience; but it also presented collaborative challenges. How could these disparate teams be brought together into a coherent whole, with a shared vision and practices?

In other words, collaboration in this case is not merely a cultural "nice to have"; it is a business necessity. The global construction industry is consolidating rapidly, and the jobs that Aecon wants to pursue are increasing dramatically in scale and complexity. "Forty percent of our revenue is now coming from larger, more complex projects, such as those valued at over $100 million," wrote CEO John Beck in 2013.[15]

So how does the company get where it needs to go? How does it make "ONE Aecon" – a phrase coined by senior management to reflect this goal, and to hasten its achievement – a reality?

The next chapter in the Aecon story, as noted, remains to be written. But, certainly, collaborative organizations are built around collaborative leaders, who – like great jazz musicians, improvisational actors, and team sport players – are interconnected through trust and skill.

Questions to Contemplate

1. To what extent are you, personally, a "collaborative" person? Are you cooperative, collegial, flexible, and open-minded?
2. In your current role, have you maximized the opportunities for collaboration within your organization?
3. Have you explored the degree of interconnectedness within your industry, between governments and your business, within your supply chain, with your customers?

Books and Articles to Read

The Decay of Command and Control Leadership Shawn Murphy (Switch & Shift, 2012)

Collaboration: How Leaders Avoid the Traps, Build Common Ground, and Reap Big Results Morten Hansen (Harvard Business Press, 2009)

Give and Take: Why Helping Others Drives Our Success Adam M. Grant (Penguin, 2014)

"When Senior Managers Won't Collaborate" Heidi K. Gardner (*Harvard Business Review*, March 2015)

Teaming: How Organizations Learn, Innovate, and Compete in the Knowledge Economy Amy Edmondson (Jossey-Bass, 2012)

Videos to Watch

"Listen, Learn ... then Lead" TED Talk by Stanley A. McChrystal (www. ted.com/talk, 2011)
"Want to Help Someone? Shut Up and Listen!" TED Talk by Ernesto Sirolli (www.ted.com/talk, 2012)
"Dare to Disagree" TED Talk by Margaret Heffernan (www.ted.com/ talk, 2012)
"How to Manage for Collective Creativity" TED Talk by Linda Hill (www.ted.com/talk, 2015)
"Improv 101 (The 'Yes, and...' Principle)" by Bob Kulhan (YouTube, 2014)

A Podcast to Listen to

Full Interview: Daniel Pink on Motivation 3.0. CBC Spark Radio Show with Nora Young (YouTube, 2010)

Notes

1 There are several versions of this quote. This one is from a 1950 letter quoted in the *New York Times* (03.29.72). But another version – written by Einstein to a distraught father who had lost a son and was seeking solace – invoked "true religion" as one way to free oneself from the "optical delusion of consciousness." See http://en.wikiquote.org/wiki/Albert_Einstein. For a facsimile of this letter, see http://www.lettersofnote.com/2011/11/delusion.html.
2 For the entire essay, see 'His Holiness the Dalai Lama Reflects on Working Toward Peace,' on the Santa Clara University website at http://www.scu.edu/ethics/architects-of-peace/Dalai-Lama/essay.html.
3 This quote can be found many places online, including http://www.old-schoolvalue.com/blog/investing-perspective/warren-buffett-quotes/.
4 Fey, Tina, *Bossypants* (Reagan Arthur/Little, Brown), 2013 reprint edition, p. 84.
5 This example is drawn from "Teaming at Disney Animation," Harvard Business School case #9-615-023, by Amy C. Edmondson, David L. Ager, Emily Harburg, and Natalie Bartlett.
6 This story is derived from an op-ed piece – "Frenemies: A love story" – by Thomas P. O'Neill, the late Speaker's son, in the *New York Times*, 10.05.12, online at http://campaignstops.blogs.nytimes.com/2012/10/05/frenemies-a-love-story/?_r=0. The younger O'Neill is actually arguing that the Reagan–O'Neill relationship was less collegial than is remembered, but the facts he presents argue with equal (or greater) force toward the opposite conclusion.
7 See the CBS news summary of the disaster, and Ham's interview six months later, in "NASA official breaks her silence," by Jarrett Murphy, 08.04.03, at http://www.cbsnews.com/news/nasa-official-breaks-her-silence/.
8 This quote is from an *Orlando Sentinel* article published on 03.23.03, by Michael Cabbage and titled "NASA managers missed chances to take closer look for tile damage," online at http://www.billnelson.senate.gov/newsroom/news/nasa-managers-missed-chances-to-take-closer-look-for-tile-damage.

9   See the Stephenson profile and interview in Gerard Seijts's *Good Leaders Learn* (Routledge, 2014), p. 100.

10 See the Honoré profile and interview in Gerard Seijts's *Good Leaders Learn* (Routledge, 2014), pp. 199–201.

11 See this clip from "Coach Carter" (2005) online at https://www.youtube.com/watch?v=1g82D68N-ys.

12 See the complete *Duke Today* interview in "Duke employees show how Coach K's qualities of teamwork emanate beyond basketball," by Brian Roth, 2015, at http://today.duke.edu/showcase/coachklessons/.

13 See the Cope profile and interview in Gerard Seijts's *Good Leaders Learn* (Routledge, 2014), p. 314.

14 Although author Gerard Seijts has researched the company, this material is mainly taken from the company's website (www.aecon.com).

15 From Beck's written answers to a survey, "Top contractors report," by Jim Barnes, 06.01.13, online at http://www.on-sitemag.com/news/oh-canada-opportunities-and-challenges-in-the-canadian-construction-industry/1002422051/?&er=NA.

6   Humanity

In the summer of 2014, two men in Austin, Texas, came up with an idea for a homemade social science experiment. The older of the two was a homeless man named Sandy Shook – grey-haired, tall but slightly stooped, and fiftyish – who had been living on the street for years due to a long-running battle with depression. The other was videographer Joseph Costello – several decades younger than Shook, and a regular contributor to the Quiet Assassins YouTube channel.[1]

The set-up was simple. First, they filmed a disheveled-looking Shook asking passersby for spare change under a variety of pretexts: a little short on a bus ticket, a quarter short for a cup of coffee, a buck short on a Subway sandwich, and so on. He didn't succeed very often. Then Costello arranged for Shook to get a haircut, a "business casual" outfit (charcoal-grey slacks, a light-grey sports coat, brown loafers, and a white button-down shirt), and a non-functioning cell phone. Now looking something like a slightly over-the-hill Liam Neeson, he held the non-functional cell phone up to his ear and accosted pedestrians, using more or less the same pitches: coffee, bus ticket, Subway sandwich, and so on. This time, he was notably more successful.

Why were the people on the street that day far more inclined to help the distinguished-looking Shook than the disreputable-looking one? Most likely, they believed the well-dressed executive's story, and they didn't believe the panhandler's. They were more inclined to be generous to someone who probably didn't need the money than they were to someone who probably did.

One thing that's interesting about this experiment is that it touches on humanity on three key levels: in personal relationships, in the workplace, and in society. Those street-level encounters were a series of one-on-one interactions. The injection of the executive persona – in the form of the dressed-up Sandy Shook – invokes the hierarchy of the office environment. And the disparity between the disheveled Sandy Shook and most of the passersby reminds us of our human obligations on a societal level.

A particularly touching moment in the video came when "executive Sandy" tried to get a young man who was passing by – who himself looked to be in disarray – to give him a quarter. The young man, certain that he had a quarter somewhere, dug deep into the pockets of his frayed trousers. Although he failed to find a coin, he seemed determined to help. Both Shook and Costello broke out of character, and Costello wound up giving the young man money instead.

The fact is, we humans are selective in our humanity. We are predisposed to trust people who look like us, and act like us. Conversely, we are equally predisposed to be "inhumane" to people we find odd, or unsettling, or scary. And on some level, we know this, and we're usually not proud of it. For example, we tend to hire the people with whom we're personally comfortable and not hire those who put us a little bit on edge. (This is known as the well-documented "similar-to-me" effect.) Most of us feel guilty saying no to panhandlers. Sure, some of them are probably not in such tough shape, and don't really need that quarter or that dollar; maybe some of them are just unwilling to find and keep a steady job. But surely some of them do need help.

So is humanity still humanity when it's selective? What part of our humanity justifies the type of judging that we fall into – and does that false selectivity ultimately undermine our capacity for judgment? Can a true leader get by on intermittent humanity? Does humanity lead to a leader being "soft," sentimental, and lacking in judgment? What is humanity, anyway?

When you demonstrate humanity, you have a genuine concern and care for others, and you can appreciate and identify with others' values, feelings, and beliefs. You have a capacity to forgive, and not hold grudges. You understand that people are fallible, and you offer opportunities for individuals to learn from their mistakes.

In this chapter, we explore some of the key elements of humanity – on the right-hand side of Figure 6.1, below – and look at how the dimension of humanity complements the other dimensions of leader character.

First, let's look at one of the most compelling examples of humanity in recent history – the story of Nelson Mandela – and consider what this example teaches us.

Touching Their Hearts

Born in 1918, Rolihlahla Mandela was a member of the Madiba clan in a village in the Transkei region in southeastern South Africa.[2] While in grade school, he acquired the Christian name "Nelson," in keeping with the custom of the time. He received a good education with no notable bumps along the road – until, that is, he was expelled from the University College of Fort Hare for participating in a student protest.

The protest was a harbinger of things to come. In 1944, a year after finishing college, Mandela joined the African National Congress (ANC). As the ANC grew more radical in the 1950s, Mandela gained an ever-higher

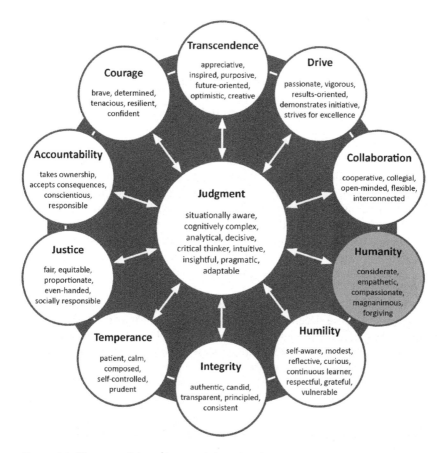

Figure 6.1 Character Dimensions and Associated Elements

profile – and drew the attention of the apartheid government. He was first arrested in 1955, and arrested again in 1962. Two years later, at age 46, he was sentenced to life imprisonment on notorious Robben Island.

It was a brutal, spirit-crushing place: "the harshest, most iron-fisted outpost in the South African penal system," as Mandala later wrote.[3] He and his fellow prisoners slept on straw mats, crushed boulders to make gravel, quarried lime for the island's roads, and shivered through the cold South African winters. Mandela was initially allowed to have only one visitor and receive only one letter every six months, and – like his fellow prisoners – was denied any news of the outside world. He was prevented from attending the funerals of his mother and his eldest son. Although during his long imprisonment he was offered at least three conditional releases, he refused to compromise with the government.

Ultimately, Mandela spent 18 years on Robben Island. Throughout those long years, he remained respectful – if wary – of his jailers. But because he was an established leader, he was singled out for abuse by a succession of commanding officers (as the head wardens were called). One of the most notorious of these was a colonel named Piet Badenhorst, with whom Mandela clashed regularly. When Badenhorst's time to be rotated off the island finally arrived, he called Mandela to his office. To Mandela's astonishment, Badenhorst said that he wanted to wish the ANC leader and his fellow prisoners good luck. As Mandela later wrote:

> Badenhorst had perhaps been the most callous and barbaric com-
> manding officer we had had on Robben Island. But that day in the
> office, he had revealed that there was another side to his nature, a side
> that had been obscured but that still existed. It was a useful reminder
> that all men, even the most seemingly cold-blooded, have a core of
> decency, and that if their heart is touched, they are capable of chan-
> ging. Ultimately, Badenhorst was not evil; his inhumanity had been
> foisted upon him by an inhuman system. He behaved like a brute
> because he was rewarded for brutish behavior.[4]

It was a key insight – that a corrupt system can inspire inhumane behavior even in otherwise decent people – and it was an insight that was possible only because of Mandela's own humanity. Mandela was prepared to see Badenhorst as a person with a "core of decency," who was neither inherently evil nor irredeemable.

Gradually, the times caught up with Nelson Mandela. In 1982, he was transferred to Pollsmoor Prison in Cape Town. Over the next six years, the conditions of his imprisonment were gradually relaxed – in part because the government needed a prominent member of the ANC with whom to negotiate.

Mandela's 27 years of imprisonment ended on February 11, 1990. Now began the task of rebuilding a nation, amidst rising tensions and ever-increasing levels of violence between and within the races. Sitting across the table from South African President F. W. de Klerk, Mandela participated in the talks that led to the end of white minority rule.

The deal was struck. In 1993, Mandela and de Klerk shared the Nobel Peace Prize for heading off what could have been a catastrophic civil war, pitting race against race. And in May 1994, Mandela was inaugurated as South Africa's first democratically elected president. His brief inaug-ural address included thanks both to the freedom-fighters who had pre-vailed and to the security forces – so long the face of oppression – who had secured the democratic elections that many had believed could never take place.

"None of us acting alone can achieve success," he said toward the end of his remarks. "We must therefore act together as a united people, for national reconciliation, for nation building, for the birth of a new world."[5]

All in all, it is a stirring – almost mythic – tale of humanity rewarded. But it's fair to ask: Does such humanity have a role to play in the conduct of business? Does it reside in people with fewer superhuman characteristics and achievements?

Rhoda Panice was a small-business owner – widowed at 34 with two young children, one of whom was severely disabled – who struggled to keep her toy, bicycle, and nursery furniture retail business going. Located in a heavily working-class neighborhood in Manchester, in the U.K., the business made 70 percent of its sales to single-parent families, or households in which one parent was unemployed or permanently disabled. They would buy something for the upcoming Christmas, have it put away, and pay for it one or two shillings each week. In about half the cases, the gift wasn't paid for before Christmas ... but Panice made sure that the gift was always delivered before the holidays.

It was part of a bigger picture. Panice extended credit to those who could not pay on time, and wrote off the debts of those who could not pay at all. She never turned anything over to a collection agency. Why? Because her fundamental humanity would allow for nothing else. She saw no reason why people who had little in the way of material goods could not have some dignity in their lives.

At the other end of the spectrum, in terms of corporate scale and scope, we find George Cope – the aforementioned CEO of Bell Canada – who has committed himself and his company to the cause of mental health. When questioned whether this falls within the purview of the leader of a publicly held company, Cope is quick to point out that his personal efforts – as well as the voluntary, extra-curricular efforts of employees – are being spent on the cause. At the same time, he has no hesitation in arguing that great companies should embrace great societal needs.

Similarly, Ed Clark at TD Bank Group was a corporate leader in promoting equal opportunities for the LGBT community, long before it was common or popular to do so; Guy French of Warner-Lambert embraced the cause of disabled and very sick children through sponsorship of a summer camp; and Maple Leaf Foods, one of Canada's largest food-processing companies, commits itself and its employees (again on a voluntary basis) to the support of food banks in various communities, and is frequently in the forefront of providing food aid for disaster relief efforts.

Of course, the leaders who do these things are acting for many different and varied reasons, but the common thread is the fundamental sense of humanity that is baked into their characters. By engaging others in their organizations and setting examples for other business leaders, moreover, they are helping to develop a broader base of business leaders who are not afraid to let their essential humanity shine through.

Character Elements: What Goes into "Humanity"?

Looking back to Figure 6.1, you can see that there are five character elements that contribute to the dimension of humanity. When you exhibit humanity, you are:

Considerate: You make the effort to understand what others are experiencing, thinking, and feeling. You acknowledge and appreciate others' viewpoints even when you disagree with them.

Certainly, Nelson Mandela's determination to get inside the heads and hearts of his oppressors was a major contributor to his ultimate success. And even after vanquishing apartheid, Mandela practiced consideration. In 1995, in the six-week period when the South African rugby team, the Springboks, were contending for the World Cup, Mandela pleaded with his countrymen to support the team. Blacks and whites alike were astounded: The springbok (a kind of gazelle) had long been the emblem of apartheid. When the Springboks won the World Cup, Mandela – wearing a green and gold cap and jersey that displayed the Springboks' logo – mounted the winner's platform and shook the hand of the blond Afrikaner, François Pienaar, who had led the team to victory.

Pienaar – who had been taught by his parents that Mandela was a thug and a terrorist – later recalled the impact of Mandela's gamble:

> I'm still gobsmacked when I think back to the profound change that happened. We started obviously with a great leader with a fantastic vision who realized that sport is important for the Afrikaner white community and [that this was a way] to earn their respect and trust.[6]

Consideration doesn't require a world stage; it can also be manifested in the understated but determined gesture. In 1994, Bruce Farrer – an English teacher at Bert Fox Community High School in Fort Qu'Appelle, Saskatchewan – gave his ninth-grade English students an unusual assignment. He had them write ten-page letters to themselves speculating on what they would like to be as grown-ups. He had originally intended to have the students keep the letters themselves, but was afraid that many would be lost over time. So he held on to the letters, with the promise that he would return them to their authors at a date they chose in the seemingly distant future: typically 10, 20, or 25 years later. (The students had to provide their home addresses, as well as those of relatives who seemed unlikely to move around.) The following year, he repeated the assignment, and again took home a bundle of handwritten letters. By the time he reached retirement age in 2002, he had five large boxes filled with letters, which he carefully set aside.[7]

A few years later, he began making good on his promise to those long-ago classes of ninth graders who had chosen a ten-year return date. Every year since then, he has spent several weeks doing online detective work, tracking down the letter-writers and returning their work. From the start, the recipients were moved and astonished – even awed. "I was just feeling honored and grateful," one former student (now a teacher himself) commented. "Amazed and inspired at the work of Mr. Farrer."

Few in Farrer's position would have bothered with, or perhaps even remembered, those letters that had been written so long ago. And few people would have criticized him if he had decided not to follow through on his end of the bargain: After all, he was retired, and most of the learning had occurred in the writing of those essays. But Farrer was determined and considerate, to an extraordinary degree.

That same consideration was nothing new, of course; it had long characterized his teaching: "I always felt like an individual [in your class]," another former student wrote in an online tribute, "and that my opinion counted! Thank you again."[8]

Empathetic: You are sensitive to others' values, feelings, and beliefs. You readily put yourself in others' shoes.

Al Braatz is the captain of Station 9 of the London, Ontario, Fire Department, which serves the south side of the city. Braatz has been in the London fire service for a quarter-century, and is widely respected for his leadership skills. Citywide, all new recruits to the department go through the same basic training; but Braatz puts new arrivals at Station 9 through an additional training exercise of his own design. He assembles everyone on duty at a conference table, and tells the rookie that he wants him or her to tell the group something personal about himself or herself – something important, some accomplishment that he or she is proud of, which will give the team some insight into what makes him or her tick. Braatz further explains that everyone at the table will do the same thing, in turn.

In many cases, the new recruit worries that he or she is being set up. (Fire stations are notorious for elaborate practical jokes.) In addition, many of the new recruits are "Type A" personalities – eager to jump into dangerous situations and accomplish heroics – so they are doubly disinclined to engage in touchy-feely exercises. But Braatz persists:

> In an organization, people are defined by their accomplishments, and should be recognized for them. So right off the bat, in the station, the new recruits learn a little bit about their colleagues. And most importantly, when you get a tip to be successful from a person, it spurs even more conversation. People build upon that sharing, and then it becomes not only a tip but a training session. By the end of that session, and it takes several hours, that person feels like he has been tucked under a wing. I want to give them the green light to be an active member of the team. They are now part of something.[9]

Through his exercise, Braatz not only demonstrates empathy; he also teaches empathy – and even the oldest veteran around the table gets the benefit of a refresher course in empathy. Everyone is "tucked under a wing."

Compassionate: You demonstrate care for others, and actively promote their well-being within and outside the organization.

Antoni Cimolino, artistic director of Canada's Stratford Festival, straddles the line between creative leader and business executive. In both roles, he sees the need and the opportunity to lead with compassion. He demonstrates that compassion for his employees in part by taking an interest in their success – and by helping those successes to happen. As he comments:

> You need to stop and say, "Look, I'd like to see your work. I'd like to understand what you do better," and then ask your colleagues about who is showing talent and a real gift. For the senior leader in the organization to cut through the ranks and talk to someone several levels down who shows promise is a major empowerment and gift to that young person.[10]

And – Cimolino emphasizes – it's a gift that the leader has to follow up on. When compassionate leaders create opportunities for younger people, they have to take responsibility for those opportunities after the fact. In other words, they not only have to open the door, but also help the younger person make his or her way through that door and achieve success.

Societies have the power to enable leaders and their organizations to be successful. Conversely, leaders without compassion are increasingly finding out that their businesses are at odds with societal expectations. Thus it is no surprise that many organizations are now embracing social causes. Coca-Cola aims to improve access to water for 2 million people in Africa; in 2010, Bell Canada Enterprises announced that it would be contributing $50 million to mental health programs; and the Kellogg Company aspires to donate a billion servings of cereal and snacks by the end of 2016 to help solve hunger in the United States.

Magnanimous: You remain "big-spirited," generous, and forgiving, especially toward rivals or those who are less powerful.

Or more powerful, as was the case for Nelson Mandela. "Mandela had the great gift of magnanimity," one of his jailers, Christo Brand, later wrote of the period toward the end of Mandela's 27-year imprisonment, when the government of F. W. de Klerk began negotiating with him. "His people were being beaten and arrested and detained without charge. Some of them were little more than children. His own wife and daughters were suffering. Yet he was able to produce a smile and a handshake for the very people who were ordering this."[11]

Magnanimity is not turning the other cheek prematurely, or endlessly. Mandela made demands of, and extracted concessions from, his jailers. He showed spine – a major part of his leader character. And yet, even as he cataloged the injuries inflicted on his people by their white rulers through the Truth and Reconciliation Commission, and sought redress, he looked for a "core of decency" in those oppressors.

In the workplace – as in much of life – magnanimity means the forgiving of old grudges. It means looking past affronts, real and imagined, so that respectful and productive conversations can take place. It means showcasing your own humanity, and that of others around you, in a way that bureaucracies and hierarchies are structurally inclined to thwart.

Forgiving: You respond to mistakes with patience and understanding. You give people a chance to learn and improve. Singling out and blaming people for things that go wrong – and things always do go wrong – wastes important learning opportunities.

Author Kevin Eikenberry distinguishes among three kinds of forgiveness: forgiveness of self, of others, and of situations.[12] Self-forgiveness, he writes, is a prerequisite to learning from our mistakes; it also allows us to leave the past behind and move into the future. Forgiveness of others – the conventional sense of the word – is essential to productivity and happiness: If we waste our energy on recriminations and trench warfare, we stop making progress. And finally, we have to "forgive" situations that are beyond our control. Dams burst; brakes fail; hurricanes happen. If you find yourself saying "if only" a lot, Eikenberry suggests, "you likely have a ways to go in this area."

In a sense, forgiveness is selfish: You forgive, in part, to rid yourself of lingering negative feelings or emotions, and open the door to personal development and growth.

These five character elements work together to support humanity. Empathy is critical to develop a capacity to relate to others. Compassion builds on empathy and extends it in the service of promoting well-being in others. Being considerate requires both empathy and compassion. Although a word that is not often used, magnanimity means that a person acts in a way that is big-spirited, rising above the inevitable fray inherent in difficult circumstances – which often requires forgiveness of oneself and others.

Humanity Complementing Other Dimensions

It is easy to see how humanity complements other dimensions. For example, humanity provides a depth of connectivity to others that brings with it knowledge, awareness, and understanding, which in turn informs justice, fosters collaboration, and provides an important source of inspiration for transcendence.

Humanity ensures that integrity is not construed in a narrow sense, so that candor in challenging conversations – for example – is not invoked simply in the service of self-interest. And those who act with consideration, or display magnanimity or forgiveness, are likely to be more successful in creating confidence and resiliency in others.

Humanity in the Absence of Other Dimensions

Having a strong sense of humanity without temperance may leave one very vulnerable. Why? Because temperance provides the self-regulation needed when you find yourself in charged situations that may lead to personal or structural conflict.

Having a strong sense of humanity without drive and accountability leads to unfocused effort or unrealized potential. You can be more concerned with maintaining good interpersonal relationships than getting the task done. People may see you as too friendly and a pushover, unable to make the tough decisions.

Justice offers balance to humanity, since it helps to bring perspective to the natural complexities that surface as you try to deepen your sense of humanity. Humanity without humility is difficult to develop, as you need to be self-aware of your tendencies in your daily interactions with individuals. It is only through reflection on experiences, and an openness to learning, that we can improve.

Reclaiming our Humanity

Chris Abani is a novelist, poet, essayist, screenwriter, and playwright who grew up in Afikpo, Nigeria in the 1980s.[13] He and many others in his age cohort were determined to bring down the military dictatorship that then ruled the country. Imprisoned three times by the Nigerian government, he transformed his harrowing experiences into a series of powerful novels, including *GraceLand* and *The Virgin of Flames*.

"What I've come to learn is that the world is never saved in grand, messianic gestures," he told a TED conference in Monterey, California in February 2008, "but in a simple accumulation of gentle, soft, almost invisible, everyday acts of compassion."[14]

He discussed "*Ubuntu*" – a concept of the South African Nguni Bantu people – which translates literally into "human kindness," but more generally refers to a sense that all humanity is joined by a universal bond of sharing and reciprocity. There is no way for us to be human, Abani argued, without relating to other people: "The only way for me to be human is for you to reflect my humanity back at me."

Recently, Martin Pistorius – the author of *Ghost Boy*, who was trapped in his body with a neurological disorder for a decade – wrote about what he had learned from the experience. As he was returning to consciousness, he was aware of others; however, those around him assumed he had no awareness. The exception was his massage therapist, who always spoke to him as if he was aware – and, perhaps not coincidentally, was the first to sense he was responding.

Being unable to respond and yet still aware of others taught Pistorius a lot about humanity. "I think being seen and having another person validate your existence is incredibly important," he explained, "not just for me in that moment, but for everyone. In a sense it makes you feel like you matter." Asked what he learned about human nature in those years he was trapped, he responded, "That everyone has a story, their own struggles, challenges, and insecurities. People, some more than others, put on a mask that they present to the world."[15]

Humanity is a critical dimension of leader character. It needs to be honored and exercised in our personal lives, in the workplace, and in society.

Questions to Contemplate

1. To what extent have you managed to reflect your own, personal humanity in what you do for work, and how you behave in the workplace?
2. Do you treat others with whom you work – even those with whom you have significant disagreements or conflict – with compassion?
3. When you have had to do something really tough – like firing an employee, or laying off people for whom you have no work – have you considered how they will be affected by this, and how they will feel about it? And have you looked for ways to protect their sense of dignity and self-respect, despite the reality of their loss?

Books and Articles to Read

Six Habits of Highly Empathic People Roman Krznaric (Greater Good Science Center, 2012)

Why Compassion in Business Makes Sense Emma Seppala (Greater Good Science Center, 2013)

"Why We Need Kind and Compassionate Leaders" Ray B. Williams (*Psychology Today*, August 2012)

Resonant Leadership: Renewing Yourself and Connecting with Others Through Mindfulness, Hope, and Compassion Richard E. Boyatzis & Annie McKee (Harvard Business Press, 2005)

Building Leaders the West Point Way: Ten Principles from the Nation's Most Powerful Leadership Lab Joseph P. Franklin (Thomas Nelson, 2007)

The Art of Forgiveness, Lovingkindness, and Peace Jack Kornfield (Bantam, 2008)

Leading with Kindness: How Good People Consistently Get Superior Results William F. Baker & Michael O'Malley (AMACOM, 2008)

"The Human Moment at Work" Edward M. Hallowell (*Harvard Business Review*, January-February 1999)

Humanise: Why Human Centred Leadership is the Key to the 21st Century Anthony Howard (John Wiley & Sons, 2015)

Videos to Watch

"The Power of Empathy" (RSA Shorts, YouTube, 2013)
"A New Story for Business" by R. Edward Freeman (YouTube, 2013)
'Truly Human Leadership" TEDx Talk by Bob Chapman (www.ted.com/talk, 2012)
"Everyday Leadership" TED Talk by Drew Dudley (www.ted.com/talk, 2010)
"Clinton: Lessons Learned from Mandela" (YouTube, 2006)
"Why aren't we more compassionate?" TED Talk by Daniel Goleman (www.ted.com/talk, 2007)

Notes

1 See the *San Francisco Globe* article and video – "An amazing social experiment on homelessness in America," 08.02.14, at https://sfglobe.com/?id=2324starting, and an article on the experiment on myfoxaustin.com, "Video of Austin homeless experiment reaches millions of viewers," 08.09.14, at http://www.myfoxaustin.com/story/26241287/video-of-austin-homeless-experiment-reaches-millions-of-viewers.
2 This biography is principally derived from the Nelson Mandela Foundation at https://www.nelsonmandela.org/content/page/biography.
3 From *Long Walk to Freedom,* by Nelson Mandela (Back Bay Books, 1995).
4 From *Long Walk to Freedom*, by Nelson Mandela (Back Bay Books, 1995).
5 The full text is online at the African National Congress's website at http://www.anc.org.za/show.php?id=3132.
6 See *The Guardian's* 12.08.13 write-up of the episode, "Francois Pienaar: 'When the whistle blew, South African changed forever,' by David Smith," online at http://www.theguardian.com/world/2013/dec/08/nelson-mandela-francois-pienaar-rugby-world-cup, and a NZAUTV video at https://www.youtube.com/watch?v=O1VuGEcYV4k. A Hollywood movie, *Invictus*, was also based on the stirring story.
7 Farrer's story was summarized in a 03.31.14 article by the CBC News, "20 years later, Sask. teacher mails student-penned letters," online at http://www.cbc.ca/news/canada/saskatchewan/20-years-later-sask-teacher-mails-student-penned-letters-1.2592962.
8 Definitely watch this video, and read the comments that accompany it, from which this quote is taken: http://www.aboveandbeyond.ca/bruce-teacher-letters-students/.
9 This story is an excerpt from Gerard Seijts's 06.18.14 blog on "Leadership in the fire-fighter service," online at http://www.ivey.uwo.ca/leadership/for-leaders/leadership-blogs/2014/06/leadership-in-the-fire-fighter-service/.
10 This section is derived from the chapter on Cimolino in *Good Leaders Learn* (Routledge, 2014), by this book's co-author Gerard Seijts, p. 350.
11 From *Mandela: My Prisoner, My Friend*, by Christo Brand (Thomas Dunne Books, 2014).
12 See Eikenberry's 09.08.14 blog – "Three types of forgiveness and why they matter to us as leaders" – at http://blog.kevineikenberry.com/leadership-supervisory-skills/three-types-forgiveness-matter-us-leaders/.

13 See Abani's website at http://www.chrisabani.com/about-chris/.

14 See Abani's TED video at https://www.ted.com/talks/chris_abani_muses_on_ humanity#t-76042.

15 See Sarah MacWhirter's 02.25.15 story in the *Globe & Mail* – "Ghost boy: Trapped in his own body, Martin Pistorius always had hope," online at http://www.theglobeand-mail.com/life/health-and-fitness/health/ghost-boy-trapped-in-his-own-body-martin-pistorius-always-had-hope/article23202679/.

7 Humility

We can think of many situations where strong egos have contributed to the success of individuals and the organizations they lead. For example, Steve Jobs at Apple, Jack Welch at General Electric, and Jamie Dimon at JP Morgan: All would be described as having pretty healthy egos, and enjoying great business results in their time at the helms of the organizations they led.

But, sadly, there are also many examples in which outsized, uncontrolled egos have got leaders into trouble. Especially in the wake of the 2008 financial crisis, many stories circulated about ego-driven CEOs and executive teams whose actions prior to the meltdown put their organizations, shareholders, and indeed the global economy at risk. Chuck Prince at Citibank, John Mack at Morgan Stanley, James ("Jimmy") Cayne from Bear Sterns, and Dick Fuld of Lehman Brothers will be remembered as CEOs who were victims of their own out-of-control egos.

We argue that without some measure of humility, leaders can fail through overconfidence, arrogance, and hubris. Indeed, those people who may determine your fate in the business world – your board of directors, your regulators, your key shareholders – are constantly on the lookout for those signs of arrogance in you and your management teams.

What is Humility?

Humble people let their accomplishments speak for themselves. They acknowledge limitations, understand the importance of thoughtful examination of their opinions and ideas, and embrace opportunities for personal growth and development. They don't consider themselves to be more important or special than others. They are respectful of others, and understand and appreciate the strengths and contributions of others. And finally, humility is the key to continuous learning, for without it, people don't feel the need to learn. Andy Grove, one of the founders of Intel, wrote a biography with the title *Only the Paranoid Survive*. We would submit that Grove was not paranoid but surely understood that in the fast-moving tech world, arrogance, hubris, or any sense of invulnerability would surely lead to downfall.

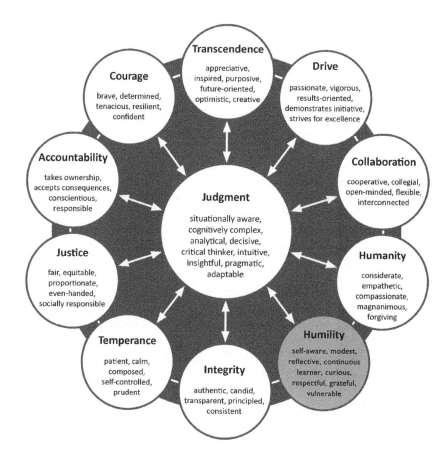

Figure 7.1 Character Dimensions and Associated Elements

In this chapter, we explore the key elements of humility – in the lower right corner of Figure 7.1 – and look at how the dimension of humility complements the other dimensions of leader character.

First, let's look at some examples of humility – or the lack thereof – and consider what those examples teach us.

Sports, Politics, and Business: Any Room for Humility?

One of the strangest things about lack of humility is that it may lead people to make colossally bad decisions, and then to compound more bad decisions on top of the first one, either on the assumption that they know what is best, or that the rules don't apply to them. "I'm too smart to get caught," as this logic goes; "and even if I get caught, I'm too important to be held accountable for my actions."

For example, take the case of Lance Armstrong, the professional road racing cyclist and captain of the U.S. Postal Service team who won the Tour de France an astounding seven consecutive years between 1999 and 2005. A role model to many individuals, Armstrong was accused in 2011 of using illegal performance-enhancing drugs (PEDs) for much of the previous decade. He strenuously denied the allegations. But in 2012, the United States Anti-Doping Agency (USADA) banned him from cycling for life, and stripped him of his seven Tour de France victories, ruling that Armstrong had engaged in "the most sophisticated, professionalized and successful doping program that sport has ever seen."[1] Not only had Armstrong used PEDs, concluded the USADA, but he had coerced his teammates to do so as well. The emerging details – including furtive blood transfusions in covert mobile laboratories – became more and more repugnant.

Armstrong continued to assert his innocence, attacking and even suing his accusers at every opportunity. Then, in January 2013, in a complete about-face, he confessed to all the charges during an on-camera interview with Oprah Winfrey – during which he referred to himself as a "bully" who "expected to get whatever he wanted and to control every outcome."[2]

Even this confession drew fire: a measure of how far from grace Armstrong had fallen. He told Oprah that he stopped doping in 2005 – a claim that, if true, might mean that the relevant statute of limitations had expired, and that he could escape prosecution. If he was trying to be contrite, and show humility, he failed. One of his accusers – who had been singled out for abuse by Armstrong for years – responded to the interview by saying that Armstrong "doesn't know how to tell the truth, and how to say he's sorry."[3]

In the political realm, the classic example of "I'm too smart to get caught and I'm too important to be held accountable" is Gary Hart, the former U. S. Senator from Colorado. In 1987, Hart was far out in front in the race for the Democratic nomination for President – and given that he was favored to win the general election over the likely Republican nominee, he stood to be the next U. S. president. Then word got out that he was having an affair with a 29-year-old commercial actress from Miami. When pressed by reporters, he snapped, "Follow me around. I don't care. I'm serious. If anybody wants to put a tail on me, go ahead. They'd be very bored." They did put a tail on him, and quickly turned up ample evidence of the affair. Hart's campaign imploded. Rather than moving into the White House, he became a sordid political footnote.[4]

More recently, Toronto Mayor Rob Ford ran into trouble for – among other things – his lack of humility.[5] The first signs of trouble in Ford's character emerged publicly in April 2006, when – as a sitting city councilor – he was escorted out of a Maple Leafs hockey game for shouting obscenities. First he denied even being at the game, but then admitted that he had been, and apologized for his behavior. Despite this incident, and evidence of previous substance abuse in the late 1990s, Ford was elected mayor of Toronto in 2010, and pursued a generally populist agenda.

Early in 2013, rumors started to circulate that Ford was a crack cocaine user. He flatly and repeatedly denied the rumors – but in November admitted that he had indeed used the illegal drug, "probably in one of my drunken stupors." Then, at the very moment when some humility was called for, Ford castigated the press corps for "not asking the right questions," which enabled him to conceal the truth for many months. The backlash to this and other revelations was intense, and the city council began stripping him of his powers. When in January 2014 he announced his intention to run for re-election, he brushed aside the white-hot controversy over his personal conduct. "I've been the best mayor that this city's ever had," he boasted.

Ford never saw himself as constrained by the rules that govern most people in the public eye. The stunning side story was that Ford had many supporters who suggested that what he did in private simply didn't matter, as long as he delivered on his cost-cutting election promises. What these supporters failed to understand was that lack of humility impacts judgment, and acts as a ticking time bomb embedded in the decision-making of the organization.

At this point, perhaps we need some relief from out-of-control egos. One example we can point to is that of Narayana Murthy, former CEO and executive chairman of Infosys Limited, the global software consulting company headquartered in Bangalore, India.[6] Murthy co-founded the company in 1981, ran it as CEO until 2002, and served on its board until 2013. Infosys was, and is, an astounding business success story. More than any other single company, Infosys invented the global delivery model that led to India's huge success as a center for IT services outsourcing. The company was listed on NASDAQ in 1999, and over the past two decades has been the best-performing stock on the benchmark S&P BSE Sensex. While that index recorded an aggregate nine-fold gain over those 20 years, Infosys became 64 times more valuable.[7]

Murthy is extraordinarily accomplished in his own right. He was the first Indian winner of Ernst & Young's World Entrepreneur Award (2003). A 2005 study conducted by the Economist Intelligence Unit ranked him as among the "world's ten most admired chief executives." He was listed as one of the "12 greatest entrepreneurs of our time" by *Fortune* in 2012. He has led key corporate governance initiatives in India, and serves as an IT advisor to several Asian countries. He serves on the boards of the Ford Foundation, the Rhodes Trust, the Indian School of Business, and the United Nations Foundation, and – in the corporate sector – has served on the boards of both HSBC and Unilever. He was chairman of the International Institute of Information Technology in Bangalore between 2002 and 2007; and – reflecting his interest in education – he has served on the boards of Cornell University, the Singapore Management University, INSEAD (in Paris), the Wharton School of Management, and the Stanford Business School. He has been awarded honorary doctorates from more than two dozen universities in India and abroad. He also is a billionaire.

And every night, when he goes home – away from the fanfare, hoopla, awards, deference, and power – Murthy makes a point of helping clean the bathrooms at his home.[8]

Why does he pick up a toilet brush? He explains that he isn't just hoping to make his wife happy. Taking a lesson from Gandhi, he tries to perform tasks that might be considered beneath his elevated station in life – as a reminder that all contributions to society should be valued. "In the corporate context," he says, "it shows that you have respect for everybody's contribution." Murthy believes that sustainable success requires CEOs to recognize that there are people who are smarter than they are, and who – given the chance – can do things better. "Once you have that humility," he explains, "once you have that openness of mind, even when you are doing well, it is possible to learn from people who are doing better than you both within the organization and outside the organization."

But simply recognizing that you can benefit from other people's honest opinions isn't enough, Murthy observes, because most employees won't risk disagreeing with the boss. As a result, the biggest challenge a leader has is to create channels for feedback and keep them open. "The day a leader closes those feedback channels," he says, "is the day when a leader's power starts diminishing and he or she starts doing things that are completely wrong."

At Infosys, Murthy actively promulgated one key rule: "You can disagree with me as long as you are not disagreeable." Among other things, this openness to polite opposition allowed him to learn what employees really thought about his leadership style. For example? "Many colleagues have come to me and said I am too sales-oriented; and that I value the contribution of sales people much more than the contribution of other people. That was a big revelation to me."

In response, Murthy asked for examples, which employees supplied. He then talked with them about why sales people were so important to the company: If nobody bought Infosys's products and services, there would be no Infosys. "They seemed convinced," Murthy recalls, "[but] from that day onward, I listened to everybody with the same level of attention."

Character Elements: What Goes into "Humility"?

Looking back to Figure 7.1, you can see that there are eight character elements that combine to foster humility. When you are humble, you are:

Self-aware: You are mindful of your own feelings, thoughts, values, motives, reactions, and behavior. Self-awareness helps people to become more successful in their interactions with people.[9] It provides a critical feedback loop to learn.

For example, Carol Stephenson – former dean of the Ivey Business School at Canada's Western University, and a former executive in the telecom sector – believes that self-awareness comes in part through seasoning.[10] "The more experienced you get," she says, "the more self-aware you become. I say to the younger leaders, just chill out a little bit and learn more about yourself. Learn what you're good at, find out what you're not so good at, and don't be afraid to say that you're not good at something."[11]

Modest: You don't unduly call attention to your own accomplishments.

One example of deflecting – and managing – praise comes from Kiran Mazumdar-Shaw, chairman and managing director of Biocon Limited, and one of the true pioneers of the Indian biotechnology industry. She was celebrated by both *Forbes* and *Times* as one of the world's 100 most powerful women. She shrugs off such accolades, citing a key influence in her life: "My husband keeps me grounded. And he always reminds me of a very important saying, and I keep using that saying a lot: 'People that mind don't matter and people that matter don't mind.'"

Celebrity, she explains, teaches you to act in a certain way – pampered, celebrated, spoiled – and that behavior is counterproductive. "Whereas if you're humble, and you're not expecting to be treated in a special way, but just give your best, you end up getting recognized." People shouldn't do things because they want to wind up on the *Forbes* list, she adds; they should wind up on the *Forbes* list because they want to do things.

Reflective: You frequently examine your mental models and thinking habits to cultivate constructive thought patterns and conduct. This can be undertaken in real time, or it can be a more measured process.

Charles Brindamour is CEO of Intact Financial Corporation, the leading provider of property and casualty insurance in Canada. He began his career as an actuary, which may hint at the origins of his methodical approach to reflection. "I reflect all the time on the impact I have on others," he says. "It's a constant, ongoing introspection on the impact you have on others – in situations, in meetings, and when we debate projects – and on the impact I have on others over a period of time. I step back, look at the past year or two, and have this inner dialogue – probably more than I should! – on the impact I have on others. I assess whether it was calibrated properly, and whether it had the desired impact. I consider whether or not it was constructive, whether the other party was open to the feedback, and so on."

For Brindamore, reflection is inseparable from leadership: "I spend a lot of time, including informal time, reflecting on the impact I've had on others – and therefore, on leadership."[12]

Continuous learner: You seek and enjoy new opportunities to learn and grow on a continuous basis. Good leaders never lose their impulse to learn new things. They know that once they do, complacency sets in – a dysfunctional tendency that tends to undercut performance.

Antonio Cimolino, artistic director of Canada's Stratford Shakespeare Festival, emphasizes that you don't have to go looking for opportunities to learn; you mainly have to recognize and take advantage of them when they present themselves to you. "There's something to be learned every day," he explains, "both by looking in the mirror at yourself and by looking at the people around you." And while you can readily see ways that others can improve themselves, "it is better to start with yourself."

Curious: You demonstrate a genuine fascination with a wide variety of topics. You express a keen interest in seeking out new information and novel experiences, and approach these learning opportunities with an open, inquisitive, non-judgmental attitude. Obviously, curiosity is closely linked to continuous learning, cited just above. The curious person finds a broad range of ideas and contexts interesting, and is humble enough to "park his or her ego" and venture into the unknown.

One compelling example is Purdy Crawford – a Canadian lawyer, businessman, and philanthropist who died in 2014 at the age of 82. Born a coal miner's son in Nova Scotia, and educated in a two-room schoolhouse, Crawford began his professional life as a lawyer in the late 1950s with the firm of Osler Hoskin & Harcourt, helped the Ontario provincial government draft new securities regulations, moved into the business sector as president and CEO of Imasco, Ltd. – where he spent a decade – and eventually made his way back into law. Along the way, Crawford achieved minor-celebrity status for his habit of sending selected magazine and newspaper articles – which came to be known as "Purdy's Picks" – to an ever-growing list of friends and associates.

One businessperson whom Crawford mentored remembered him as a "good listener and a ferocious reader." Crawford – that friend recalled – would never read the 12-page summary of a legal decision if he could get his hands on the entire document.[13] His powerful brand of curiosity, and his willingness to explore realms that were foreign to him, sparked similar excitement in those around him.

Respectful: You treat others with dignity, especially when providing feedback. You remain tolerant, civil, courteous, and constructive with others.

One of the lessons that we can take away from both the Gary Hart and Rob Ford stories is that public displays of disdain are rarely likely to work in your favor – especially if it's the press corps toward which you are being disdainful. On the positive side of the ledger, we have Narayana Murthy's account of "negotiating" with his subordinates to accommodate their concerns, even when he wasn't entirely convinced by their arguments.

Grateful: You sincerely acknowledge and appreciate others' contributions. You feel thankful for the things you have received in life. Genuine gratitude serves humility, because we lose our sense of self-importance when we have a deeply felt appreciation for even the smallest things around us. Here is one simple "gratitude exercise": Imagine all the things that had to happen so that you could have a piece of paper on the table in front of you. That humble piece of paper connects you with an incredible range of people over multiple generations, as well as with the natural world. All those people, places, and resources deserve your gratitude – and humility.

One of the strangest aspects of the sorry tale of Lance Armstrong was how willing he was to abuse the teammates who helped make his cycling victories possible. First he compelled them to join him in the drug abuse; then, when the truth started to leak out, he turned on them savagely.

Contrast this with the story of Chris Martin IV, who in 1983 faced the imminent closure of the Nazareth, Pennsylvania-based guitar company founded by his great-great-great grandfather in 1833. Martin called a meeting with his employees, who knew full well that the company was on the cliff edge. Martin thanked them for being patient with the company, which hadn't given them a raise in years. Then he challenged them to get back to making the great guitars that he knew they were capable of making – and promised them that if the company survived, they would share in any future profits. It worked. Since that dark period, Martin has rebounded, and has paid out millions of dollars in profit-sharing checks.[14]

Vulnerable: You let others see your true self.

John Furlong, the former CEO of the Vancouver Olympic Committee, credits his father with teaching him the importance of being open and vulnerable. "We've tried to teach you right and wrong," his father told him at one point; "and we've tried to give you what you need to navigate through the world." Then, as Furlong recalls, his father added: "These things are not going to be enough, however, unless you're prepared to step out of the crowd, be a little bit more vulnerable, risk a little bit more humiliation, and do more than the people around you." If he did so, the senior Furlong concluded, he would have "a fighting chance to be an inspired human being."

Obviously, these character elements work together to support humility. Being reflective is critical to self-awareness. When you are grateful for what you have, it helps bring perspective to where you fit in the bigger picture. This sense of your relative place in the world is particularly powerful when you are a continuous learner. Being grateful and a continuous learner will support a sense of modesty and reduce the inclination to act in a self-serving manner. These elements, in turn, foster being respectful of others.

Humility and a Strong Ego

As suggested above, Jack Welch – the former chairman and CEO of General Electric – is more often associated with ego than with humility. But it was Welch who was fond of pointing out that "the operative assumption today is that someone, somewhere, has a better idea; and the operative compulsion is to find out who has that better idea, and put it into action fast."

Acknowledging that others are doing it better is a form of humility – and it was this attitude that enabled GE under Welch to adopt the ideas that others had developed, such as Six Sigma from Motorola, quick inventory turns from American Standard, kaizen methodologies from Toyota, and others. The whole "Workout" system at GE was driven by the fundamental belief that innovation in productivity could be driven by the ideas and energy of people who were not in formal leadership positions at GE and that the job of the leadership was to enable, encourage, and empower these people to make change.

Ben Bernanke – chairman of the Federal Reserve during the 2008 financial crisis, and a former economics professor at Princeton – and Henry (Hank) Paulsen, Secretary of the Treasury and former chairman at Goldman Sachs, both had strong egos. (They could not have reached their lofty positions without a healthy sense of self-regard.) But when the crisis unfolded, they both realized that they did not have the answers. Their fundamental humility made them reach out to others, listen to what they had to say, and fashion solutions on the run. And when those solutions turned out to be less than perfect, that same fundamental humility allowed them to recognize problems early, correct course, and pursue different solutions.

Humility Complementing Other Dimensions

Without humility, your ego can take over and result in decisions and actions that are clouded by a sense of self-importance. It can result in an approach to humanity and collaboration that is motivated by self-interest, which in the long run can destroy relationships, and cause leaders to be rejected by their followers and other stakeholders.

Furthermore, justice and courage may become skewed by this sense of self-importance. Humility takes integrity to a deeper level because as you become more reflective and self-aware, shortcomings in the realm of integrity – such as authenticity and candor – are revealed.

Last, it would be hard to be held accountable if one had no humility. Those who duck their responsibilities will lose the respect of their peers, those whom they report to, those who work for them, and the general public.

Ultimately, an out-of-control ego hurts its owner the most. At a recent golf tournament, Rory McIlroy, the world's top-ranked player, hooked a shot into the water … and his 3-iron quickly followed. He had let the frustration of two days of poor play get the better of him.

At the end of his round, he made a point of expressing regret for his action, apologizing to the assembled spectators for his failure to be a good role model. "It wasn't one of my proudest moments," he admitted. "I wouldn't encourage kids to do it. It felt good at the time, but I don't feel good about it now." He showed drive and lacked temperance; but ultimately, his humility assured the world that he didn't see himself as someone to whom the rules of etiquette don't apply.

Humility in the Absence of Other Dimensions

Of course, we caution against excessive humility, because this may lead to self-abnegation – a failure to celebrate personal strengths – which may undermine the self-confidence that a leader must have to become and stay successful.

Humility without courage, drive, and transcendence may make you overly passive. These other dimensions of character provide a sense of purpose and energy. They ensure that humility is arising from confidence, rather than a lack of confidence. Consider the great things accomplished by Mother Teresa, a woman of great humility. Her humility was clearly supported by the other dimensions of character, and captured by her statement that "if you are humble, nothing will touch you, neither praise nor disgrace, because you know what you are."

Transcendence brings an expansive quality to humility, so that it doesn't become narrow in its application, running the risk that you limit what you believe is possible. Rather, strength of humility – when coupled with dimensions like transcendence and drive – can be incredibly liberating, because it helps us to be open to ideas and approaches that feel almost beyond reach. While humility helps to check ego, accountability prevents you from disconnecting from the role you need to play. There are many people who hide behind being shy, or not wanting to be in the spotlight; however, when they discover that accountability demands it, they speak up and share their point of view. In other words, they learn to strengthen their humility.

Humility and the Gifts of Imperfection

One of the all-time most watched videos on TED.com – with more than 18 million views – documents a talk given in 2010 at TEDx Houston by a researcher and social worker named Brené Brown.[15] Brown, based at the University of Houston's Graduate College of Social Work, studies (in her words) vulnerability, courage, worthiness, and shame.[16] She is the author of two #1 *New York Times* best-selling books: *Daring Greatly* and *The Gifts of Imperfection.*

Brown argued in Houston that healthy and happy people – people she defined as "wholehearted" – have four key attributes: the courage to be imperfect, the compassion to be kind to themselves and to others, and connection with others, as a result of authenticity. "They were willing to let go of who they should be," she told her audience, "in order to be who they were."

We are imperfect, says Brown, and we are wired for struggle, and we are worthy of love and belonging. But we have to let ourselves be "seen" – deeply seen. We have to practice gratitude. We have to stop yelling, and start listening.

Nowhere in her talk did Brown use the word "humility." But it is the implicit undertone in all that she advocates: listening, learning, showing respect, being vulnerable, acknowledging, and struggling against imperfection.

And, as a result of that process, getting a little less imperfect. "There is nothing noble in being superior to your fellow man," Ernest Hemingway wrote. "True nobility is being superior to your former self."

Questions to Contemplate

1.   Are my ego strengths accompanied by humility? Do I keep my ego in check, so that I can learn from my mistakes and appreciate the strengths and value of others?
2.   When making important decisions in life or work, do I make sure to get the inputs of others, no matter how right I think my own inclinations are?
3.   Do I ensure that I am not cutting myself off from people who are at a different level or status than I am – especially customers, suppliers, employees, and shareholders – who may have valuable inputs that I may not be getting?

Books and Articles to Read

Daring Greatly: How the Courage to Be Vulnerable Transforms the Way We Live, Love, Parent, and Lead Brené Brown (Gotham, 2012)

Giving One Pause: Learn How Cultivating Humility can Drive Success, Even in the Most Time-, Budget-, and Attention-Stressed Workplaces Nance Guilmartin (ASTD, 2010)

"The Paradox Of Humility In American Business And Society" Doug Guthrie (*Forbes*, November 2013)

"Expressed Humility in Organizations: Implications for Performance, Teams, and Leadership" Bradley Owens, Michael Johnson, and Terence Mitchell (*Organization Science*, 24 (5), November 2012)

Judgment Calls: Twelve Stories of Big Decisions and the Teams that Got Them Right Thomas H. Davenport and Brook Manville (Harvard Business Review Press, 2012)

Thinking, Fast and Slow Daniel Kahneman (Anchor Canada, 2013)

"The Moral Bucket List" David Brooks (*New York Times*, December 4, 2015)

Videos to Watch

"The Power of Vulnerability" TED Talk by Brené Brown (www.ted.com/talk, 2010)

President Obama: "I'm Really Proud of All of You." (YouTube, 2012)

Notes

1 See the BBC's summary, "Lance Armstrong: Usada report labels him 'a serial cheat'," 10.11.12, online at http://www.bbc.com/sport/0/cycling/19903716.
2 The quote is from a *USA Today* summary of the interview, "Lance Armstrong to Oprah: Story was 'one big lie'," by Brent Schrotenboer, 01.18.13, at http://www.usatoday.com/story/sports/cycling/2013/01/17/lance-armstrong-oprah-winfrey-confession/1843641/. The interview can be seen at http://www.oprah.com/own/Lance-Armstrong-Confesses-to-Oprah-Video.
3 See, for example, the 01.18.13 ABC News story by Neal Karlinsky and Anthony Castellano, online at http://abcnews.go.com/US/lance-armstrong-lied-oprah-cover-crimes-investigators/story?id=18245484.
4 For an excellent summary of the Hart affair and its long-term impact on American politics, see Matt Bai's article in the 09.18.14 edition of the *New York Times* at http://www.nytimes.com/2014/09/21/magazine/how-gary-harts-downfall-forever-changed-american-politics.html?_r=0. Bai's premise is that Hart's downfall fundamentally changed the relationship between American politicians and the media.
5 For an interesting summary of Ford's rise to power and fall from grace, see the Star.com's timeline, "Rob Ford: Accomplishments and Controversies," 09.17.14, at http://www.thestar.com/news/gta/2014/09/17/rob_fords_highs_and_lows_at_toronto_city_hall.html.
6 Unless otherwise noted, this section is derived from Gerard Seijts's *Good Leaders Learn* (Routledge, 2014).
7 Statistics from George Smith Alexander's 12.07.14 BloombergBusiness article, "Infosys co-founders sell about $1 billion of stock," at http://www.bloomberg.com/news/2014-12-08/infosys-founders-said-to-sell-about-1-billion-of-stock.html.
8 This section also draws upon Gerard Seijts's column in the 11.30.12 edition of *BW/Businessworld*, online at http://www.businessworld.in/news/web-exclusives/a-legacy-of-leadership/656851/page-1.html.
9 Van Velsor, E., Taylor, S., and Leslie, J. B., "An examination of the relationships among self-perception accuracy, self-awareness, gender, and leader effectiveness," *Human Resource Management*, 32 (1993), 249–263; Church, A., "Managerial self-awareness in high-performing individuals in organizations," *Journal of Applied Psychology*, 82 (1993), 281–292.
10 In the spirit of full disclosure, the authors point out that Stephenson is their former boss, in the unique hierarchy of academia.
11 From Gerard Seijts's *Good Leaders Learn* (Routledge, 2014).
12 Ibid.
13 From Crawford's obituary, "Respected business leader Purdy Crawford dies at 82," by Janet McFarland, in the 08.12.14 *Globe and Mail*, online at http://www.theglobeandmail.com/report-on-business/veteran-canadian-businessman-purdy-crawford-dies/article20007010/.

14 See, for example, Jack Boulware's 04.10.09 blog, "C. F. Martin Guitars," online at http://www.jackboulware.com/writing/cf-martin-guitars.
15 See the TED talk at http://www.ted.com/talks/brene_brown_on_vulnerability?language=en#t-587388.
16 See Brown's website at http://brenebrown.com/about/.

8 Integrity

In this chapter, we explore the dimension of integrity, which you will see depicted at the bottom of Figure 8.1. What do we mean, and not mean, by integrity? What are its key behavioral elements? How do these elements complement one another to create integrity? How does integrity complement the other ten dimensions?

Integrity is derived from the Latin word *integer*, or "wholeness." When we refer to a building's structural integrity, we're talking about the ability of that building to hold itself together under a load – including the load of its own weight – without collapsing. Personal integrity shares a fundamental quality with structural integrity: It can't come and go. It has to be there whether people are looking or not – or you risk a calamity.

Let's look at an example of integrity in action. It focuses on a Canadian woman who – operating largely out of the limelight – has exerted a powerful influence on dozens of corporations.

Integrity in the Boardroom

Eileen Mercier is a professional independent director and former management consultant. Her career includes 40 years of general management experience in the forest products, financial services, integrated oil, and communication industries. She was one of Canada's first female professional directors. She is or has been a member of the board of organizations such as the Ontario Teachers' Pension Plan, Intact Financial Corporation, Teekay Corporation, and University Health Network. She was named one of the "Top 25 Women of Influence" by *Women of Influence* magazine in 2011, and one of "Canada's Most Powerful Women: Top 100" by the Women's Executive Network in 2012.

In that same year, the Toronto *Globe and Mail* published an article about her, which depicted her as competent, principled, candid, and consistent:

> For the past 16 years, she has been a blunt and vocal conscience on more than two dozen boards, challenging executives and directors when she believes salaries are exorbitant, financial results opaque, or corporate behavior too risky...

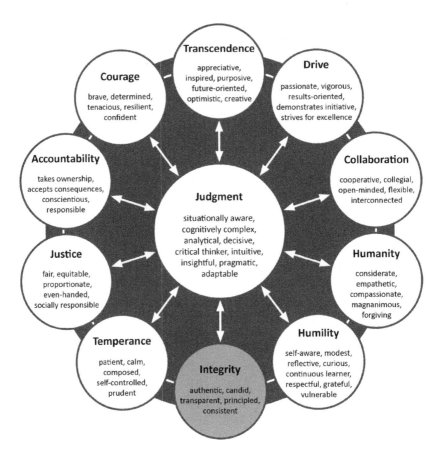

Figure 8.1 Character Dimensions and Associated Elements

In the clubby world of Canadian business it is rare to see a prominent director break ranks. It is particularly unique to hear the criticism
emanate from the small and self-conscious ranks of female directors.
To Ms. Mercier, however, it is her status as an outsider that frees her to
challenge boardroom orthodoxy.[1]

In a recent interview, Mercier cited a variety of influences that collectively
shaped her worldview. Her father taught her to never be afraid of anything.
Her mother told her to give the toughest jobs to the busiest people. In
the 1970s, when she was a very junior staffer at the TD Bank Group,
then-president and CEO Allen Lambert asked her to stop by the executive
suite (where she had never been before) so she could give him her opinion on
a pair of paintings that the bank had just purchased. He seemed genuinely
interested in what she had to say, she recalls, and that lesson – about how
to engage and inspire young people – stuck with her. Early in her years of

board service, she learned about the importance of "chemistry" within a group: If the chemistry isn't right, you know you can't continue.

One episode brings these various lessons together:

> I'm not shy about talking about issues, including ethical ones. I'll give you an example. One of the companies of which I'm on the board has quite a big operation in Brazil. The internal auditors discovered an issue involving a loan. At the Audit Committee meeting I asked a follow-up question about the event. Management told us that the perpetrator was still there. This was three or four days after they had found out about the transgression.
>
> I asked to get the CEO of that business on the phone. We were about nine hours away from where he was at the time, and I said, "I don't care what the time is, get him on the phone." So we got him on the phone, and I said, "What are you thinking? What kind of a message is that? This person has to be out of there, and everybody needs to know what happened, and why."

The episode illustrates an important aspect of Mercier's leader character. She knew instinctively what had to happen – this person has to be out of there – and it wasn't happening. Rousting out the faraway (and presumably sleepy) CEO, she asked him a series of pointed questions, and – based on his bad answers – quickly got to the outcome she knew was needed. You don't have to know everything, she says, but you have to stand for something.

Character Elements: What Goes into "Integrity"?

As Figure 8.1 indicates, we have identified five character elements that are illustrative of the integrity dimension. When you have "integrity," you are:

Authentic: You make decisions and take actions that are true to your personal values and beliefs. People see your actions as sincere and genuine. A prime example of an authentic leader is Michael McCain (see Chapter 11) and how he led Maple Leaf Foods through a food-poisoning crisis, an existential challenge by activist investors, and the capital-intensive restructuring of the company's manufacturing and distribution networks. At all times, he shared his concerns, vision, values, sense of risks, and potential rewards with his shareholders, employees, directors, and other stakeholders. As a result, people felt they had come to know the real Michael McCain, and therefore trusted him.

Candid: You strive to be truthful and straightforward with yourself, and with others. You remain forthright even in difficult situations without being mean-spirited.

Candor is essential to achieving long-term success. For example, as explained in *Forbes*, Warren Buffett, CEO and chairman of Berkshire Hathaway, counts on his vice-chairman, Charlie Munger, to point out flaws in his own reasoning. Said Buffett: "If I talk it through [with him], it's because deep down I know I might be doing something dumb, and he'll tell me."[2]

Jack Welch at General Electric saw candor as a source of competitive advantage, because candid people deal with reality, "seeing things as they are, not as they were or wish them to be." Jeff Immelt, his successor at GE, carried the same principle forward; his personal style is very different from Welch's – it is certainly less blunt – but it is no less effective.

Transparent: You remain open and honest in your relationships and communications. You allow others to see what you truly value, believe, know, and intend, including those things with which you are struggling. Recently, Howard Schultz, the CEO of Starbucks, said that: "I think the currency of leadership is transparency. You've got to be truthful. I don't think you should be vulnerable every day, but there are moments where you've got to share your soul and conscience with people and show them who you are, and not be afraid of it." He modeled this behavior during the 2008 financial crisis, when more than 12,000 Starbucks employees lost their jobs.

Principled: You demonstrate high personal and professional standards.

Dominic D'Alessandro was the president and CEO of Manulife Financial, a major Canadian insurance company and financial services provider.[3] In 2005, the company got "hoodwinked" into recommending one of the Portus Alternative Asset Management Inc.'s products to its clients. Quite predictably, Manulife was hit with a class-action lawsuit alleging that it had "failed to conduct proper due diligence on Portus before it entered into a referral agreement with the hedge fund operator."[4] The company immediately promised to refund thousands of investors who had lost money in their investment – almost $235 million.

Jeffrey Gandz asked D'Alessandro if it would be possible to write a case on the decision to refund investors who had lost money in their investment. His response: "It will be the shortest business case study ever written." Why? His answer: "It was just the right thing to do."

Consistent: You practice what you preach. And you walk that talk across situations – including both good and challenging times, over the long haul.

Eileen Mercier's story underscores this longitudinal dimension of integrity. Over the long term, integrity doesn't just "count"; it's all-important. "In business as in life," as she puts it, "in the final analysis, it is really all you have. Don't lend it to any company or individual that you do not trust. Your reputation must be your first, last, and most important consideration." Her story also hints at the difficulties that are sometimes associated with integrity: If the chemistry isn't right, you know you can't continue.

If you encounter wrongdoing in a given context, then you either need to exercise your integrity through voicing your concerns and take subsequent action, or – if your personal values and convictions no longer fit with those of the people around – you need to exit the situation.

Integrity and Ethics

Many people use the words "ethics" and "integrity" interchangeably. But as we see it, using those words as if they meant more or less the same thing washes out some very important and useful distinctions.

"Ethics" is a set of guidelines for right or wrong, and thus provides a roadmap for decision-making and action. What is considered to be ethical will vary from person to person, and group to group. For those who have well-developed ethical frameworks, it helps them to find "a bright moral line" that guides their decision-making. Even though they sometimes choose to step over that line, they almost always know that they are doing so. When they do so – acting in ways that are inconsistent with their internal ethical codes, or more public codes to which they have visibly ascribed – then they are considered to lack integrity.

Integrity Complementing Other Dimensions

People with high levels of integrity tend to reveal the other dimensions of their character. When integrity is lacking, it becomes difficult – or indeed, impossible – to be truly collaborative; indeed, it may be necessary for individuals to oppose the actions of others, thereby creating open conflict. Displays of authentic anger threaten temperance, and candid comments – unless they are very skillfully conveyed – can be considered lacking in compassion.

Being self-effacing can be appropriate, up to a certain point; but in a corrupt organizational context, integrity may have to trump humility.

Integrity is a major underpinning element for accountability. This is what Eileen Mercier demands in those boardrooms: People in positions of authority need to take responsibility for their actions, which is one kind of integrity. When they don't, the people around them have to call them out: a second kind of integrity.

And finally, integrity also helps to inform justice, and may serve as a motivating force for drive and courage. When you have integrity, you are able and willing to act on those dimensions.

Integrity in the Absence of Other Dimensions

Can integrity stand alone? Maybe your first reaction is to imagine an individual of such sterling integrity that he or she could live a character-filled life on the strength of that integrity alone.

We suggest not. Without humanity and collaboration, integrity can become dogmatic and rigid. There is a subtle but important difference between being right and self-righteous. As one of our colleagues used to say: "Trying to be right is a noble purpose, but self-righteousness becomes annoying, and the minute you turn sanctimonious, people begin to tune you out." Harry Potter's Professor Dumbledore put it this way: "People find it far easier to forgive others for being wrong than being right."

Courage and drive are critical to exercising integrity, given that being principled and candid on a consistent basis is not easy. Engaging in vigorous debate in the search for organizational excellence is critically important for any leader who wishes to contribute. But it takes courage to say things people do not want to hear, or expect to hear, in person. Narayana Murthy, one of the co-founders of Infosys, insists that ideas should be judged based on data and facts. He tells his colleagues that they can disagree with him as long as they don't become disagreeable. Many whistleblowers describe "living through hell" as they exposed wrongdoing and cover-ups at high levels in governments and corporations.

And finally, accountability ensures that you are prepared to live with the consequences that sometimes arise from acting with integrity. Nobel Laureate Malala Yousafzai is the Pakistani activist for human rights and female education. She nearly paid the ultimate price for her principled stand, her candor, and her transparency when the Taliban tried to kill her in 2012. She continues her activism, despite ongoing threats against her life.

Integrity on its Own: Not Necessarily the Winning Formula

Let's look at a second example of a woman who – like Eileen Mercier – was willing to demonstrate integrity in a tough situation. In the wake of the financial meltdown on Wall Street that began in 2008, the Federal Reserve Bank of New York (the Fed) adopted a new watchdog policy: In the case of banks deemed too big to fail, the Fed would station bank examiners on site to monitor those banks' activities and help keep them out of trouble.

One of those newly hired federal bank examiners was a young woman named Carmen Segarra, who was placed at Goldman Sachs between November 2011 and May 2012.[5] Highly educated – with degrees from Harvard (BA), Columbia (MA in French cultural studies), and Cornell (law) – Segarra spent 13 years working at a succession of financial firms, where she brought her legal and language skills (fluent or conversant in five languages) to bear on a variety of complex legal and regulatory challenges. When the Fed went looking for a new kind of watchdog, Segarra – most recently a senior counsel at Citibank – seemed a perfect fit.[6]

After a few months, she concluded that Goldman lacked a comprehensive, company-wide policy sufficient to head off conflicts of interest. Such a policy had been recommended by a federal advisory letter, but was not required by law. Goldman didn't like her finding – and evidence suggests that her bosses at the Fed didn't, either. Perhaps anticipating trouble, Segarra began taping her conversations with her Fed supervisor, also embedded at Goldman: a collection that eventually grew to comprise some 46 hours of tape. While the tapes of discussions among the Goldman-based Fed officials don't indicate any flat-out wrongdoing on their part, they paint a picture of shady dealings at Goldman, and of a group of regulators who had been effectively "captured" by the bank they were supposed to be monitoring.

Segarra formally refused to tone down her opinion about Goldman's lack of a conflict-of-interest policy – a request made by her supervisors – and also refused to destroy all supporting documents. A week later – in May 2012 – she was fired by the Fed. In 2013, Segarra filed a lawsuit against her now former employer for wrongful termination as a whistleblower. The case was dismissed in the spring of 2014 without a ruling on its merits. As U.S. District Judge Ronnie Abrams saw it, because no federal law had been broken, Segarra didn't meet the definition of a whistleblower.[7] (Again, the advisory letter from the Fed was only that: advisory.) Judge Abrams's own impartiality was soon called into question, in part because her husband was then serving as a legal advisor to Goldman. Not surprisingly, Segarra's lawyers filed an appeal.[8]

"It remains to be seen whether [Segarra] can really come out a winner," writes Yves Smith in a lengthy and thoughtful blog post, the main focus of which was to take journalists to task for their allegedly lazy coverage of the Segarra case.[9] "Reputable institutions close their ranks against people who refuse to knuckle under the pressure to conform, and Segarra has made it clear she has way more grit than most."

Yes, Segarra demonstrated principled and consistent behavior, which are among the fundamental building blocks of integrity. At the same time, she can be faulted on the equally important elements of authenticity, candor, and transparency. (Surreptitiously taping dozens of hours of conversations with your bosses is a pretty good definition of "furtive," which seems the opposite of authentic, candid, and transparent!)

But even if she met all the standards of integrity – which we would argue she did not – she appears to lack other dimensions of leader character that might have helped her succeed in what turned out to be a lonely crusade. For example, based on our best knowledge, we would argue that she came up short on the dimensions of collaboration (at times failing to be open-minded); temperance (evidently lacking the patience that might have enhanced her ability to influence and persuade); and humility (her actions regularly verged on arrogance).

Exercising integrity along with the other dimensions helps ensure that the stance you take incorporates other points of view without being co-opted by them. It helps to ensure that justice is not just done, but is seen to have been done. Yes, in cases where there is widespread corruption, whistleblowing and the mechanisms to support it are definitely necessary; in most situations – even some very challenging ones – they can be handled without resorting to whistleblowing.

The Standard You Walk Past

Let's end this chapter on a more upbeat note.

Integrity is about walking the talk. It's about being honest and transparent in your business dealings, and holding others to the same standard. It's about bringing the organization's values to life in your own behavior. It's about refraining from asking others to do things that are morally objectionable – and calling others out when they stray.

In June 2013, public allegations surfaced regarding a series of unacceptable behaviors by active members of the Australian Army.[10] Allegedly, a group of officers had produced and distributed material that demeaned women, using both Department of Defence computer systems and the internet. The members of this group secretly photographed themselves having sex with women, and then emailed those photos to a variety of recipients.

Even aside from the content of the revelations, their timing was horrendous. Only three months earlier, the Australian Army had launched a new campaign to recruit more women soldiers. A great deal of work had gone into making the army more female- and family-friendly. Now, all that work was in jeopardy.

A key player in that effort at institutional transformation had been Chief of Army and Lieutenant General David Morrison, a second-generation Australian Army officer whose father had distinguished himself both in Korea and Vietnam. Morrison had joined the army in 1979, rising steadily through the ranks over the ensuing three decades. Personable, businesslike, and forthright, the phrase most often used to describe him was straight-shooter. "He's got integrity a mile deep," as one of his former commanders put it, "and he calls it like it is."[11]

What did Morrison do, when confronted with allegations of sordid and criminal behavior in the ranks below him – allegations that, if true, would strike at the heart of the army he was trying to build? First he held a press conference. "It's on me," he told the assembled reporters – and by extension, the nation. "I'm responsible for this. I'm the chief of the Australian Army. The culture of the army is in my hands during my tenure, and I am doing as much as I possibly can to improve it."[12]

Then he went on TV. Staring – glaring – directly at the camera, he delivered a three-minute, straight-from-the-heart statement.[13] First he spoke to his fellow Australians, assuring them that the alleged misdeeds were in direct contravention to every value that his army stood for. Then he spoke directly, unblinkingly, to the perpetrators, and any sympathizers they might have.

> Those who think that it's OK to behave in a way that demeans or exploits their colleagues have no place in this army ... If that does not suit you, then get out. You may find another employer where your attitude and behavior is acceptable, but I doubt it. The same goes for those who think that toughness is built on humiliating others. Every one of us is responsible for the culture and reputation of our army, and the environment in which we work. If you become aware of any individual degrading another, then show moral courage and take a stand against it...
>
> I will be ruthless in ridding the army of people who cannot live up to its values. And I need every one of you to support me in achieving this. The standard you walk past is the standard you accept. That goes for all of us, but especially those who by their rank have a leadership role ... If you're not up to it, find something else to do with your life. There is no place for you amongst this band of brothers ... and sisters.

The video went viral. It attracted particular attention in the U.S., where Congressional leaders were then grilling American military leaders about allegedly increasing levels of sexual abuse and violence within the U.S. military.

We again want to underscore a core message, well stated by Morrison: "The standard you walk past is the standard you accept." Integrity is about not walking past an unacceptable standard, as the actions of Ellen Mercier and David Morrison loudly declare. Integrity is about being authentic, candid, transparent, principled, and consistent. It is about owning the problem. It is about setting and communicating the *right* standard.

Questions to Contemplate

1. Do you walk the talk? Are you authentic, candid, transparent, principled, and consistent?
2. When you see wrongdoing in your organization, do you challenge it or ignore it?
3. Do you (sometimes) veer toward being self-righteous when dealing with wrongdoing and are there ways in which you could minimize this possibility while still speaking up and speaking out?

Books and Articles to Read

"Want to Create a Culture of Integrity? Take Baby Steps" Dan Ariely (*The Company Ethicist*, 2013)
  "Why We Lie" Dan Ariely (*The Wall Street Journal*, May 26, 2012)
  Trustworthiness And Integrity: What It Takes And Why It's So Hard Michael Josephson (Josephson Institute, 2011)
  Integrity: The Courage to Meet the Demands of Reality Henry Cloud (Harper Business, 2009)
  Integrity: Doing the Right Thing for the Right Reason Barbara Killinger (McGill-Queens University Press, 2010)
  Sincerity and Authenticity Lionel Trilling (Harvard University Press, 1972)
  True North: Discover Your Authentic Leadership Bill George and Peter Sims (Jossey-Bass, 2007)

Videos to Watch

"Create Candor in the Workplace" Jack Welch (Stanford Graduate School of Business, YouTube, 2009)
  "Our Buggy Moral Code" TED Talk by Dan Ariely (www.ted.com/talk, 2009)
  "What We Don't Understand About Trust" TED Talk by Onora O'Neill (www.ted.com/talk, 2013)
  "Golden Balls – £100,150 Split or Steal?" (YouTube, 2008)
  "Golden Balls – The Weirdest Split or Steal Ever" (YouTube, 2008)
  David Morrison's PSA to the nation and to his troops (YouTube, 2013)

Notes

1 In the 05.13.11 edition of the *Globe and Mail*, "Eileen Mercier: It's all about multitasking," by Jacquie McNish, online at http://www.theglobeandmail.com/report-on-business/careers/careers-leadership/eileen-mercier-its-all-about-multitasking/article4263126/?page=all.
2 This example is taken from a 2014 *Forbes* article, "5 counterintuitive habits of truly authentic leaders," written by Maseena Ziegler; see http://www.forbes.com/sites/maseenaziegler/2014/06/22/5-counterintuitive-habits-of-truly-authentic-leaders/.
3 John Hancock is the U.S. unit of Manulife.
4 This example is derived from an 03.04.05 article by Sinclair Stewart and Paul Waldie, "Manulife guarantees Portus investments," in the *Globe and Mail*; online at http://www.theglobeandmail.com/report-on-business/manulife-guarantees-portus-investments/article976787/.
5 Much of this story is derived from a ProPublica/*This American Life* joint investigation, summarized online in the ProPublica website in an 11.17.14 article by Jake Bernstein, at http://www.propublica.org/article/the-carmen-segarra-tapes; and a related article, 10.28.13, also by Bernstein, "So who is Carmen Segarra? A Fed whistleblower Q&A," online at http://www.propublica.org/article/so-who-is-carmen-segarra-a-fed-whistleblower-qa.

6 Yves Smith's 09.29.14 article, "Fed whistleblower Carmen Segarra, Snowden, and the closing of the journalistic mind," on the *Naked Capitalism* website, online at (http://www.nakedcapitalism.com/2014/09/ fed-whistleblower-carmen-segarra-snowden-closing-journalistic-mind.html) also presents a recent and balanced summary of the Segarra affair.

7 Judge Abrams's rationale is summarized in a 04.23.14 Reuters piece by Jonathan Stempel, "NY Fed wins dismissal of lawsuit by examiner who faulted Goldman," online at http://www.reuters.com/article/2014/04/23/nyfed-goldman-lawsuit-idUSL2N0NF28P20140423.

8 See Tyler Durden's 09.28.14 *Burning Platform* column on the Segarra affair – "I am putting everything in Goldman Sachs because these guys can do whatever the hell they want" – online at http://www.theburningplatform.com/tag/ carmen-segarra/.

9 From Smith's 09.29.14 article cited above, at http://www.nakedcapitalism. com/2014/09/fed-whistleblower-carmen-segarra-snowden-closing-journalistic-mind.html.

10 This section is derived, except where otherwise noted, from "The Cultural Battle of the Australian Army," Ivey Publishing Case #9B13C035, written by Paul Bigus in 2013.

11 Paul Toohey, "Meet the Man behind Lieutenant General David Morrison," news.com.au, 06.22.13, online at http://www.news.com.au/lifestyle/meet-the-man-behind-lieutenant-general-david-morrison/story-fneuzufi-1226668094794.

12 From Toohey's 06.22.13 article cited above, at http://www.news.com. au/lifestyle/meet-the-man-behind-lieutenant-general-david-morrison/ story-fneuzufi-1226668094794.

13 See the video at https://www.youtube.com/watch?v=SSR19QL8ZvI.

9   Temperance

"Temperance" is a word that – because of its vaguely antique connotations – falls oddly on contemporary eyes and ears, like high collars and hoop skirts. Actually, the word dates back to the time of the ancient Greeks, to whom it meant "self-control." In the Bible, temperance took on a somewhat narrower meaning: exercising control over one's desires and passions – and in particular, over one's sensual appetites.[1]

The word was appropriated in the early 1800s by reformers across the English-speaking world who advocated moderation in the consumption of alcohol.[2] The temperance movement inevitably overlapped with the abstinence movement – meaning total abstention from alcohol – and when extreme anti-alcohol measures like Prohibition in the U.S. failed, "temperance" fell into disrepute.

We think this is unfair, and unfortunate. We need temperance, broadly defined, in our constellation of leader character dimensions – as the events leading up to the financial meltdown in the last decade so dramatically underscored. The word, and the concept behind it, deserve a new lease on life.

What is temperance? Temperate people conduct themselves in a calm, composed manner. They maintain the ability to think clearly and respond reasonably in tense situations. They complete work and solve problems in a thoughtful, careful manner. They are prudent – resisting excesses, and staying grounded.

In this chapter, we explore some of the key elements of temperance – highlighted in Figure 9.1, below – and look at how the dimension of temperance interacts with other dimensions of leader character.

First, let's look at three examples of temperance – and intemperance – in action.

Temperance: Good for Business and Tennis?

Dennis "Chip" Wilson is a serial entrepreneur who has been celebrated as one of Canada's most creative business practitioners in the late twentieth and early twenty-first centuries.[3] In 2004, for example, he was named Canadian Entrepreneur of the Year for Innovation and Marketing by

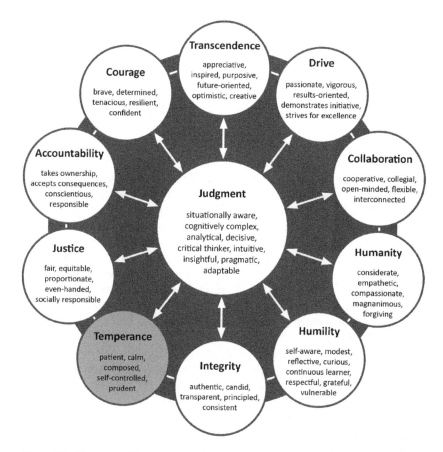

Figure 9.1 Character Dimensions and Associated Elements

Ernst & Young. Five years later, the Alberta School of Business gave him its Henry Singer Award, which recognizes "an exceptional business leader in the retailing and services sectors." With his wife Shannon, he also has emerged as a creative philanthropist, supporting children's education in Ethiopia and several highly visible causes in Vancouver and British Columbia.

What's interesting about Wilson, for the purposes of this chapter, is how over the course of his impressive career he not only has mastered business challenges, but also has created other problems by losing control over his emotions, and his tongue.

In 1980 – the year he graduated from the University of Calgary – Wilson founded Westbeach Snowboard Ltd., a surf, skate, and snowboard vertical retailer. He served as its CEO until 1995, when the private equity group to whom he had sold Westbeach ran out of patience with the company's lack of profitability:

I remember being in Hong Kong and getting a fax conveying the fact that I had been removed as CEO and that they had decided to put in their own CEO. I did the predictable. I complained. I jumped up and down. I called my lawyers. And then, you know, I just settled down and started to reflect.

What Wilson realized, upon reflection, was that his board of directors – which had been imposed upon him by his venture capitalists – was right. The directors were older, more experienced individuals who were interested in giving back their knowledge in life and to mentor and to teach. It was time for him to get out of the way. He then started another company, Lululemon Athletica Inc., which grew out of his enrolling in the first commercial yoga class offered in Vancouver. Wilson loved the experience, but hated the experience of wearing cotton clothing while sweating and stretching his way through class. Already experienced with technical athletic fabrics, in 1998 he opened a combination yoga studio and store in Vancouver, selling clothes specifically for yoga – and also offering advice and counseling in the ways and benefits of yoga. The company enjoyed rapid growth, selling apparel for yoga, running, dancing, "and most other sweaty pursuits."[4] Today it operates more than 250 stores in North America, Australia, and New Zealand.

As the leader of Lululemon, over the next decade or so, Wilson went down a road roughly similar to the one he had traveled at Westbeach: from pioneering entrepreneur to somewhat disaffected manager, sometimes prone to blurting out what was on his mind without considering the consequences. In 2013, for example, Lululemon came under fire when some of its women's yoga pants turned out to be unexpectedly transparent under workout conditions; Wilson's public response was that some women's bodies simply weren't appropriate for Lululemon's products. In the ensuing firestorm, one analyst – citing Wilson's misstep – downgraded Lululemon's stock, and Wilson was savaged in the media. Eventually, and despite being the founder and largest shareholder in the company, he was pressured to resign from the board.

Now let's look at a contrasting case from a very different venue. On Saturday, July 5, 2014, 20-year-old Canadian tennis star Eugenie Bouchard stepped onto Centre Court at Wimbledon for her women's final match with Petra Kvitova. For Bouchard, it was the definition of a high-stress event: at stake were £1,760,000 and the coveted Rosewater Dish, with millions of spectators worldwide tuned in for the televised final.

Even though Bouchard hadn't lost a set on her trip to the finals, tennis insiders suspected that she would be outgunned by the formidable Kvitova, the six-foot-tall Czech who already had one Wimbledon championship (2011) behind her.[5] Those who liked Kvitova's chances were right: She crushed Bouchard in the shortest women's final in 31 years. Bouchard played well, but Kvitova played brilliantly – perhaps the match of her career: "magical stuff," in the official Wimbledon write-up, and a "pummeling," per commentator John McEnroe.

Throughout, however, Bouchard maintained an amazing degree of self-control. She didn't appear angry, frustrated, or demoralized; instead, she kept playing her own game, hoping that Kvitova would come down to earth. As it turned out, that didn't happen. In the wake of Bouchard's crushing defeat, she was ushered into a small room to await the trophy-presentation ceremony. It turned out to be the engraver's room, meaning that she had to watch Kvitova's name – instead of her own – get engraved on the champion's Rosewater Dish.

Throughout the ordeal of the match and post-match ceremonies, Bouchard kept her cool. In the obligatory interview after the awarding of the trophies, she seemed almost upbeat. "I like Wimbledon," she said calmly. Asked if she could have played better, she started to agree, but then backed up and started over. "Sometimes your opponent just plays better than you," she said, "and that's what happened today." Would she abandon her celebrated self-control, and indulge in the junk food that she had foresworn in preparation for Wimbledon? "I'll definitely have dessert tonight," she responded. "I haven't had dessert for a while, so I'll have some brownie or something tonight." Was it cruel to have to sit in the engraver's room before the presentation? "Maybe a bit," she acknowledged. But she got to have her picture taken with the men's doubles winners, so all in all, "it's pretty cool."[6]

England was charmed by this sustained display of good sportsmanship, which in this case is synonymous with self-control. Well after the match was over – and as a steady rain fell – fans stood on nearby Henman Hill chanting, "We still love you, Genie!"

And finally, let's look at the example of Halla Tomasdottir, whose temperate approach to financial services in Iceland stood in stark contrast to the approaches of most other Icelandic financial firms – and which ultimately served as a beacon of hope when her country's economy collapsed in 2008.

Iceland had been enjoying a boom in the five or so years preceding that collapse. The currency soared, and money began flowing into the country. Feeling confident – to what turned out to be an intemperate degree – Iceland's banks began wooing British and Dutch investors to high-interest online accounts. When three of Iceland's biggest banks (Kaupthing, Glitnir, and Landsbanki) failed spectacularly in 2008, it turned out that the guarantees on those accounts were essentially worthless, and the British and Dutch governments had to repay their citizens using taxpayer money.[7] Meanwhile, the high-flying krona collapsed, and the Icelandic economy suffered through a staggering contraction – a reversal that some observers called the worst national financial crisis *ever*. "It seems likely that never before had a country managed to amass such great sums of money per capita," wrote *Der Spiegel*, "only to lose it again in a short period of time."[8]

"It actually got so bad that somebody put our country up for sale on eBay," joked Tomasdottir in her TEDWomen 2010 talk. "Ninety-nine pence was the starting price and no reserve."[9]

Tomasdottir and a colleague, Kristin Petursdottir, founded Audur Capital in Reykjavik in 2007. Both had been investment bankers in the U.S. and had experienced firsthand the giddy, irrationally exuberant mood then prevalent on Wall Street. Convinced that the global financial party – which by that point had fully engulfed tiny Iceland – was bound to end, they set up Audur, a boutique investment bank explicitly designed to take a more prudent and temperate approach. "We believed that we had a set of values," Tomasdottir explains, "and a way of doing business that would be more sustainable than what we had experienced until then."

Those values, she adds, were "feminine values." She and her colleagues at Audur conducted what they called "emotional due diligence," as well as the financial equivalent. They engaged in straight talk with their clients, including straight talk about the ever-increasing risks in the investment environment. They argued in favor of long-term profits that took into account social and environmental benefits. And while she doesn't blame men, as a gender, for the giant economic swoon that began in 2008, she does believe that a "lack of diversity, and sameness, leads to disastrous problems."

Her prescription, going forward? "We need to start embracing the beauty of balance," she says. "That's the only sustainable future."

Balance paid off well at Audur, which successfully protected its own capital and that of its clients throughout the meltdown. Audur also emerged as a leader in the Icelandic rebuilding effort, teaming up with the singer Björk to create a fund aimed at sustainable growth – and investing the first 100 million krona (approximately $826,000) in that fund.[10]

Character Elements: What Goes into "Temperance"?

As Figure 9.1 indicates, there are five character elements that contribute to the temperance dimension. When you exhibit temperance, you are:

Patient: You recognize that not everything that needs to be accomplished can be done immediately. You deal with frustrations without becoming anxious, agitated, or angry.

Dennis Wilson has gotten [gotten] better at this, over the course of his career. Early on, he told people what to do, demanded results, and was frustrated when he didn't get them. Reflecting on his time at Lululemon, he says, "The business has turned into something where I can't tell anyone how to do anything in the company. I have to be happy with the results of mentoring and teaching people, and actually letting them make their own mistakes at some levels. So, it is an evolution."[11]

Calm: You stay cool, collected, centered, and balanced. You don't display feelings of nervousness, anger, or other strong emotions.

One of the enduring images of the terrorist attacks in New York on September 11, 2001, was Mayor Rudy Giuliani's temperate public persona, particularly when he addressed the media. He urged calm, and – under the unblinking eye of the national television spotlight – he was reassuring. In the process, he became "America's mayor."

Interestingly, in Giuliani's later life – when he was out of office and therefore not required to demonstrate public leadership – he made some remarkably intemperate comments impugning Barack Obama's patriotism. The comments probably contributed to the political deadlock in Washington, probably made it more difficult for Obama to do his job, and certainly undercut Giuliani's own stature in the public eye.

Composed: You maintain your presence of mind and focus, especially in challenging situations. "I'm still holding my head up," said Eugenie Bouchard in the post-match interview. "I feel like I've come a long way and I'm proud of what I've achieved not only this week but this year as well. So, you know, life is good, and I'm just going to keep working. That's what you have to do: just go back to work."[12]

US Airways Captain Chesley Sullenberger showed great presence of mind when his plane – departing from New York's LaGuardia Airport on January 15, 2009 – collided with a flock of birds just minutes into the flight and lost power in both engines. Audiotapes of the conversation between Sullenberger and air traffic controllers documented the "astounding composure" of Sullenberger as he calmly glided his aircraft into a water landing on the Hudson River, thereby saving the lives of all 155 passengers and crew aboard.

Self-controlled: You remain disciplined and stay on track. You control strong emotions like anger or disappointment, especially in difficult situations. Germany's Chancellor Angela Merkel, a former research scientist, has become one of the most powerful women in the world. She has been in charge of Europe's biggest economy since 2000, and sets the political tone in the continent. She led Germany and Europe through a succession of daunting financial, economic, and political crises – and throughout the years, has been the epitome of self-control.

Prudent: You demonstrate vigilance, care, and thought in your work. Halla Tomasdottir emphasized risk awareness as a cornerstone of her firm's work, and that was one key reason why Audur experienced no loss of capital – either its own, or that of its investors – during the meltdown of 2008.

Warren Buffett, one of the richest men in the world, is known for his prudence. He still lives in the same home (in Omaha, Nebraska) that he purchased in 1958 for $31,500. His prudence extends to his investment strategy, the engine of his wealth creation. He is widely quoted to the effect that "the less prudence with which others conduct their affairs, the greater the prudence with which we should conduct our own affairs."

Temperance Complementing Other Dimensions

Let's look again at Figure 9.1 to remind ourselves of the eleven dimensions of leader character. Does temperance complement the other dimensions – and if so, how?

The expansiveness and momentum associated with transcendence, drive, and courage often require a tempering and regulation. This tempering can prevent recklessness in the case of courage and drive, or disconnection from reality in the case of transcendence. The spectacular failure of U.S.-based retail giant Target in Canada serves as a case in point. The company's senior leadership team never understood the Canadian marketplace and its competitors, and as a result of "blind enthusiasm and skewed assumptions," 133 stores were opened almost all at once … and subsequently closed. Less than two years later, Target filed for liquidation in Canada.

Temperance helps to regulate emotions that may run high as you exercise humanity and collaboration in order to deepen your connections with others. There's a fine line to be struck between being empathetic with a colleague and being too deeply drawn into that colleague's out-of-control emotional dramas. Similarly, there's a balance to be struck between shrugging off the evening news entirely and taking it too much to heart – to the extent that it becomes too upsetting to watch. Temperance can help in both cases.

The discipline associated with temperance brings a rigor to the other dimensions and in particular helps in providing the regulation needed when judgment dictates to dial-down on one of the dimensions. We should never forget that our words are just like toothpaste: Once they escape the tube, you can't push them back in.

Temperance in the Absence of Other Dimensions

Temperance can become very narrow without transcendence, courage, and drive. Temperance tends to slow down and restrain actions, while these other dimensions tend to accelerate and expand the possibilities. Without justice and humanity, temperance can become a practice of minimizing and resorting to what you can do without regard to what you need to do.

People who take temperance to an extreme can become obstructive within their organization – throwing up cautions and roadblocks to a paralyzing degree. Transcendence and drive are the antidotes to this kind of excessive caution (just as temperance is the antidote to them). Think of the roles played by the Finance and Legal departments in most companies: They are the voices of reason and temperance. Now think of how many times they are the embodiment of frustration for people who are trying to get things done. Courage and drive are sometimes needed to win your arguments with Finance!

Clearly, the character elements work together to support temperance. Having self-control enhances the ability to remain calm and composed in difficult situations. Being prudent enables self-control, and both are critical for patience. Being calm fosters the peace of mind that supports patience and self-control.

Cultivating Temperance

Earlier, we stressed the importance of being able to think clearly and respond reasonably in tense situations – to exercise self-control. Can that ability be cultivated? The answer appears to be "yes."

Columbia University-based psychologist Walter Mischel has been studying self-control since the late 1960s, in part by following a cohort of children from infancy to adulthood.[13] Among his many celebrated findings: Four-year-olds who can successfully resist one marshmallow today in favor of two marshmallows tomorrow – in other words, children who can delay their gratification – are more likely to graduate from college and less likely to become overweight. Based on his research, the children's television series *Sesame Street* in 2013 developed a sequence of skits in which Cookie Monster – long famous for his lack of self-control around cookies – is persuaded to be more temperate about cookies so that he can gain entry into the "Cookie Connoisseurs Club."

In a recent interview, Mischel observed that the lessons of his research pertain not just to young people (and Cookie Monsters), but to people of all ages:

> The good news is that this cognitive and emotional skill set is eminently teachable, particularly early in life. It's great in preschool; it's great within the first few years of life. It's great to adolescence even. And it continues to be a skill set that can be developed even when we're quite mature adults.

How, exactly? Mischel points to the development of the executive function, which is (simply stated) the brain's capacity to analyze, organize, decide, and execute. In most people, the frontal part of the cortex of the brain develops around the age of puberty, and this is when executive function begins to kick in.

Successful executive function depends on two building blocks: 1) the ability to perform executive tasks (including cognitive control skills), and 2) the motivation to do so. Cookie Monster adopted several strategies to enhance his ability to resist cookies (such as putting a mental frame around nearby cookies and pretending that they were only pictures of cookies, or by imagining that the cookies were actually smelly fish); the Cookie Connoisseurs Club provided the incentive or motivation.

Translating this sequence of ideas into the language of this chapter: Temperance is a quality that can be cultivated, assuming that you develop your brain in certain ways, and that your incentive structure allows you – and better yet, persuades you – to act in temperate ways. Taking the second challenge first: Think of how Halla Tomasdottir and Kristin Petursdottir structured Audur Capital's incentives to foster temperance among their colleagues and their investors – and thereby to sidestep the global meltdown that they saw coming.

How do we develop our brains to promote temperance? One proven way is through meditation, which reduces stress and promotes emotional stability.[14] Researchers have determined that in the brains of people who meditate, the prefrontal cortex – that is, the region of the brain responsible for attention and control – tends to be thicker than it is in the brains of people who don't meditate.[15]

How does meditation work its magic? Most likely, every meditator would answer that question differently; but to generalize, it promotes the ability to be fully present in the moment. This is a habit of mind, which provides a focus for tackling challenges. In effect, meditation inoculates you against stress. Stressful moments activate the fight/flight response, which releases adrenaline, which in turn floods your brain with distracting thoughts. Successful athletes use breathing techniques to maintain their self-control – which can be considered a real-time stand-in for a deeper meditative state.

Stepping out onto Centre Court at Wimbledon is clearly a stressful moment, and Eugenie Bouchard had large reserves of self-control to draw upon. Dennis Wilson and his wife Shannon have recently launched a website promoting the advantages of meditation for business people.[16]

"Treasure your grey tissue," the site advises. Then it poses and answers two rhetorical questions: Where are you? Start there. What time is it? Start now.

When it comes to cultivating temperance, this is the best possible advice.

Questions to Contemplate

1. As a leader, do you display temperance at the right times, in the right places?
2. Even when seething inside, can you project calmness?
3. What is your personal risk appetite? Have you developed your own approach to taking risk, or playing it safe? What are you prepared to lose in your search for positive returns in your work and your life?

Books and Articles to Read

The Secret to Mastering Patience John Baldoni (Inc.com, 2012)

The Willpower Instinct: How Self-Control Works, Why It Matters, and What You Can Do to Get More of It Kelly McGonigal (Avery Trade, 2013)

How to Stay Cool, Calm & Collected When the Pressure's On: A Stress-Control Plan for Business People John Newman (AMACON, 2007)

Breakdown of Will George Ainslie (Cambridge University Press, 2001)

Mastery Robert Greene (Viking Adult, 2012)

Emotional Intelligence 2.0 Travis Bradberry and Jean Greaves (TalentSmart, 2009)

Videos to Watch

"Controlling our Willpower" by Kelly McGonigal on *The Agenda* with Steve Paiken (YouTube, 2012)

"Why we all need to practice emotional first aid" TEDx Talk by Guy Talk by Winch (www.ted.com/talk, 2014)

Notes

1 See Jarrod Jacobs's interesting (undated) write-up of "Self-Control," and the six occurrences of "temperance" in the King James Bible at http://www.watchmanmag.com/0406/040623.htm.
2 The temperance movement in the U.S. is best remembered today, but there were also vigorous temperance groups in the U.K., Australia, and New Zealand. Teetotalism – complete abstention – took root in Preston, England, in 1833, as per Wikipedia (http://en.wikipedia.org/wiki/Temperance_movement).
3 This story is derived in part from the chapter on Wilson in *Good Leaders Learn* (Routledge, 2014), by this book's co-author Gerard Seijts.
4 The Lululemon website, at http://www.lululemon.com/about/, is definitely worth a visit.
5 See the official write-up by Ron Atkin, 04.05.14, "Towering Kvitova wins second Wimbledon singles title," at http://www.wimbledon.com/en_GB/news/articles/2014-07-05/kvitova_wins_second_wimbledon_singles_title.html.
6 Again, see the video and transcript at http://www.wimbledon.com/en_GB/news/interviews/2014-07-05/201407051404575524182.html.
7 See *The Guardian*'s interesting summary, "Iceland rises from the ashes of banking collapse," by Simon Bowers, 10.06.13, at http://www.theguardian.com/world/2013/oct/06/iceland-financial-recovery-banking-collapse.
8 See the 01.10.14 post-recovery retrospective article by Guido Mingels in *Der Spiegel* at http://www.spiegel.de/international/europe/financial-recovery-of-iceland-a-case-worth-studying-a-942387.html.
9 Much of this section is derived from Tomasdottir's TEDWomen 2010 talk, including direct quotes. For a transcript of that talk, see http://www.ted.com/talks/halla_tomasdottir/transcript?language=en#t-38000.
10 In February 2009, following the collapse of the disgraced national government, Iceland elected its first female prime minister – perhaps reflecting a

national inclination to let the country's women run things for a change. See "After the crash, Iceland's women lead the rescue," in *The Guardian*, 02.21.09, by Ruth Sunderland, online at http://www.theguardian.com/world/2009/feb/22/iceland-women. For details on the BJORK fund, see John S. W. MacDonald's 12.31.08 article, "Bjork to rescue Iceland's economy?" online at http://observer.com/2008/12/bjork-to-rescue-icelands-economy/.

11 Seijts, Gerard, *Good Leaders Learn* (Routledge, 2014), p. 304.

12 From the Wimbledon transcript cited above, at http://www.wimbledon.com/en_GB/news/interviews/2014-07-05/201407051404575524182.html.

13 See the excellent December 2104 review by Lea Winerman, "Acing the marshmallow test," of Mischel's 2014 book, *The Marshmallow Test*, in the American Psychological Association's magazine, *Monitor on Psychology*, at http://www.apa.org/monitor/2014/12/marshmallow-test.aspx.

14 Even simple breathing exercises go a long way toward developing self-control. See, for example, Mary and Corey Crossan's 07.08.14 article in the *Huffington Post*, "Leaders should learn to engage the moment like Genie Bouchard," on athletes' approaches to self-control, referencing Eugenie Bouchard, at http://www.huffingtonpost.ca/ivey-business-school/eugenie-bouchardwimbledon-b_5568521.html.

15 Researchers at Massachusetts General Hospital, for example, found that even an eight-week program in "mindfulness training" led to structural changes in the amygdala. See "Mindfulness meditation training changes brain structure in eight weeks," 01.21.11, at *Science Daily*, online at http://www.sciencedaily.com/releases/2011/01/110121144007.htm.

16 The site – http://www.whil.com/ – asserts that "a leader's 'soft skills' are every bit as important as pure processing power if not more so."

10 Justice

It started in September 2011, in Zuccotti Park – a nondescript little plaza in Lower Manhattan, near Wall Street. A more or less leaderless group of young people gathered to protest unfairness, inequality, an unlevel playing field, greedy money-managers, the dominance of the so-called "1 percent," the influence of Corporate America on democracy on the U.S.: pick your target. A tent city sprang up. And despite the relative incoherence of the protest, dozens of similar encampments – all sharing the prefix "Occupy" – popped up in downtowns across the country.

In an era in which inequality of incomes, wealth, rights, and opportunities is being highlighted as never before, the challenges for leaders to establish and maintain justice and fairness within their organizations has never been greater. Followers look to their leaders for both distributive and procedural justice, as well as the feeling that they are being treated with respect and dignity in the ways that such justice is dispensed. They want their leaders to be fair, even-handed, and proportionate in the ways they dispense rewards and punishments. As a result, there is increased pressure on leaders to be socially responsible for their actions that affect the societies within which they operate.

We consider justice to be a critical character dimension, because it influences the contextually influenced behaviors on which people will judge their leaders.

Take the case of WestJet Airlines Ltd.'s (WestJet) effort to launch a second airline, to be named Encore, under its corporate wing.[1] Founded in 1996, WestJet held a 36 percent share of the Canadian air travel market, second only to Air Canada, which held 40 percent. It had almost 10,000 employees and 105 planes serving over 85 destinations in North America, Central America, and the Caribbean. WestJet had been consistently ranked one of the most profitable airlines in the world, and had grown its revenues at an annual average of 10.7 percent over nearly two decades of operation. Using only one aircraft type, the Boeing 737, and a restricted number of airports, the company could operate very effectively and efficiently on its chosen route structure.

Part of its success had been the low fares it could offer customers. But the company also won and retained customers through its high service levels, thanks in part to an empowered and motivated workforce. WestJet was regularly held up as a textbook example of successful two-way communication and employee engagement. On numerous occasions, the company was named as one of Canada's Top Employers and Best Places to Work, and it had received many awards for its much-admired corporate culture. To cite just one example: Hierarchy within the company was minimized, with everyone – from pilots to flight attendants – cleaning the planes between flights.

WestJet's senior leadership team referred to the airline's customers as "guests," and encouraged the company's employees to take the initiative, when necessary, to ensure a guest's satisfaction. WestJet employees participated in the company's profit-sharing program, and – thanks to a generous Employee Share Purchase Plan (ESPP) – they had the option to put up to 20 percent of their earnings toward WestJet stock, and all such contributions were matched 100 percent by the company. As a result, many employees were not just satisfied workers, but also were proud owners of the company.

But, by 2009, WestJet's management faced a difficult challenge. Its leadership recognized that future profitable growth required it to deviate from its single aircraft type, restricted airport usage, and limited route structure. It was going to need to add a second aircraft type for short-haul operations, many of which would originate from secondary airports and would feed traffic to its longer-range aircraft operating out of major airports.

This analysis led to a decision in 2012 to buy 25 new Bombardier Q400 jets – 78-passenger planes that were ideally suited to the short-haul runs that WestJet was now planning to offer. Passenger volumes could be maximized through a feeder-strategy, connecting smaller airbases to the fleet of 737s. In addition, the Q400s were more technologically advanced and fuel-efficient than the 737s; on at least some routes, therefore, it would make sense to replace the 737s with the new, smaller planes.

This development forced to the surface a fundamental question: Would the new fleet be considered simply an extension of the existing corporation, or would it be set up as a fully owned subsidiary? WestJet's senior management favored the latter, since that would allow for a different compensation plan for newly hired pilots and flight attendants thus keeping costs down for the regional airline. They therefore came up with a plan for a wholly owned subsidiary, to be known as "Encore." Consistent with WestJet's corporate values, they put this plan to an employee vote. Following a lot of explanation for taking this "second airline" approach, WestJet's existing employees approved the creation of the new regional airline by a whopping 91 percent. The support was more in principle than in support of any actual specifics. Notably, pay rates for new employees were not discussed in the context of this vote.

WestJet management tried to blur the lines between the two companies, hoping that the older company's culture and sterling reputation would transfer over to the new one. But several lines that were drawn clearly worked directly against this outcome. First, Encore's employees were paid less for essentially the same work. Second, the Employee Share Purchase Plan at Encore was less generous: Employees at the new airline could only put up to 10 percent of their salaries into the plan (again, with a 100 percent match from the company).

Encore employees wore the same uniforms as their WestJet counterparts – and the colors of the two fleets of airplanes were identical – but pay and benefits were different. Obviously, many of Encore's new employees resented the compensation differentials. But so, too, did some of WestJet's workers. As one commented:

> That was a big cultural problem, not just for those who moved over to Encore but for everybody at WestJet, even if it didn't affect you directly … It's part of what makes WestJetters unique … They are very conscious about their fellow WestJetters, and they want them to be treated well. They are very vocal when they think there has been an injustice somewhere in the company.[2]

One irony in the WestJet/Encore story is that the parent company was simply being held to its own high standards. A less generous and conscientious organization might have implemented exactly the same policies and got away with them, because no one expected any better of it. Similarly, an organization that didn't worry much about fairness wouldn't attract employees who would become very vocal when they perceived an injustice somewhere in the company. But for a company like WestJet to drift away from justice – or at least appear to do so – was deeply troubling to people who had a personal investment in justice.

In the end, WestJet management made adjustments to provide Encore flight attendants with a minimum guaranteed number of paid hours, and more flexibility and predictability around scheduling that would allow them to get a second job. Management also explained to the employees that the benefits package, profit-sharing, and Employee Share Purchase Plan was more generous than other regional airlines, such as Air Canada Express, Porter Airlines, and Sunwest Aviation.

The Reference Point for Justice

Obviously, senior leaders – both in business and in other sectors – tend to have a different reference point for what is fair than do non-managerial employees. WestJetters and Encore employees chose WestJet as their point of reference; WestJet's management chose its budget airline as theirs. In many labor relations issues, the parties selectively and self-servingly choose their frames of reference. So do compensation committees of boards of directors when deciding how to pay their senior executives. So also do provinces, states, or municipalities when deciding how to pay their people, what levels of service to offer to taxpayers, how to set tax rates, and so on. When this selective comparison happens, injustices are frequently perceived, and may be difficult to explain away.

At the micro-level, people think about appropriate rewards for performance, and penalties for non-performance, up to and including the behaviors that justify suspension or termination and the factors that might mitigate rewards and punishments. These points of reference may be based on historical precedent, organizational practice, or an individual's sense of what is right, what is proportionate to the level of the performance, or the egregiousness of the offense.

This kind of justice can be broken down into several dimensions.[3] For example, there is distributive justice, which refers to the perceived fairness of the outcome one receives (e.g., compensation, promotion, etc.) relative to the inputs one has made (e.g., effort, working hours, qualifications, etc.). There is also procedural justice, meaning that the processes whereby key decisions are made can be relied upon to be fair, to have been based on sound criteria, accurate measurement, and unbiased assessment. Finally, there is interactional justice, which has to do with the way individuals or groups are treated as those key decisions are made. Are they treated with respect? Are the explanations offered timely, specific, and true?

When you are individually, personally just, you strive to ensure that individuals are treated equitably and fairly, and that consequences (positive or negative) are commensurate with contributions (or transgressions). You remain objective, and keep personal biases to a minimum when making decisions. You provide others with the opportunity to voice their opinions on processes and procedures, and you provide timely, specific, and candid explanations for decisions. Finally, you seek to redress for wrongdoings inside and outside the organization to the best of your ability.

Character Elements: What Goes into "Justice"?

Looking at Figure 10.1, below, you can see that there are five character elements that contribute to the dimension of justice. When you exhibit justice, you are:

Fair and equitable: You ensure that consequences are appropriate to the circumstances.

Of course, the challenge here is twofold: first, to decide whether or not a given issue should be held up to the fairness standard; and second, to decide what fairness means in that particular context.

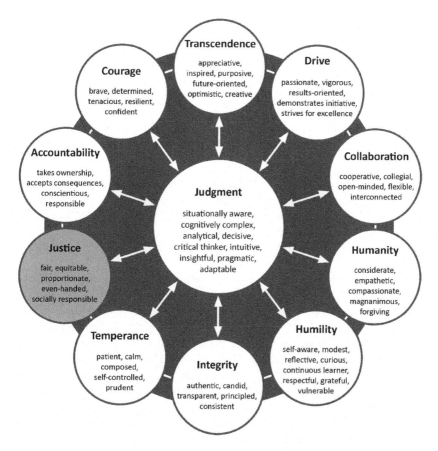

Figure 10.1 Character Dimensions and Associated Elements

Costco's much-celebrated co-founder and CEO, Jim Sinegal, has established a reputation for focusing the fairness spotlight on a wide range of issues – including issues that many CEOs would prefer to leave in the shadows.[4] Despite his company's impressive returns in recent years, including a doubling of its share price, Sinegal pays himself a relatively modest $350,000 annual salary. We say "relatively modest" because we live in an era in which a bank CEO might make 350 times as much as a front-line employee. Where did that number come from? Sinegal decided that he shouldn't be paid more than a dozen $30,000-a-year employees. (Multiply $30,000 by twelve, and then round down.) He also steers clear of the business-royalty trappings cherished by many high-ranking executives. He answers his own phone. His employment contract with Costco is a single page, and – in one clause – clearly spells out how the board of directors can get rid of him if they conclude he's neglecting his duties.

Does distributive justice pay? Costco's turnover rate is a fifth that of arch-rival Walmart – and, in fact, is the lowest among all large retailers. Multiple benefits accrue, starting with lower training costs, and continuing with a workforce that carries a message of goodwill out into the world. "Imagine that you have 120,000 loyal ambassadors out there who are constantly saying good things about Costco," Sinegal once observed, "It has to be a significant advantage for you."[5] And one way to recruit, retain, and inspire those ambassadors is to treat them fairly. Justice may be an altruistic concept, but it may also be a source of sustainable corporate performance.

Procedural justice: You apply due processes and appropriate standards for all. You remain open and transparent in procedures.

Anne Mulcahy was the CEO of Xerox in the early 2000s, when that venerable company was on the brink of disaster.[6] When she took over in 2001, the company recorded a loss of $94 million. Four years later, Xerox announced profits of $978 million.

It was anything but an easy path. Along the way, she cut the company's workforce by 30 percent, and shut down its desktop division. But she began her tenure by *listening* to people – beginning with a three-month world tour in which she picked the brains of employees, customers, and business sages like Warren Buffett. And she thought of procedural justice as unfolding along multiple time frames. And at the same time that she was swinging a very broad sword, she was also encouraging Xerox's remaining employees to think about 30-year careers with the company – in other words, careers much like her own. "The whole experience changes if the company takes the responsibility," she explained, "and the employee comes in with an attitude that long-term relationships are great."[7]

Proportionate: You ensure that responses and outcomes are commensurate with the circumstances, and you ensure that rewards or sanctions fit the situation.

The late Frank Batten – the Virginia-based media magnate who was the moving force behind the Weather Channel – prided himself on running his several companies on basic principles of fairness. One day, however, he got a rude awakening. He had undertaken to write a first-person strategic history of the Weather Channel, which involved interviewing a number of employees, both active and retired. One of those interviewees was a technical specialist who had developed much of the early technology that made the Weather Channel possible. This individual was also an early dabbler in the World Wide Web, and he had the foresight to reserve the "weather.com" URL for the company – a seemingly small act that helped generate huge profits for the company in subsequent years. (During Hurricane Sandy's 2012 rampage, for example, weather.com logged 960 million page-views in only three days, and advertising revenues soared accordingly.[8]) But at a critical juncture, this farsighted individual had been rudely shoved aside by a group of outside technicians – he was told he was "too anchored in the past" – and he resigned in quiet protest.

The abrupt departure reflected a principled stand, but it also had significant consequences for him, in terms of near-term compensation and longer-term retirement pay. Through his book research, Batten discovered that his company had done wrong by this individual – a thirty-year veteran of the larger corporation – and undertook to make him whole. This was only just, Batten felt, given the technician's major contributions to the company.[9]

Even-handed: You remain impartial and unbiased in the treatment and judgment of others.

Abraham Lincoln has been celebrated for a whole host of admirable traits, including – notably – his even-handedness. At no time was this more visibly displayed than in the first week of April 1865, when Lincoln traveled down the Potomac to visit Richmond: the Confederate capital that had fallen on April 3rd. Walking the streets of the vanquished city, Lincoln acknowledged the cheers of blacks who considered him their liberator – simultaneously celebrating the Union's great victory and comforting the former slaves who had suffered so much.

On the front lines, he celebrated the courage of Union troops. But then he made a point of visiting a field hospital to shake hands with wounded Confederate soldiers. Upon his departure, he asked a military band to play *Dixie*. "That tune is now Federal property," he joked. "It belongs to us, and, at any rate, it is good to show the rebels that they will be free to hear it again."[10]

Socially responsible: As a leader, you are aware of injustices inside and outside the organization, and seek to redress them.

An obvious recent example in the corporate sector came when Starbucks CEO Howard Schultz decided to spark a discussion about race relations in the United States. It was not a new concern for Schultz: As far back as the 1990s, Schultz had launched an aggressive effort to make the executive offices of his company more representative of the population of the U.S.[11] But the social turmoil in late 2014 arising out of the shooting death of Michael Brown – an 18-year-old black man – in Ferguson, Missouri, prompted Schultz to do some soul-searching. In December, Schultz launched a series of six town hall meetings across the country at which he invited his employees to talk candidly about race. It was a highly emotional set of meetings for Schultz, who decided that he had to take the conversation outside of the company and engage a broader public.

On March 17, 2015 – with the approval of the company's board of directors – baristas began writing the words "Race Together" on coffee cups in 12,000 Starbucks stores across the U.S.[12] Reaction was immediate – and pretty consistently negative. TV commentators blasted Schultz for being out of touch – or worse, for cynically exploiting tumultuous race relations in the U.S. for commercial gain. Customers grumbled about already long waits getting longer as baristas took the time to explain the somewhat ambiguous inscription. A week later, the coffee-cup campaign was quietly interred, although Schultz and the company insisted that the larger "Race Together" initiative would continue.

"We're playing a long game here," Schultz explained to a LinkedIn writer, "and I'm deeply committed to the long game."[13] He reiterated his strong belief that if the 115,000 U.S. employees of Starbucks could benefit from frank discussions of race relations, then the 60 million Americans that his company served each week – and, by extension, the larger society – could also benefit from those discussions. "All we've tried to do is demonstrate to the country and to our people and our customers that we can be better," he said. "And that we want to make an investment in our society."

In the 1990s, Ed Clark, CEO of TD Bank Group, also became aware of the systemic and individual discrimination on the basis of sexual orientation within his own and other organizations. He led the effort to create a non-discriminatory working environment for LGBT individuals within the TD Bank Group through empowering task forces and individuals to identify problems and engineer and implement solutions, creating an environment in which everyone could achieve their maximum potential regardless of gender identification or sexual preference. Not stopping at his own organization, Clark spoke out clearly and often to other business groups, taking the view that leadership does not stop at your own organization and that a large, influential organization has the responsibility to try to shape society for the better.

As you can see, the elements of justice work together and can challenge each other in the course of their development. For example, being equitable is supported by being even-handed; and even-handed contributes to being proportionate. Being equitable and fair, even-handed and proportionate are worthwhile goals but may also be challenging to achieve.

Justice Supporting Other Dimensions

Justice provides important motivation that fuels courage to step up and initiate action, and to drive until the goal is achieved. Collaboration is enhanced when people feel they are given voice and treated with respect during debate and problem solving – in other words, when both procedural and interactional justice are present.

Justice ensures that accountability is not superficial, but takes into consideration the variety of interests at stake in any given situation. For example, for leaders' actions to be sustainable, they must be perceived as equitable. If they are not, resistance and opposition may form. This may be true at the individual level, if a dismissal is considered unjust; and also at a group level, when employees decide that the company is being unjust, and take work action such as a strike or work-to-rule. It can also happen at a societal level, when citizens feel that a company is violating societal norms or mores, and react by boycotting its products or services, or refusing to apply when the company is seeking to hire. At the extreme, this can lead to political or regulatory actions that can severely damage or even cripple an organization and render leaders ineffective.

Justice in the Absence of Other Dimensions

To demonstrate justice, leaders require many of the other dimensions of leader character. Without humanity and humility, for example, a leader seldom bothers to understand how others may see things, or considers that they have a right to be consulted and given a say in the matter. Without temperance, a leader may rush to implement what is to him or her "the obvious course" without even considering the consequences on employee engagement and satisfaction, turnover, and militancy in labor relations.

Without courage, drive, and accountability, you may not have the capacity to even consider or tackle the myriad of challenges associated with being a just leader. For example, different stakeholders offer various and sometimes contradictory views on the course of action to take and the role of justice, as in the case of Anne Mulcahy and Howard Schultz. On the other hand, temperance and judgment are essential, since focusing on justice in isolation of other relevant considerations may – as in the case of WestJet and Encore – lead to suboptimal decisions.

Justice May be in Our Genes

Skeptics of the idea that leader character comprises justice might invoke the old canard that "nice guys finish last." The individual and company stories presented in this chapter argue strongly to the contrary. "Nice guys" – fair individuals – who are also creative strategists and skilled operators often finish first, and probably sleep well at night.

Other skeptics might argue that justice is a "nice to have" – something that a business or a society can embrace when times are good, but must necessarily go on the back burner when times get tough. A crisis can call forth behavior that may well hurt individuals unfairly, but which protects the organization and helps it endure over the longer run.

But what if justice actually runs deeper than that? What if it resides in our blood and bones?

Emory University primatologist Frans de Waal makes a convincing case that empathy – a foundation of justice, since it implies seeing the world through another person's eyes – may be a genetic trait of both primates and humans.[14] We are conditioned to think in terms of the survival of the fittest – the Darwinian model of bitter evolutionary contest – but according to de Waal, that may be only half the story. We survive not just by competing, but also by cooperating. Reciprocity also comes into play: We help others today in the expectation that they will return the favor tomorrow.[15]

In one celebrated experiment, de Waal's team put chimpanzees in adjacent cages – fully visible to each other – and offered a bucket of red and green tokens to one of them. If that chimp handed a red token to the human attendant, only that chimp would get food. If it handed a green token to the human, both chimps would get fed. The "choosing chimp" consistently chose the empathetic path – unless the non-choosing chimp behaved aggressively toward him, in which case the choosing chimp tended to hand over a red token, thereby punishing bad behavior.

Another experiment – this one involving two capuchin monkeys from the same extended family – tested the animals' sense of fairness. As a reward for performing a simple task, they gave both of the monkeys (again in adjacent cages, and visible to each other) cucumbers. In the next round, they continued to give one monkey cucumbers as a reward, but began giving the other monkey grapes for the same task: a much preferred food, among capuchins. As a videotape of the experiment illustrated, as soon as this inequitable behavior began, the disadvantaged monkey began hurling the proffered bits of cucumber back at the researcher in fury, grabbing the bars of the cage and rattling them in apparent fury, and otherwise eloquently displaying its sense of justice betrayed.

"This is basically the Wall Street protest, that you see here," de Waal joked, at the end of the videotape. But continuing in a more serious vein, he described several pairs of monkeys in which the "favored" monkey – the one getting the grapes – actually began turning down the grapes when it realized that its fellow monkey was being shortchanged by the system. This, in de Waal's view, was further evidence that primates have the benefit of an "evolved morality": one that helps them cooperate to survive.

The logical extension is clear: Humans, too, have the benefit of an evolved morality. And by another logical extension, the individual who embodies and taps into our innate sense of justice is likely to be a highly effective leader.

Questions to Contemplate

1. When you decide to build a reputation for justice, or even to talk about justice in organizations being a good thing, what risks are you taking? What constraints are you putting on how you, personally, act and speak? How you will deal with others in your organization?
2. When you decide to adopt a strategy such as WestJet's, how far do you have to go to maintain a reputation for justice? Is it even possible?
3. When you see an injustice taking place within your organization, what do you do about it? What are your options? How do you choose between them?

Books and Articles to Read

Are You Just a Leader or a Just Leader? Deborah Mills-Scofield (Switch & Shift, 2014)

"Defining Respectful Leadership" Niels van Quaquebeke and Tilman Eckloff (*Journal of Business Ethics*, 91 (3) 2010)

"Justice Take Up Battle Over Exxon Valdez" Linda Greenhouse (*New York Times*, February 28, 2008)

"Why It's So Hard to Be Fair" Joel Brockner (*Harvard Business Review*, March 2006)

"Fair Process: Managing in the Knowledge Economy" W. Chan Kim and Renee Mauborgne (*Harvard Business Review*, January 2003)

Justice: What's the Right Thing to Do? Michael J. Sandel (Farrar, Straus and Giroux, 2010)

The Divide: American Injustice in the Age of the Wealth Gap Matt Taibbi (Spiegel & Grau, 2014)

Videos to Watch

A Few Good Men "You Can't Handle the Truth" (YouTube, 1992)

"Justice' with Michael Sandel (Harvard University) (YouTube, 2009)

"Does Money Make You Mean?" TED Talk by Paul Piff (www.ted.com/talk, 2013)

Craig Kielburger Case Video Series: Ian O. Ihnatowycz Institute for Leadership (Ivey Business School, 2012)

Notes

1 This story is a condensed version of "Ferio Pugliese: leading WestJet's new regional carrier Encore," Ivey Publishing case #9B15C008, written by Robert Way under the direction of Gerard Seijts and Professor Jean-Louis Schaan.

2 From the above-cited case.

3 This summary is derived from the informative Wikipedia entry on organizational justice, at http://en.wikipedia.org/wiki/Organizational_justice. In this section, it draws on the equity-theory work of J. S. Adams and G. S. Leventhal.

4 See, for example, *Business Insider*'s 02.25.10 list by Glen Stensberry of "10 Business Leaders You Should Strive to Emulate," online at http://www.businessinsider.com/10-examples-of-excellent-business-leadership-2010–2?op=1.

5 Find more Jim Sinegal quotes at the "Believe – Evan Carmichael" website: http://www.evancarmichael.com/Famous-Entrepreneurs/1107/Jim-Sinegal-Quotes.html.

6 Mulcahy showed up on numerous lists of top business leaders in subsequent years, including *Forbes*'s 2012 list, 07.24.12, by David K. Williams, "Top 10 list: the greatest living business leaders today," online at http://www.forbes.com/sites/davidkwilliams/2012/07/24/top-10-list-the-greatest-living-business-leaders-today/.

7 From *Contemporary Business*, by David L. Kurtz and Louis E. Boone (South-West, 2008).

8   That was also 41 million unique visits. See Laura Stampler's 10.29.12 *Business Insider* article, "Weather.com's traffic is exploding and these advertisers are reaping the rewards," onlines at http://www.businessinsider.com/weathercoms-traffic-is-exploding-and-these-advertisers-are-reaping-the-rewards-2012-10.

9   This story comes from Batten's *The Weather Channel* (Landmark Communications, 2002).

10   From Marc Robinson's *The American Play: 1787–2000* (Yale University Press, 2010). The story is also told online at http://abrahamlincolnsclassroom.org/abraham-lincoln-in-depth/abraham-lincoln-and-music/.

11   This initiative is described in his book, *Pour Your Heart Into It* (Hyperion, 1999).

12   See the company's explanation of the program, and related videos and print stories, in an 03.17.15 blogpost on the company website, "Race together: conversation has the power to change hearts and minds," online at https://news.starbucks.com/news/race-together-conversation-has-the-power-to-change-hearts-and-minds.

13   See Daniel Roth's 04.11.15 LinkedIn interview with Schultz, online at https://www.linkedin.com/pulse/howard-schultz-isnt-giving-up-race-together-daniel-roth.

14   See CNN's 01.19.13 write-up of de Waal's work by Elizabeth Landau, "Morality: It's not just for humans," online at http://www.cnn.com/2013/01/19/health/chimpanzee-fairness-morality/.

15   See de Waal's charming TED talk on moral behavior in animals at https://www.youtube.com/watch?v=GcJxRqTs5n.

11 Accountability

The first hints of trouble arrived at headquarters on August 7, 2008, when a distributor for Maple Leaf Foods – the biggest supplier of fresh and processed meats to Canadian retail outlets – called in a report.[1] A public health official had been in touch with the distributor about several of the company's sliced meat products, and it appeared that an investigation was in the offing. Within the week, the Canadian Food Inspection Agency (CFIA) told Maple Leaf that it was investigating three meat products that had been packed in the company's Toronto plant. The company told its distributors that the CFIA was investigating illnesses that might possibly be related to its products. The three products were put on hold – with orders to neither ship nor sell – and Maple Leaf prepared for a recall.

The president and CEO of Maple Leaf, Michael McCain, received a late-night call on Saturday, August 16th. The CFIA had determined that listeria monocytogenes had been discovered in two Maple Leaf products. This is the bacteria that causes listeriosis: a serious infection that begins with the ingestion of the bacterium – usually through the consumption of tainted foods – and quickly spreads beyond the gastrointestinal tract. Typical symptoms include fever, aches, diarrhea, but more severe complications – including convulsions, and even death – sometimes ensue. Pregnant women are at particular risk, with infections during pregnancy sometimes leading to miscarriage, stillbirth, premature delivery, or a life-threatening infection of the baby *in utero*.[2] However, the CFIA was not yet able to link the DNA fingerprints between the human listeriosis cases and the Maple Leaf products.

At McCain's directive, the company initiated a voluntary recall of all products made on the suspected lines at the plant, and press releases explaining the potential threat to public health were issued. As the investigation widened, the company could do little more than wait for further developments. Those developments came quickly, with the CFIA telling Maple Leaf on August 19th that a possible link existed between one of its products and the death of a person. In response, Maple Leaf immediately shut down its Toronto plant and recalled 191 products. Four days later, a definite link was established between the strain of listeria monocytogenes found in Maple Leaf products and the illnesses and deaths.

McCain then undertook to explain to the public his company's position. Looking weary and worried, wearing a button-down blue shirt, no tie, and no suit coat, he looked directly into a camera and talked for just over a minute to Canadians. He pointed out that although listeria is a bacterium that is common in the environment, this was not a common circumstance. "Tragically," he said, "our products have been linked to illnesses and loss of life." In fact, hundreds of people had been made ill, and, by the time the crisis ended in October, 23 people would be dead. McCain simply offered his deepest sympathies to those who had taken ill and to the families of those who had lost loved ones. He said that Maple Leaf's 23,000 employees were dedicated to food safety – "but this week, our best efforts failed, and we are deeply sorry." He came across as sincere and deeply concerned.[3]

One YouTube reviewer observed that McCain looked nervous. "Of course he looks nervous," another responded. "He just ignored a roomful of highly paid lawyers who told him that if he told the truth – that the company's systems broke down – he'd probably get sued for a lot of money. I don't know him, but in this case, he sure was a stand-up guy."

As it turned out, that was the consensus that emerged in the wake of the crisis: that McCain was indeed a stand-up guy, and that – despite this catastrophe – Maple Leaf could indeed be trusted. How was the situation turned around? McCain was a constant and calming presence, coming across as both transparent and decisive.[4] The company destroyed tens of millions of dollars' worth of product. In a series of press conferences and news releases, Maple Leaf described what it was learning from the ongoing investigation, and also explained the steps it was taking to correct problems as soon as they were identified. It invited the media into the offending plant. It settled a class-action lawsuit in record time.[5] Partially in response to these and similar measures, McCain was named CEO of the Year for 2008 by the Canadian press.[6]

It is instructive to contrast this story, and its outcome, with a similar challenge faced by another Canadian food producer – XL Foods Inc. – in 2012.[7] In that year, a dozen consumers of beef products produced by XL Foods were taken ill, and their illnesses were traced back to the company's plant in Brooks, Alberta. This time, the culprit was E. coli: again, a common enough bacterium that is easily controlled by attention to sanitation, but one that can quickly get out of control in an unsanitary food-processing plant.

What ensued was the largest beef recall in Canadian history. In the case of XL Foods, though, no one stepped forward in the Michael McCain role. Its co-CEOs, Brian and Lee Nilsson, preferred to work through junior staff.[8] And in marked contrast to the Maple Leaf approach, XL Foods basically ducked for cover, letting the CFIA take the lead in informing the public about the latest developments in the unfolding crisis.

Interestingly enough, the language used by XL Foods in its press releases was not substantially different from that used by McCain, in his role as company spokesperson. "All members of the XL community deeply regret the illness caused by the consumption of beef products," read one such press release. The company took "full responsibility" for the safety of its plants and products. But the near-total absence of any individual stepping up and owning the problem greatly undercut the apologetic language. In a highly unusual step, the company put recordings of its press releases on its media phone line – thus reinforcing the impression of a company that was out of touch, and out of reach.

Some have said that Maple Leaf – which sells branded products – simply had to do more than XL Foods, whose products are packaged and branded by other companies. Others have pointed out that because Maple Leaf is a public company and XL Foods is private, different sets of rules applied in the two crises. Still others have argued what is in effect the opposite case, suggesting that Maple Leaf's and XL Foods' public faces were both reflections of cynically conceived legal strategies – in other words, "we'll say and do what we have to say and do to get out of this alive." This is an interpretation that McCain hotly denied at the time, and subsequently continued to deny. "Going through the crisis," he told reporters, "there are two advisers I've paid no attention to. The first are the lawyers, and the second are the accountants."[9]

When you are accountable, you accept responsibility for your decisions and actions. (You don't hide behind lawyers and accountants.) You are willing to step up and take ownership of challenging issues. You reliably deliver on expectations, and you can be counted upon in tough situations. You do this promptly when any problem arises. In 2015, Blue Bell Ice Cream had to recall all of its ice cream products from U.S. distribution. While it used many of the same words as Maple Leaf Foods in making the recall, it delayed several weeks – some press reports said months – acknowledging the problem and taking accountability.

In this chapter, we explore the key elements of accountability – on the left-hand side of Figure 11.1 – and then look at how the dimension of accountability complements the other dimensions of leader character.

Let's begin by looking at four character elements of accountability. What does "accountability" look like?

Character Elements: What Goes into "Accountability"?

Looking at Figure 11.1, overleaf, you can see that there are four character elements that contribute to the leadership dimension of accountability. When you exhibit accountability, you:

Take ownership: You personally engage the salient, important, and challenging issues.

George Cope has been president and CEO of BCE Inc. and Bell Canada – Canada's largest telecommunications company – since 2008. In that role, he has helped shape and implement the company's strategy for

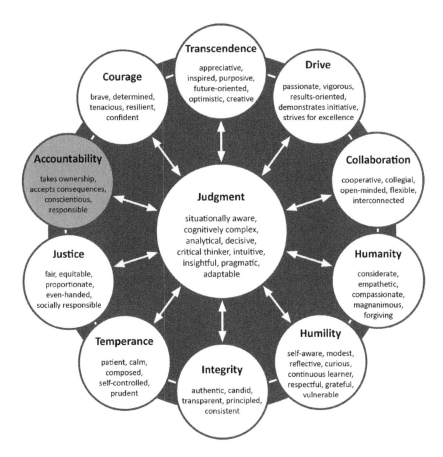

Figure 11.1 Character Dimensions and Associated Elements

growth in a turbulent era. In 2012, Bell attempted to buy Astral Media: a $3 billion deal that would have greatly expanded its footprint in Quebec, and given Bell access to a rich library of new content. Bell argued before the Canadian Radio-television and Telecommunications Commission (CRTC) that this kind of industry consolidation was necessary, in the face of increasing competition from global players like Netflix.[10] Astral was a willing partner to the purchase – having initially floated the idea to Bell – and most industry observers thought that it was a done deal.

But the CRTC, worried about the increased media concentration that would result from the proposed acquisition, blocked the proposed acquisition – a serious blow to Bell's expansion plans.[11] Cope stepped forward to accept responsibility for the defeat:

> I insisted that I be the one out there in public when our original bid to purchase Astral Media Inc. fell through, not the head of our media

division. It was my duty to explain what happened, and what we'd do to move forward.[12]

Cope owned that very public failure. (One newspaper account from the period was entitled, "How George Cope got his bell rung.") But from Bell's perspective, at least, the story has a happy ending: In 2013, the CRTC accepted a revised proposal from Bell to purchase Astral, and the deal went forward.

Accept consequences: You acknowledge the responsibility to justify your decisions, actions, and outcomes. You are willing to be held accountable.

This was a key lesson of the Maple Leaf listeriosis crisis. "We were accepting of our accountability," Michael McCain told an interviewer in 2011, three years after the fact. "We were decisive in our actions to address the challenges, and we were transparent and open with the various stakeholders about what had happened, and what we were going to do to correct it."[13]

Sometimes this exercise of personal responsibility takes the form of consequences avoided. Arkadi Kuhlmann – introduced in Chapter 1 – is the founder and CEO of ZenBanx, Inc., a financial services and technology firm that offers a multi-currency mobile banking account.[14] Earlier in his career, however, he ran a trading company – a firm that he says candidly had a lot of dealings with "bad people" and did things that, while technically legal, seemed wrong in principle. Although sorely tempted, Kuhlmann ultimately backed away from the moral cliff edge:

> I think the only thing that held me back was not because I was overly virtuous, but I think I was scared that, if I went there and did that, I couldn't reverse it. What I've learned as a leader is that life is a blackboard that you cannot erase. Everything counts. There's no such thing as a time-out. There's no such thing as "it doesn't count." There's a blackboard and it'll never be erased.

We write on the blackboard every day – and we're accountable for those writings. Yes, says Kuhlmann; people deserve second chances. But it's simply not okay for a leader to knowingly misbehave, and count on being forgiven. "It's okay to fail," he says. "It's okay to win. But you can't cross the [moral] line."

Act in conscientious ways: You are dependable and reliable. You are consistently attentive, and perform your duties thoroughly and well.

This kind of behavior can range from the unheralded to the heroic. In the latter category is the conduct of the staff of the Taj Mahal Palace and Hotel in Mumbai when that iconic, 103-year-old facility was attacked by ten terrorists on November 26, 2008. What ensued was a sustained bloodbath, with ten terrorists with automatic weapons and grenades killing 175 people over the course of two horrific days.[15]

The 500 registered guests in the hotel – and the 600 or so additional guests attending functions or eating in the facility's restaurants – would have been entirely at the mercy of the terrorists, except for the actions of the 600 staff members who were on duty that night. Those staff members tended to be young, and many were relatively new to the Palace payroll. Because they were employees, they knew the locations of all the back stairways and emergency exits. In other words, they knew how to save themselves, if they chose to run.

As it turned out, nobody ran. Every single employee stayed on site to help as best they could: helping guests escape, and then – in some cases – running back into the besieged complex to try and rescue more people. The switchboard operators who had been spirited out of the building voluntarily returned to their posts, serving as a central communications post – and meanwhile, calling guests in their rooms and telling them how to best protect themselves.

One young female employee, Mallika Jagad, was helping to run a banquet for senior executives of Unilever in a sixth-floor function room. She and her fellow employees kept the 65 banquet-goers calm – lying on the floor, behind locked doors – for an entire night. Just before dawn, though, the banquet hall started filling with smoke from fires raging in the adjoining hallways. The only way out was through the windows. The staff attracted the attention of firefighters with a ladder truck, who broke in through the plate-glass windows and started a rescue operation. The employees insisted that all the guests escape down the ladders first. "I was looking after the function," explains Jagad. "I was responsible. I could have been the youngest in the room – and I know at one point I was the youngest in the room – but I was doing my job."

In a second, less successful effort, during an apparent lull in the siege, a group of chefs and other kitchen staff attempted to take a large group of guests down a back stairwell and out into an alley. The chefs lined up in a sort of human chain, urging the guests to move quickly through the darkness. But two terrorists discovered the escape attempt, and opened fire. A half-dozen chefs were gunned down.

But that was the tragic exception. Through the heroic efforts of the hotel staff, most guests – and ultimately, most employees – escaped the carnage. Why? Observers have pointed to the family-like quality of many Indian workplaces, in which strong interpersonal bonds can be formed. The larger Indian culture also teaches people from an early age to honor guests – a way of honoring God. But most important was a cadre of people who knew how to do their jobs well, and decided to carry out their duties under the worst circumstances imaginable.

Act in responsible ways: You acknowledge personal obligations as part of your role. You stand answerable for decisions and actions.

Linda Hasenfratz was named CEO of Linamar Corporation in 2002. The business was founded in 1964 as a single lathe in her father's basement; today, this global manufacturing enterprise manufactures precision products in 48 plants around the world.[16] Key product lines include powertrain components – which Linamar supplies to vehicle manufacturers – and aerial work platforms for the construction industry and related businesses.

Before joining the corporate staff – and ultimately earning the CEO's title – Hasenfratz held a wide range of positions in the company: machine operator, operations manager, general manager of several divisions, chief financial officer, and COO. This far-ranging experience not only gave her an intimate perspective on many parts of the business; it also helped her overcome skepticism about being the founder's daughter, and earned her a network of supporters across the company.

That credibility, experience, and network served her well in the recent financial crisis. As she recalls:

> We faced dark days in 2008–2009. Automotive is a big part of our business. Two of our top five customers were on the brink of bankruptcy. Automotive volumes had gone from 17–18 million units a year to 8 million. Our heavy truck business was down dramatically. Our [aerial work platform] business fell 80 percent. These were just shocking changes.
>
> The crisis really required my team and me to step up … It required us to go above and beyond [on] the communications side … We went out of our way to over-communicate with our employees, investors, customers, and suppliers. We told them, "Here's what's happening. Here's what it means to you. Here's what we know. There are things we don't know … "
>
> I remember going to visit with investors. I've always tried to visit our investors in Toronto and Montreal each quarter. I didn't stop doing this during the crisis. I remember the investors told me, "You are the only CEO we've seen in months." They really appreciated those visits because they were scared, too…[17]

Those investors certainly had reason to be scared: The company's stock had plunged from $12 a share in 2007 to as low as $2 a share in the midst of the crisis.[18] But the willingness of Hasenfratz and her colleagues to stand up and be answerable – even when they didn't have all the answers – helped quell the panic. Meanwhile, management's willingness to make painful decisions, such as cutting the workforce from 12,000 to 7,000, helped ensure survival. When good times returned, Linamar hired 10,000 people in three years. Today, the company employs some 19,000 people worldwide, and (as of this writing) the share price hovers in the high 70s.[19]

These four character elements work together to create accountability. For example, being accountable requires individuals to take ownership and accept the consequences for the actions initiated under their leadership. Individuals who demonstrate conscientiousness, and acknowledge the personal obligations associated with any role, take ownership and accept the consequences of their actions.

Accountability Complementing Other Dimensions

Accountability ensures that the expansiveness that comes from courage, drive, and transcendence – as well as the connectivity that arises from collaboration and humanity – are anchored in a personal willingness to take ownership, accept consequences, and bear responsibility.

Accountability therefore increases performance. It also brings a rigor to how you behave: a self-discipline that complements integrity and temperance. For example, a sense of accountability to the development of the next generation of leadership helps a leader to be candid during performance management conversations. Accountability is also related to personal learning and development: Both humanity and accountability are required to truly learn from mistakes through personal reflection and setting improvement goals.

Accountability in the Absence of Other Dimensions

Accountability relies on the other dimensions to inform what it is you take ownership for. Without humanity and transcendence, you can accept ownership and responsibility but fail to account for a broader range of interests. Without courage and drive, you may lack the strength to exercise accountability. Humility and integrity help to ensure that being accountable occurs in a way that is not self-interested.

Conversely, taking the whole world on one's shoulders typically results in burn-out. Dimensions such as collaboration, temperance, and judgment may help prevent this from happening.

Accountability: The Small Stuff is the Big Stuff

Is accountability its own reward? No and yes. Previously (in Chapter 7), we met John Furlong, the former CEO of the Vancouver Olympic Committee. Furlong played a key role in bringing the Olympics to that city in 2010, logging more than 1.2 million miles on airplanes in a far-ranging international effort to bring the Games to his home city. In his book *Patriot Hearts*, he recounted a touching story of accountability rewarded.[20]

The quest started at the turn of the new century, with the critical vote scheduled to be held at a meeting of the International Olympic Committee (IOC) in Prague in 2003. At one point on his quest to land the Olympics for Vancouver, Furlong decided that the time had come to write personal thank-you notes to all the members of the IOC with whom he had met. It was an arduous task that he wasn't looking forward to, but he finally forced himself to begin writing the letters during his endless succession of flights. As he recalls:

> I carried the letters in batches in my briefcase. As I was working, the flight attendants knew what I was doing and they left me alone to write. I was getting fed up with my own words, my hand hurt, and I was tired when the attendant arrived with a tray of water, accidentally spilling the whole thing over me.
>
> I wanted to throw her off the plane! She got towels, but the damage had been done. She was heartbroken.
>
> I threw away a number of letters and started over. It was painful. But, after I had mailed them, and then started receiving phone calls from people who were so touched by the letters that they were going to support us, it meant a lot. Writing these letters was an important detail and every single detail matters. I had finished the task and it was a burden off my shoulders, but I didn't know for sure how it would play out. Then, of course, we won by three votes in Prague.
>
> Here is the real lesson: We can choose to make the effort or not. Much of the time, I think we ignore what needs to be done and accept less than the very best. I tried with the Games not to allow anyone to do that.

We've all been there: looking for a rationalization as to why we can't, or won't, or shouldn't be held accountable. Furlong had a ready-made excuse, when the hapless flight attendant dumped a tray of water on his work: "Hey, I tried; but it clearly wasn't meant to be. I'll find some other way to follow up with those IOC members." Parenthetically, we can only imagine the embarrassment that flight attendant – presumably responsible and accountable – must have experienced, in the wake of the spill!

Accountability may reside in the small details: the letters written over, painfully. But it may ultimately manifest itself in the three votes that change the course of sports history. Don't cut a corner, advises John Furlong – not now, not ever! Make the effort. Do what you know needs to be done, even if no one else will know what you did or didn't do.

Because, ultimately, you will know.

Accountability and Control

No one would seriously debate the concept that people should be accountable for the things they control. But what about accountability for things that they don't control?

For many years, there was a prevailing ethic that people in senior roles held themselves accountable for everything bad that happened within their organizations. This was reflected in the doctrines of "ministerial responsibility" in government: the idea that if something happened on your watch, whether you personally did it or could have stopped it being done, you were accountable. More recently, this seems to have waned, leading to – among other things – egregious cases of executive pay becoming decoupled from both corporate performance and shareholder returns.

At this point, let's return to Michael McCain, the CEO at Maple Leaf Foods. In 2013, a serious outbreak of porcine epidemic diarrhea led to the destruction of millions of pigs in the U.S. and Canada, sending hog prices skyrocketing and resulting in very poor operating results for Maple Leaf Foods.

This was clearly something beyond the company's control. Some argued that the system for calculating cash bonuses and stock rewards should be adjusted for 2013 and 2014 to take into account this "beyond our control" situation, and reward the executives and managers who struggled through it even though they hadn't met their individual or collective goals.

McCain would hear none of it. "We are accountable for delivering results to our shareholders," he said, "and we did not deliver. There will be bad years like this, and there will be good ones when we deliver plan and beyond. We earn bonuses when we make or exceed plans. When we don't, we won't."

Accountability is in part about defining the rules of the game, and then playing by those rules – in good times and bad.

Questions to Contemplate

1. Do you hold yourself fully accountable for the successes and failures with which you are associated, directly (through control) or indirectly (through your leadership in your organization)?
2. Is this accountability ethic embraced throughout your organization, and is it manifested in behaviors toward all stakeholders (customers, shareholders, suppliers, etc.)?
3. Do you run "postmortems" on decisions that did not result in good outcomes in which you accept accountability, and then lead the learning process so they don't happen again?

Books and Articles to Read

"Enforcing a Culture of Accountability: Q&A with Culture Architect Robert Richman" Courtney Buchanan (*The Company Ethicist*, 2013)

How Real Leaders Demonstrate Accountability Michael Hyatt (2012)

"Self-Accountability Empowers Solopreneurs" (*Ideavist*, February 28, 2011)

"Two Concepts of Accountability: Accountability as a Virtue and as a Mechanism" Mark Bovens (*West European Politics*, 33 (5), 2010)

QBQ! The Question Behind the Question: Practicing Personal Accountability at Work and in Life John G. Miller (Putnam Adult, 2004)

Mistakes Were Made (But Not by Me): Why We Justify Foolish Beliefs, Bad Decisions, and Hurtful Acts Carol Tavris and Elliot Aronson (Harcourt, 2008)

Videos to Watch

"Maple Leaf Foods Apology" (YouTube, 2011)
   "Milgram Experiment," Jeroen Busscher (YouTube, 2012)
   "The Psychology of Evil," TED Talk by Philip Zimbardo (www.ted.com/talk, 2008)

Notes

1 This story is derived in part from Gordon Pitts's 11.28.08 *Globe and Mail* article, "The testing of Michael McCain," online at http://www.theglobeandmail.com/report-on-business/the-testing-of-michael-mccain/article598005/?page=all.
2 See the (U.S.) Centers for Disease Control summary at http://www.cdc.gov/listeria/definition.html.
3 See this remarkable one-minute video on YouTube at https://www.youtube.com/watch?v=zIsN5AkJ1AI.
4 See these articles that support this statement: http://www.nationalpost.com/Values+Based+Leadership+Michael+McCain+Maple+Leaf+Foods/2325852/story.html; http://www.theglobeandmail.com/report-on-business/small-business/sb-growth/day-to-day/the-best-legal-advice-is-often-an-apology/article626797/; http://www.theglobeandmail.com/report-on-business/the-testing-of-michael-mccain/article598005/?page=all.
5 This detail is from Janet Davison's 10.09.12 CBC News story, "How should a company manage a meat recall crisis?" online at http://www.cbc.ca/nws/canada/how-should-a-company-manage-a-meat-recall-crisis-1.1248421.
6 See the related *National Post* column by Marty Parker, "Values-based leadership: Michael McCain at Maple Leaf Foods," 12.10.09, online at http://www.nationalpost.com/Values+Based+Leadership+Michael+McCain+Maple+Leaf+Foods/2325852/story.html.
7 See the excellent Janet Davison/CBC article, cited above, at http://www.cbc.ca/news/canada/how-should-a-company-manage-a-meat-recall-crisis-1.1248421.
8 See Leslie Boldt's interesting 10.14.12 blog on Boldt Communications, "An unmanaged issue can spell PR disaster," online at http://www.boldtcommunications.com/blog/an-unmanaged-issue-can-spell-pr-disaster/#.VQyCu0Zu8YU.
9 From the above-cited Gordon Pitts' 11.28.08 *Globe and Mail* article, at http://www.theglobeandmail.com/report-on-business/the-testing-of-michael-mccain/article598005/?page=all.
10 Both parts of this story are recounted in a *Globe and Mail* story from 06.27.13 by Simon Houpt and Sean Silcoff, "Bell's bid for Astral approved," online at http://www.theglobeandmail.com/report-on-business/bell-astral/article12861071/.
11 For the inside story on the intense lobbying that probably helped kill the deal, see the *Globe and Mail*'s 10.20.12 article by Steve Ladurantaye, "How George Cope had his bell run," online at http://www.theglobeandmail.com/globe-investor/how-george-cope-had-his-bell-rung/article4625425/.
12 See the Cope profile and interview in Gerard Seijts's *Good Leaders Learn* (Routledge, 2014), p. 310.

13 From an interview with Amanda Silliker, Canadian HR Reporter TV, online at https://www.youtube.com/watch?v=2_nZQphHq4M.

14 See the Kuhlmann profile and interview in Gerard Seijts's *Good Leaders Learn* (Routledge, 2014), p. 125.

15 This section is based in large part on Sean Silverthorne's 01.24.11 CBS news write-up, "Why Taj employees offered their lives to save guests during terrorist attack," at http://www.cbsnews.com/news/why-taj-employees-offered-their-lives-to-save-guests-during-terrorist-attack/. That story, in turn, was largely based on a Harvard Business School case, "Terror at the Taj Bombay: Customer-Centric Leadership," written in 2011 by HBS professor Rohit Deshpande. You can see Deshpande's TED talk on this subject at https://www.youtube.com/watch?v=vQGz1YRqBPw. See also Deshpande's related *Harvard Business Review* article at https://hbr.org/2011/12/the-ordinary-heroes-of-the-taj.

16 From the company's website at http://www.linamar.com/about-linamar. The company name is derived from Linda, Nancy, and Margaret: founder Frank Hasenfratz's two daughters and wife, respectively.

17 See the Hasenfratz profile and interview in Gerard Seijts's *Good Leaders Learn* (Routledge, 2014), p. 133.

18 From the company's 2007 annual report and Gerard Seijts's *Good Leaders Learn* (Routledge, 2014).

19 Results of online search, from https://www.google.com/#q=Linamar+share+price.

20 This version of the story comes from Gerard Seijts's interview with Furlong, recounted in *Good Leaders Learn* (Routledge, 2014), p. 33.

12 Courage

Individuals with courage do the right thing even though it may be unpopular, actively discouraged, or result in a negative outcome for them. They show an unrelenting determination, confidence, and perseverance in confronting difficult situations, and rebound quickly from setbacks.

What happens to an organization when the people within it show courage? Decisions are made despite uncertainty. There is opposition to bad decisions. Politics and bureaucracy wither; innovation thrives.

Conversely, what happens to an organization when people lack courage? People tend to "go with the flow" – even when the flow is based on bad decisions, and headed in a bad direction. Rather than maximizing the upside inherent in a situation, people focus on minimizing the downside. A kind of muteness prevails as people understand that the contrarian view is not welcome.

In this chapter, we explore some of the key elements of courage – depicted in Figure 12.1, below – and look at how the dimension of courage complements the other ten dimensions of leader character.

First, let's look at an example of courage in action – an example to which we'll return in subsequent sections of this chapter.

Courage Begets Courage

Our story begins at a breakfast table in Thornhill, Ontario, outside of Toronto.[1] It is the spring of 1995. A 12-year-old boy named Craig Kielburger is reading a horrifying story in the daily paper. A boy the same age as himself named Iqbal Masih has been shot to death while riding his bike in his hometown in Pakistan. Apparently, Masih has been executed for speaking out against child labor, of which he himself had been a victim from the age of four to ten.

That morning, Kielburger addressed his seventh-grade class. He told his classmates about Iqbal Masih's years of forced servitude – helping to make rugs to pay off his parents' debts. He asked the class if they were interested in doing something to help fight child labor. Eleven children raised their hands, and shortly thereafter, they began looking for charities that

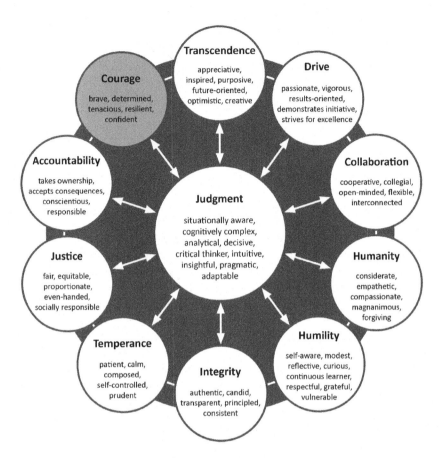

Figure 12.1 Character Dimensions and Associated Elements

might need their help. But those organizations kept saying that the twelve 12-year-olds were too young to make a difference.

So the seventh-graders took matters into their own hands. They began organizing events to raise money for an organization they had named "Free the Children." Other local kids heard about the effort, and set up chapters in their own schools. This unexpected growth was gratifying, but Kielburger – now an eighth-grader – already had a new focus: He wanted to take several weeks off from school and backpack across five Southeast Asian countries to see the child-labor situation firsthand. Not surprisingly, his parents – who didn't let him ride the subway alone – said "no." But he was relentless, and his mother finally agreed, on two conditions: He had to raise half the money himself, and he had to prove that he would be safe. He began doing odd jobs, and writing letters to potential hosts in Asia – consistently omitting his age. He also found a 25-year-old recent graduate of the University of Toronto who wanted to travel in Southeast Asia, and who agreed to serve as Kielburger's chaperone.

On his seven-week journey, Kielburger encountered exploited children living and working under appalling conditions. One day in Pakistan, after failing to get a meeting with a Canadian trade delegation that, coincidentally, was in the same city signing business agreements with Pakistani companies – and included Canadian Prime Minister Jean Chrétien – the 13-year-old Kielburger organized an impromptu press conference at the hotel where the Canadians were staying. At that session, two freed child slaves whom Kielburger had met told their terrible stories.

The result was a firestorm of press coverage. "Suddenly," Kielburger later recalled, "our fledgling charity got a huge boost that we never could have imagined."[2] The 13-year-old Kielburger soon found himself meeting with other world leaders, discussing ways to end the exploitation of children.

Upon his return to Canada, Kielburger and his band of youthful activists raised funds to support a rescue home in Pakistan for children who had been freed from slavery. But it soon became clear that simply freeing children was not enough. The economic roots of the problem – the reasons why parents sold their children in the first place – had to be addressed. In subsequent months and years, Free the Children developed a community-based approach called "Adopt a Village," which focused on four pillars of sustainability: alternative income, clean water and sanitation, health care, and education.

Since then, Free the Children has worked in more than 45 countries around the world.[3] Today, the Adopt a Village program operates in seven countries: India, Kenya, Haiti, China, Nicaragua, Sierra Leone, and Ecuador. Through its efforts, more than 1 million people have gained access to clean water and sanitation. The organization has donated some $16 million in medical supplies, and built more than 650 schools that educate 55,000 children daily. All told, some 2.3 million children around the world benefit from Free the Children's education and development programs.

In 2007 – at the age of 25 – Kielberger was named a Member of the Order of Canada by the Governor General of Canada: the country's second-highest civilian honor. He and his younger brother Marc are still actively involved in Free the Children and related causes. And in 2010, the "Craig Kielburger Secondary School" was dedicated in the town of Milton, Ontario, not far from Kielburger's hometown of Thornhill – perhaps the most appropriate honor for the young idealist and advocate for children.

It's a deeply inspiring story, all the more so in light of its unlikely origins and early evolution. We see it as a story of courage. The first chapter of that story centers on a young boy who had spent six of the first ten years of his life chained to a carpet-weaving loom, and challenged the system that had enslaved him – an act of courage that led directly to his death at the age of 12 years. The story continues forward with a second 12-year-old on the other side of the world – a stubborn kid who refused to be dissuaded by charitable organizations who told him that the most he could do to save enslaved children was turn over his parents' credit-card numbers to them. That boy, too, took enormous risks to advance a cause that had captured his youthful imagination.

Character Elements: What Goes into "Courage"?

As Figure 12.1 indicates, we have identified five character elements that contribute to the dimension of courage. When you have "courage," you are:

Brave: You do what you believe to be right, even in the face of adversity. You stand up for your personal beliefs and values, and you stand up for others.

As noted, Iqbal Masih was brave – and he paid the ultimate price for that courage. His example illustrates a key aspect of bravery: It is contagious. Masih inspired the young Craig Kielburger to take risks and stand up for others. Perhaps we can also infer that Craig's courage inspired his eleven classmates, and also enabled his parents to be brave – a prerequisite for agreeing to let a young boy head into unknown circumstances in faraway lands.

In our MBA classes, we often ask our students to think back to an occasion when someone stood up for them. Was it easy for that person to go against the herd? Is that memory sharply etched in your memory? (The answer is usually "yes.") Are you prepared to show the same kind of courage?

Determined: You display resolve, and you stay committed to seeing things through. Daily life – whether it is the life of a seventh-grader or a CEO – is hard. It is full of distractions. It tugs at us, and tempts us away from the course that we're trying to stay on. Determination keeps us on that course.

True, some undertakings are truly impossible – and that determination in the face of insurmountable obstacles may lead to escalated commitments and wasted resources. So, of course, leaders need to know the difference. But when the mission is highly improbable but not impossible, and the outcome would represent a significant improvement in the lives of others, determination is the fuel that makes it happen.

John Furlong, introduced in earlier chapters, is the former CEO of the Vancouver Olympic Committee. The project of first bidding for the 2010 Winter Olympics and then hosting it lasted some 14 years, from beginning to end. As Furlong later recalled: "I realized at the very beginning that it would take everything I had to give, and my family knew that, and we talked about it, but it was far more than that. It's an easy thing to say, but to experience something that never goes away, that lives on your pillow, wakes up on your pillow ... that was very tough."

Tenacious: This is closely related to the element of determination. You finish things, despite the inevitable obstacles, difficulties, or discouragements along the way. You work hard over extended periods, and follow through to achieve your goals.

Winston Churchill embodied tenacity, and – in one of his most famous speeches – eloquently defined it:

> We shall not flag or fail. We shall go on to the end. We shall fight in France, we shall fight on the seas and the oceans, we shall fight with growing confidence and growing strength in the air, we shall defend our island, whatever the cost may be. We shall fight on the beaches, we shall fight on the landing grounds, we shall fight in the fields and in the streets, we shall fight in the hills; we shall never surrender.

Resilient: You withstand difficult conditions, and endure. You recover quickly from setbacks. "What doesn't kill us makes us stronger," as the old saying goes.

We are reminded of the periodic *Peanuts* cartoon strip which showed Lucy persuading Charlie Brown to try one more time to kick the football that she has teed up on the ground – only to snatch it away at the last minute, causing Charlie Brown to fly up in the air and land flat on his back.[4] We may not admire Charlie Brown's judgment, but we admire his resilience.

As a more serious example, think of Silken Laumann, the Canadian rower from the 1980s and 1990s. After surviving a harrowing childhood characterized by psychological abuse, self-hatred, anorexia, and cutting, she made herself into an Olympic-caliber rower – only to suffer a dramatic accident ten weeks before her scheduled appearance in the 1992 Barcelona Games. Despite detached muscles in her leg and a shattered ankle, she captured a bronze medal that year. And her continuing self-doubts notwithstanding, she has become a motivational speaker and author of a searingly candid memoir, *Unsinkable*. "How could I help others find their inner courage," she wrote, "while holding back the real story of the self-doubt that continued to plague me?"[5]

Confident: You demonstrate self-assurance in your abilities, decisions, and actions.

Like courage, confidence can be contagious. "The only thing we have to fear is fear itself," Franklin Roosevelt famously said in his first inaugural address – and Americans took courage from that confidence. His wife Eleanor also had a prescription regarding confidence. "You gain strength, courage, and confidence by every experience in which you really stop to look fear in the face. You are able to say to yourself, 'I have lived through this horror. I can take the next thing that comes along.' You must do the thing you think you cannot do."

Of course, these five elements of courage interact with and potentiate each other. For example, bravery in the face of adversity requires the resolve that comes from determination. Resilience provides the important recovery and ability to rebound that aids tenacity. Confidence enables the bravery needed in the face of adversity. And to be determined and tenacious, you need *confidence*.

Blake Hutcheson, CEO of Oxford Properties, talks about "finishiative" as a quality for which he looks in up-and-coming managers and executives. While he respects those who demonstrate initiative, he really looks for initiative that is coupled with courage to challenge the status quo, determination to drive the initiative through to completion, get the initiative done, and resilience to continue when it's not working or problems arise, as they will, in the change process.

Courage Complementing Other Dimensions

Look back to Figure 12.1 and the eleven leader character dimensions. How does courage support the ten other dimensions?

Courage is a key enabler of the forward momentum required to achieve the sense of purpose and optimism associated with transcendence. Pope Francis has shown tremendous courage in his first years of his papacy to enact an agenda of change: a warmer, more inclusive style of governance; gender and religious tolerance; sticking up for the poorest and homeless; rooting out child abusers within the church; and signaling new tolerance for gay people and gay marriage.

There are many challenges that arise with the exercise of integrity, justice, and temperance; courage is essential to overcoming these obstacles and challenges. For example, to demonstrate openness in communication during a crisis, and to be attentive to the needs and wants of multiple stakeholder groups, not just those of the company's shareholders, requires courage. Compare the actions of Michael McCain, CEO of Maple Leaf Foods, during the 2008 listeriosis crisis – when, as described in Chapter 11, 23 people died from eating tainted cold cuts – with those of the chairman of Montreal, Maine & Atlantic Railway Ltd. Ed Burkhardt during the Lac-Megantic train disaster in Quebec, Canada.

It takes courage to display the kind of empathy and compassion associated with humanity. Conducting candid and truly constructive performance management conversations requires empathy and compassion. Candid feedback sometimes involves conflict because candor may get rejected and resented. Most of us don't like conflict and hence courage is required to conduct performance management conversations well.

And because humanity may bring with it feelings of pain, suffering, and discontent, being humane often requires the resilience associated with courage.

Courage in the Absence of Other Dimensions

On October 25, 1854, during the Crimean War, a British light cavalry unit – optimized for speed, and therefore only lightly armored – made a frontal assault against an entrenched Russian artillery battery. The "charge of the light brigade," later immortalized in a poem by Tennyson, appears to have been the result of missed communication among the British commanders. In any case, the result was a slaughter. Out of the 670 mounted troopers who entered the "Valley of Death" – Tennyson's term – 118 were killed, 127 wounded, and 60 taken prisoner. Some 335 horses were killed. When the cavalry regrouped after the catastrophe, only 195 troopers still had their horses.

"C'est magnifique, mais ce n'est pas la guerre," said French Marshal Pierre Bosquet, who witnessed the carnage. "C'est de la folie." ("It is magnificent, but it is not war. It is madness.") In other words, the troopers showed magnificent courage, but – doomed by bad intelligence, failed communications, and inept leadership – they were annihilated.

Let's look at a business story that suggests that courage alone can't make a company succeed, and that courage in excess – in other words, recklessness – may even lead to catastrophe.

By the turn of the twenty-first century, the same kinds of clean-air regulations that had been clamping down on internal-combustion engines for decades were finally starting to catch up with the diesel-engine industry.[6] The Environmental Protection Agency (EPA) wanted a 90 percent reduction in the levels of nitrogen oxides and particulates – soot – that diesel engines were releasing into the atmosphere. Truck manufacturers and original equipment manufacturers (OEMs) that made diesel engines for trucks were put on notice: Clean up your act, or face dire consequences in coming years.

The good news was the industry had time to react: The more stringent standards would be phased in gradually between 2007 and 2010. The bad news was that while there were promising technologies then under development that would allow manufacturers to meet those new standards, none had yet proven itself. Most companies were leaning toward a process called "selective catalytic reduction," or SCR, which involved the addition of a catalytic converter and a tank containing a urea solution, which broke down nitrogen oxide in outgoing emissions, converting the noxious gas into nitrogen and water.

Daniel C. Ustian, head of Illinois-based Navistar International's diesel-engine unit, wasn't convinced. Convinced that truckers would balk at the prospect of dealing with a second tank on their rigs – and paying $10,000 extra for an SCR-equipped truck – Ustian bucked the industry trend: He declined to pursue SCR, and instead embraced an alternative technology – exhaust gas recirculation (EGR) – which ran exhaust gases back through the engine to force a more complete combustion of the soot and sulfur in those gases.

If it worked, Navistar would have a clear competitive advantage. Ustian – a professional manager, rather than an engineer – decided to place a $700 million bet on EGR. It was a bold stroke, but it placed enormous pressure on the company's scientists and engineers. Could they make the technology work, and could they make it work on the EPA's timetable?

Ustian wasn't going to take "no" for an answer. As one executive later recalled:

> Dan is telling his technical people, "You've got to deliver," and they're saying, "We don't know how, but we'll try." There was a lot of tension in the technical community, from the scientists on up to the managers, about whether we should be agreeing to something we don't know how to do. Dan didn't want to hear any of it. "You're going to get it done." He's a positive thinker. He doesn't like negative thinking.

To cut a long story short, it didn't work. EGR simply couldn't meet the EPA standards. Navistar missed the 2010 deadline, and – despite some helpful exceptions and extensions from the EPA – kept failing to come up with an acceptable EGR technology. Not only did the EGR-equipped trucks still smoke too much, but now, choked down by a bad technology, they didn't work very well. Finally, in July 2012, with the company's market cap and future orders plummeting – and after losing $516 million on revenues of $6.4 billion in the first half of the year – Ustian had to do a very public and embarrassing about-face. He abandoned EGR in favor of SCR, started buying engines and after treatment systems from arch-rival Cummins, and set out to fix the damage he had inflicted on his company.[7]

Observers inside the company pointed out that Ustian's bravado in the emissions wars was nothing new. In fact, according to one manager, his whole career – and his golf game – reflected the same kind of hubris:

> He'd always take the riskier shot [in golf] … But he's a great golfer. He'd always come through. It was the same thing with work. He'd have everybody scratching their head, but he was usually right.

A month after his stunning public reversal – and amid takeover rumors and heightened scrutiny from the Securities and Exchange Commission regarding the company's accounting practices – Ustian abruptly resigned as CEO.[8] As of this writing, Navistar's future is far from certain. "I'm not thinking bankruptcy is imminent," said one financial analyst in September 2014: not exactly a ringing endorsement of a robust company.[9]

What do we take away from this story? Courage without the other dimensions – for example, temperance, humility, collaboration, or accountability – can lead to recklessness, and recklessness can lead to disaster. It's exciting – to paraphrase Field Marshall Bosquet – but it's not business. Ustian evidently worried that his company was at risk of being shoved aside by faster-moving competitors, so he "always took the riskier shot." He insulated himself from the technical people who might have provided mid-course corrections. (Engine development was done in a facility 45 minutes away from headquarters.) He limited his strategy and planning sessions to four or five participants – he didn't like big meetings – and he brooked no dissent at those meetings. In other words, he short-circuited some of the very systems that might have saved him from his own hubris.

Accountability, one of our leader character dimensions, helps ensure that the risks taken as a result of courage are ones that you are prepared to take on. Clearly, that mitigating dimension was lacking at Navistar, and it cost investors hundreds of millions of dollars and Ustian his job.

More broadly, when courage is unmodified by transcendence, it often becomes unfocused, and lacking in purpose. And when the dimensions of humanity and justice are not developed, courage may lack perspective.

The Actor and the Act

Hemingway defined courage as "grace under pressure."[10] The compelling thing about that definition is that it brings together both the *actor* and the *act*.

Leader character is a state of being – in other words, it's about the actor. We argue in this chapter that courage is a central component of leader character. We should also underscore that courage manifests itself through the act. When the time comes, the leader shows courage.

Questions to Contemplate

1. Can you think of situations in the past where you did not, in retrospect, match up to your own standards of courage? What stopped you doing so? What did you learn from those incidents?
2. What acts of courage have you seen in your personal or business life? What forces acted on those people to influence their actions?
3. How can you encourage those whom you lead to be courageous in their actions?

Books and Articles to Read

"Brené Brown: 'How Vulnerability Can Make Our Lives Better'" Dan Schawbel (*Forbes,* April 21, 2013*)*

"4 Ways to Create a Culture of Courage" Tom Rieger (*Chief Executive,* August, 2011)

"Combating Ethical Cynicism and Voicing Values in the Workplace" Mary C. Gentile (*Ivey Business Journal,* May/June, 2011)

"10 Traits of Courageous Leaders" Susan Tardanico (*Forbes,* January, 2013)

Extraordinary Circumstances: The Journey of a Corporate Whistleblower
Cynthia Cooper (Wiley, 2009)
Moral Courage Rushworth Kidder (Avon, 2006)
The Mystery of Courage William Ian Miller (Harvard University Press, 2000)
Courage, the Backbone of Leadership Gus Lee and Diane Elliott-Lee (Jossey-Bass, 2006)
Leadership and the Art of Struggle: How Great Leaders Grow Through Challenge and Adversity Steven Snyder (Berret-Koehel, 2013)

Videos to Watch

Alan Mulally of Ford: "Leaders Must Serve, with Courage" (YouTube, 2011)
Gandhi's philosophy, from the movie *Gandhi* (YouTube, 1982)
Rosa Parks' interview on the Merv Griffin Show (YouTube, 1983)
"Corruption crusader" Ken Pereira (CBC The National, 2013)

Notes

1 This story is drawn from the Craig Kielburger case series written by Mark Reno under the supervision of Mary Crossan, and published in 2012 by Ivey Publishing, including: "Craig Kielburger: a movement is born," Case #9B12M031; and "Craig Kielburger: Rescue Mission Accomplished?" Case #9B12M031B.
2 Quotes in this section are from the video that accompanies the Kielburger video series, viewable online at https://www.youtube.com/watch?v=8cvN4HE9CYs&feature=youtu.be.
3 See the organization's website at http://www.freethechildren.com/about-us/our-story/?gclid=Cj0KEQiAts-kBRCbgrXc1rnXw7MBEiQAnFqTdo4b_Nw3D6Psbnjv0e58z8SybGIsQQR88w5t0k_-o90aAoaH8P8HAQ.
4 Yes, there is an online history of the recurring football cartoon strip. See http://peanuts.wikia.com/wiki/Football_gag.
5 See the related story and a video clip of Laumann in *The Star*, 01.17.14, "Silken Laumann's new book *Unsinkable* reveals a troubled childhood," by Dianne Rinehart, at http://www.thestar.com/entertainment/books/2014/01/17/silken_laumanns_new_book_unsinkable_reveals_a_troubled_childhood.html.
6 This story is from the 08.20.12 issue of *Forbes*, "Death by hubris?" by Joann Muller, and is online at http://www.forbes.com/sites/joannmuller/2012/08/02/death-by-hubris-the-catastrophic-decision-that-could-bankrupt-a-great-american-manufacturer/.
7 See the related story, "Trouble Navistar props up its finance but now faces SEC probe," by Joann Muller, in the 08.02.12 issue of *Forbes* at http://www.forbes.com/sites/joannmuller/2012/08/02/troubled-navistar-props-up-its-finances-but-now-faces-sec-probe/.
8 An article in the 08.27.12 *Wall Street Journal*, "Navistar nabs ex-Textron CEO," by Bob Tita, provides details about Ustian's resignation, and also supplied some of the technical details included in our account. Read it online at http://www.wsj.com/news/articles/SB10000872396390444914904577615213793938568?mod=_newsreel_3.

9 From an 09.20.14 online story, "The bleeding has stopped, but Navistar is still struggling," by Meribah Knight in *Chicago Business*, online at http://www.chicagobusiness.com/article/20140920/ISSUE01/309209973/the-bleeding-has-stopped-but-navistar-is-still-struggling.
10 For an interesting commentary on the definition of courage, see "Implicit theories of courage," by Christopher Rate, Jennifer Clarke, Douglas Lindsay, and Robert Sternberg, in the *Journal of Positive Psychology*, April 2007, 2(2), 80–98.

13   Transcendence

Most businesses today pay at least some attention to the notion of a vision. Visions and vision statements are important in and of themselves. The process of arriving at a shared vision generally means that a valuable consensus is being forged – especially if it was created and ratified by those who will be guided by it. And once in place, a vision serves as reinforcement for that consensus and a lens for looking into the future. "Well," the discussion goes, "we've publicly committed ourselves to X, Y, and Z. How do those commitments square with the current crisis in customer confidence we are facing? How do they tell us to act?"

The focus of this chapter, transcendence, is bigger than that. Maybe we should start with definitions. First, there's the literal definition of transcendence, which is pretty bland. Something that is transcendent "goes beyond the limits of ordinary experience," and is "far better or greater than what is usual."[1] When you have a transcendent experience, you may draw inspiration from excellence or beauty in many arenas, including sports, music, arts, nature, and design, as well as the world of business – and you are changed by that experience of inspiration. Some businesses – including Chicago-based Metropolitan Capital Bank & Trust – deploy works of art in lobbies and other common areas to provide exactly that kind of inspiration.[2]

With transcendence, you see possibility where others who lack that character element don't see it. You have an expansive view of things – going beyond the limits of "ordinary" experience in your private or professional lives – taking into account things that are often outside the scope of vision, either because they are more peripheral or longer-term concerns. Finally, because you see more than just the realm of material existence, you transcend that experience – you "go beyond its limits" – and find a bigger purpose in life. This tends to foster optimism and release creativity.

Does a business leader have to be an aesthete, drawing inspiration from sublime works of art or the wonders of nature? While it may not be obvious that they do, such inspiration often underscores great leaps forward in business strategies, such as those described in, for example, *Blue Ocean Strategy*.[3] Do business leaders need to see possibility where others do not? Yes. Do they need to be optimistic, and foster optimism? Yes. Do they need

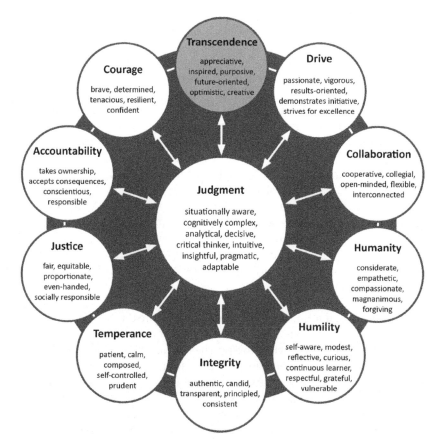

Figure 13.1 Character Dimensions and Associated Elements

to be creative, and foster creativity in others? Yes, absolutely. Although some of the elements of transcendence may seem distant from business leadership, in fact, they are all connected when the dimension comes into play. For example, creativity is cultivated through the other elements, including being appreciative, inspired, and optimistic.

The key elements of transcendence are summarized to the uppermost position in Figure 13.1. In this chapter, we explore those six elements, and look at how the dimension of transcendence supports the other dimensions of leader character.

First, let's look at an example of transcendence, and consider what this example teaches us.

Transcendence is Where You Find It: Bill and Melinda Gates

Maybe Bill Gates isn't the first person you think of when you contemplate transcendent business leaders. In his early life, at least, Gates was nerdy to the point of anti-heroic. Even today, he's more Woody Allen than he is, say, the Virgin Group's founder Sir Richard Branson. But let us make the case for Gates and his wife Melinda as transcendent individuals.[4]

William H. Gates III had some great good luck in 1980, early in his career as a software writer, when IBM decided that personal computers were not a promising market, and the operating systems that would run PCs therefore were of little interest. Big Blue decided to let Microsoft be the only authorized licensee of the disk-operating system that it had developed, up to that point. Gates secured a monopoly on the software that became known as MS-DOS, and the rest is history. "It's unusual to have so much luck in one life, I think," he reflected in 2009. "But it's been a major factor in what I have been able to do."[5]

But more than luck was involved, in this complicated tale of invention and licensing. Somehow, Gates saw around a technological corner. A little more than a decade later, Microsoft's products ran nine out of ten of the world's IBM PCs – and far more important, their far more numerous clones – and the company supplied something like half of the world's business-useful software.

Of course, Gates also encountered corners that he couldn't see around. His original partner in Microsoft, Paul Allen, wanted to create both hardware and software, but Gates vetoed the proposed hardware venture. Computing power was becoming practically free, he reasoned; why be in the business of making something that was more or less being given away?[6] As a result, Microsoft gave up the opportunity to control the user's experience from end to end – always Steve Jobs' focus at Apple – and several decades later, that decision turns out to have been a bad call. It falls to Microsoft's CEO Satya Nadella to ensure the company's continued relevance in a much-changed world.

Despite large and small setbacks, a consistent thread in Gates's public utterances and modest writings is optimism. When an interviewer asked him in 1994 how society should think about the future, he responded:

> More optimistically. As there is progress, which is partly advances in technology, in a certain sense the world gets richer. That is, the things we do that use a lot of resources and time can be done more efficiently. So people wonder, Will there be jobs? Will there be things to do? Until we're educating every kid in a fantastic way, until every inner city is cleaned up, there is no shortage of things to do. And as society gets richer, we can choose to allocate the resources in a way that gives people the incentive to go out and do those unfinished jobs.

At the time Gates gave that interview, he was already married to his former employee, Melinda French. He had always intended to give away most of his vast personal fortune, and in 2000, he and his wife established the Bill & Melinda Gates Foundation to do so in a systematic and impactful way.[7] The foundation focuses on a few large challenges: extreme poverty and poor health in developing countries, and the shortcomings of the U.S. educational system.

The very ambitiousness of the foundation's goals ensures some frustrations. For example, in 2010, the foundation assessed the impact of a huge program launched in 2005, and funded with $450 million in five-year grants. The report card was mixed, at best. One goal – to create a family of vaccines that would not need refrigeration – came up woefully short. "Back then," Gates told a reporter, "I thought: 'Wow – we'll have a bunch of thermostable vaccines by 2010.' But we're not even close to that. I'd be surprised if we have even one by 2015."[8]

At ground level, though, the foundation could point to many smaller successes that give cause for hope. For example, the foundation's much-publicized effort to eradicate polio by 2018 – in conjunction with other institutions and agencies around the world – hasn't yet succeeded, but has certainly made huge progress. In 2012, there were 223 polio cases worldwide; a year later, the number had dropped to 26.[9] And Bill and Melinda Gates continue to put their money behind their ideals: in the past 15 years, their foundation has distributed a staggering $33 billion.[10]

In a recent TED talk, Gates recalled that in his childhood, the biggest perceived threat to humanity was nuclear war.[11] Today, he asserted, the biggest threat is an outbreak of a deadly disease – an outbreak for which we're not ready. "The failure to prepare," he argued, "could allow the next epidemic to be dramatically more devastating than Ebola." The necessary preparation, Gates continued, looks a whole lot like preparing for war: a standing "army" of military personnel who are ready to be deployed – a well-trained medical reserve corps with a plan for rapid deployment, and ample reserves behind them. In addition, said Gates, we need strong health systems in poor countries – in other words, areas that are most likely to be affected. We also need to pair those two resources together effectively. To make this work, we need to conduct simulations: "germ games, not war games," as Gates put it, "so that we see where the holes are." Finally, and concurrently, we need to conduct intensive R&D to come up with the necessary preventive measures, diagnostic tools, and therapies.

Expensive? Yes. But Gates cited estimates that a recurrence of the 1918 flu pandemic today would cost the global economy something like $3 trillion – and millions and millions of deaths.

"We need to get going," he urged, "because time is not on our side." But – he concluded with an earnest and nerdy smile – "if we start now, we can be ready for the next epidemic."

Seeing around a dark corner, thinking big, and ending on a note of unembarrassed optimism: Gates transcends the threat of the moment, and inspires us to go along with him.

Character Elements: What Goes into "Transcendence"?

When you transcend a circumstance, you are:

Appreciative: You admire the character, skills, or successes of others. You enjoy beauty in things such as great design, art, music, sports, or natural beauty in the environment.

Having discussed Bill Gates at some length, it might be appropriate to cite here his longtime friend and sometimes tormentor, the late Steve Jobs. Jobs took a calligraphy course at Reed College; it had such a profound impact on him that he insisted that his revolutionary Macintosh computer include a large array of custom typefaces. Jobs was also a student of industrial design, particularly the design of great German products: Braun toasters, Porsche automobiles, and others.

When the scrappy Apple still shared a building with the well-established Sony, Jobs used to take fellow employees out to the parking lot and instruct them in the styling of the Mercedes cars driven by affluent Sony managers. "Over the years they've made the lines softer but the details starker," he explained to them. "That is what we have to do with the Macintosh."[12] To Jobs, design was law.

Inspired: You are stimulated by brilliant or timely ideas or influences.

For many people, the first person who comes to mind as an embodiment of this element is Oprah Winfrey: certainly an individual who has experienced transcendence, and has moved uncounted millions of admirers down that same path.[13]

Her childhood was intermittently nightmarish. After spending her early childhood on her grandmother's farm in Mississippi – waiting for her mother to find work and send for her – Winfrey moved to Milwaukee at age six to live with her mother. Beginning at age nine, she was repeatedly molested by family members and other visitors to the apartment. She was living on the street by age 14, and – after delivering a baby that died as an infant – she went to live with her father in Tennessee.

Vernon Winfrey provided his daughter with the structure that she had long lacked and craved. Under his watchful eye, she pulled the strands of her life together. She won a beauty contest, and earned a scholarship to Tennessee State University. But her work in radio and television drew her out of school, and eventually led her to Baltimore in 1976, where she landed her first talk show. Eight years later, she launched the program that became a nationwide sensation: *The Oprah Winfrey Show*. Incredibly, she launched a movie career in parallel with her talk show duties, and her portrayal of Sofia in *The Color Purple* earned her an Academy Award nomination.

Winfrey was more than just a performer. For example, she pushed for a national database of convicted child abusers, which in 1993 was signed into law by President Bill Clinton. In 1996 – harking back to the days when Vernon made his daughter write one book report a week – she launched an on-air book club, which quickly became an influential force in publishing. It all added up: The *Forbes* list of the fabulously rich in 2003 included Winfrey.

The plaudits rolled in. *Life* magazine named her the most influential woman of her generation. *BusinessWeek* in 2005 called her the greatest African-American philanthropist in the history of the U.S. In 2013, President Barack Obama – whose nomination as the Democratic presidential nominee in 2008 was secured in part through Winfrey's unprecedented endorsement of him – awarded her the United States' highest civilian honor: the Presidential Medal of Freedom.

Obviously, the line between inspired and inspirational quickly becomes blurred. Winfrey was, and is, both.

Purposive: You have a strong sense of personal mission or orientation in life. You find personal meaning in your work.

In 2004, an Ethiopian woman named Bethlehem Tilahun Alemu created a footwear company in her home community of Zenabwork. Her vision: that making shoes could be a platform for hope. The company's products are hand-crafted, and made almost entirely from local materials, including recycled materials. Traditional Ethiopian shoe designs are fused with artisan craft skills and contemporary design, in an effort to reach a broad and sophisticated consuming public.

The company's website is imbued with a strong sense of mission and purpose. For example:

> Africa needs far fewer charity brands and much more of its own powerful brands whose global equity it can leverage for its own good. Most importantly in the creation of the prosperity that comes from well-paid, sustainable jobs. Good jobs mean people can afford to finance their own solutions and not wait for a handout to do so.
>
> Ethiopia deeply deserves the profits, both physical, cultural, and otherwise, that come from the direct deployment of our indigenous resources into world-class finished products and brands.[14]

"Have fun," Alemu advises visitors to her company's website. Help others, and "be proud that you are making the world a better place, one step at a time."[15]

Future-oriented: You see the big picture and view things over the long term.

One of the amazing contemporary stories of future-oriented thinking in business – and one that is still very much in the process of unfolding – is that of Elon Musk. A co-founder of PayPal, the online bill-paying and money-moving service, Musk soon moved on to bigger successes. He now runs two ambitious and successful (at least in terms of current stock price) companies: Tesla Motors and Space Exploration Technologies (SpaceX).[16]

Musk is more than just the suit in the corner office; he is also a lead product developer and designer in both of his companies.[17] His pursuit of all-electric vehicles was motivated by an undergraduate vision of sustainable transport and energy production – two of the problems that are "most likely to affect the future of the world," as he noted in a TED talk.[18] In 2008, Tesla Motors produced the stunning Tesla Roadster, which sold only a small number of units but set a new standard of performance for an electric car. In 2012, the company introduced its Model S: the world's first premium electric sedan, which reached 50,000-unit sales within two years. Astoundingly, Musk had gone up against the entrenched giants of the automobile industry – and in a small but critical niche, had succeeded.[19]

SpaceX, founded in 2002, builds advanced rockets and spacecraft. Its goal? To revolutionize space technology, "with the ultimate goal of enabling people to live on other planets."[20] Musk's visions of the future might be dismissed as simply that – visions – except that he has an uncanny ability to deliver on them. For example? In December 2010, SpaceX became the only private company ever to return a spacecraft from low-Earth orbit. A year and a half later, the company again registered a first for a private company when its Dragon spacecraft docked with the International Space Station, exchanged cargo, and returned safely to Earth. Since then, with the retirement of the space shuttle fleet, Dragon has been relied upon by NASA to resupply the space station.

Optimistic: You find real positives in situations, often where others do not. Despite challenges, you remain confident about the future.

"We're both optimists," Bill and Melinda Gates recently wrote in an open letter posted on the foundation's website. "We believe by doing these things – focusing on a few big goals and working with our partners on innovative solutions – we can help every person get the chance to live a healthy, productive life."[21]

Oprah Winfrey, too, has staked a strong claim to optimism. As one of her biographers observed:

> In one forum or another – in speeches, writings, and programs – Oprah expresses her belief that it is the journey that matters. Despite the fact that her big life has provided almost everything anyone could want, her optimism suggests that the best is yet to come.[22]

Psychologists have suggested that depressed people see the world more realistically than optimistic ones – that optimists are, to some extent, deluded.[23] But if that's true, optimism is an empowering delusion, and one which – as in both the Gates and Winfrey examples – encourages the optimist to transcend current reality, and strive for a better world.

Creative: You generate unique and original ideas. You find practical, innovative solutions and ways to do things.

Sanjit Bunker Roy grew up as a privileged child in India: elite private schools, three-time national squash champion, and so forth.[24] Then, in 1965, he took a trip into the rural landscape of Palamu District Bihar and was appalled at the poverty he saw there. He decided that he wanted to give something back, and he told his family that he was going to dig wells in a village for five years. They were distraught, but he was determined. Once in the village context, he began appreciating the skills and wisdom of the local people, who – although desperately poor – had found ways to survive.

In 1972, Roy and a local farmer named Meghraj established the Social Works and Research Center to bring together urban knowledge and rural wisdom.[25] In an abandoned tuberculosis sanatorium in the village of Tilonia, they began a process of exchange and mutual education that continues to this day. Gradually, the idealistic graduate students from the city began to be replaced by ambitious local youth, and the "Barefoot College" was born. It was a new approach to educating the rural poor: one that would offer to poor people a curriculum that reflected their special needs and interests. Traditional academics were banned from the Barefoot College – in fact, people who held advanced degrees were not permitted to join the faculty.

In 1986, in the village of Rajasthan, the Barefoot College drew on the talents of local designers and builders to construct its first campus. But the college's impact and reputation were already extending far beyond these modest quarters. The hard-won wisdom that the Barefoot College was accumulating was being applied across a host of societal problems. To cite just one example: The school's leaders drew on their own experiences in Rajasthan to train villagers from across India and neighboring countries to use solar power to electrify their villages. Next, the Barefoot College went to Africa, training grandmothers in solar energy techniques. (Roy finds women in general, and grandmothers in particular, far more reliable allies than most men.) After a visible success in electrifying a village in Sierra Leone, the national government asked the Barefoot College to train 150 more grandmothers to scale the operation up.

"Don't listen to the World Bank," Roy told a TED audience in 2011. "Listen to the people on the ground. They have all the solutions in the world." But it was more than listening: It was also finding creative ways to apply those solutions.

These six character elements – appreciative, inspired, purposive, future-oriented, optimistic, and creative – form the character dimension of transcendence.

Being appreciative, for example, means that you notice things that others do not and that can be a great source of creativity. When you allow appreciation and creativity to inspire you, particularly in the service of something you find purposeful, it can fuel a sense of optimism. This sense of possibility can enhance your capacity to see potential future states and the bigger picture. Optimism can open your heart and mind, and allow you to more fully appreciate the world around you.

Transcendence Complementing Other Dimensions

Transcendence brings to every dimension an expanded scope of possibility. It provides the force of stretch and reach that are critical for courage and drive. This expanded perspective helps to ensure that dimensions such as justice, humanity, and collaboration continue to grow over time. To dimensions like humility and temperance that require restraint, transcendence brings a sense of meaning and motivation.

Transcendence in the Absence of Other Dimensions

Transcendence in the absence of support from other dimensions can lead to not being grounded in reality. The dimensions of temperance and accountability are critical to providing the self-regulation that helps keep you grounded. Transcendence or vision without drive is just a hallucination, as Thomas Edison once observed. And to bring transcendence into focus and reality often requires the conviction and courage that true innovators bring. Reflection and compassion – elements of humility and humanity – feed transcendence.

Romeo Dallaire is a retired Canadian general who led the United Nations peacekeeping force in Rwanda during the 1994 genocide. In that role, he witnessed unspeakable horrors. He is also a former senator, and – in the course of his farewell speech to the Senate – he reflected on his experiences, and also addressed Canada's place in the world and the dire situation in Africa:

> If we are to overcome the challenges facing the world today, we need transcendent leadership with the deepest conviction and the most honourable of intentions. In other words, we need statesmanship. There is a dearth of statesmanship, of taking risk, demonstrating flexibility, innovation and humility. The question is: When will Canada finally answer the call again?[26]

Again, we see the subtle interplay among many elements that is needed to achieve transcendence.

The Transcendental Club

Sometime around 1836 – the dates are a little fuzzy – an ordained Congregationalist minister named Frederic Henry Hedge organized a loosely knit but like-minded group of New Englanders into what was first called the "Hedge Club" but soon became known instead as the Transcendental Club.[27] Its initial membership roll was impressive, including such luminaries as Ralph Waldo Emerson, Margaret Fuller, Nathaniel Hawthorne, Walt Whitman, Henry Wadsworth Longfellow, and Henry David Thoreau.

Very simply stated, the Transcendentalists wanted more inspiration than the stuffy and straight-laced Protestant denominations of the day afforded them. They wanted to validate understanding that came to them not only through their five senses – the day-to-day experience of life – but also through their personal experience of divinity through transcendent experiences.

The result of this openness, this questioning, and this willingness to look around corners led to an incredible outburst of creativity, in what was still the small and somewhat isolated literary community of Boston. *The Scarlet Letter, The House of Seven Gables, Moby-Dick, Uncle Tom's Cabin, Walden,* and *Leaves of Grass*: All rushed off the pens of the Transcendentalists between 1850 and 1855. Having given themselves permission to transcend the present, and to think for themselves, they created great things. Transcendence was idealism, and freedom. As Whitman wrote:

> You shall no longer take things at second or third hand, nor look through the eyes of the dead, nor feed on the spectres in books, You shall not look through my eyes either, nor take things from me, You shall listen to all sides and filter them from your self.[28]

And these are common threads across the stories told in this chapter, as well: idealism and freedom, underpinning and fueling creativity. Great business leaders are members of their own Transcendental Club. They manage, at one and the same time, to keep their heads above the horizon and their feet on the ground.

Questions to Contemplate

1. What or who has ever made you think beyond what you thought were the bounds of possibility? How did they do that?
2. Could you lead a process of visioning in your organization that would lift people's ideas beyond their own sense experience? How would that work for you in your context?
3. What experiences could you give yourself and your employees that would get them to "think bigger and more broadly" about what could be done to move your organization to a new, higher trend-line?

Books and Articles to Read

The Ten Faces of Innovation: IDEO's Strategies for Defeating the Devil's Advocate and Driving Creativity Throughout Your Organization Tom Kelley and Jonathan Littman (Crown Business, 2005)

Learned Optimism: How to Change Your Mind and Your Life Martin E. Seligman (Vintage, 2006)

Start with Why: How Great Leaders Inspire Everyone to Take Action Simon Sinek (Penguin Group, 2009)

"Compelling Visions: Content, Context, Credibility and Collaboration" Jeffrey Gandz (*Ivey Business Journal*, March/April, 2009)

The Art of Possibility: Transforming Professional and Personal Life Rosamund Stone Zander and Benjamin Zander (Penguin, 2002)

Videos to Watch

"How Top CEOs Cope with Constant Stress" Interview with Justin Menkes (*Harvard Business Review*, YouTube, 2011)

"Why Great Ideas Get Rejected" TED Talk by David Burkus (www.ted.com/talk, 2013)

"Why We Do What We Do" TED Talk by Tony Robbins (www.ted.com/talk, 2006)

"The Transformative Power of Classical Music" TED Talk by Benjamin Zander (www.ted.com/talk, 2008)

"How Great Leaders Inspire Action" TED Talk by Simon Sinek (www.ted.com/talk, 2009)

"Embrace the Shake" TED Talk by Phil Hansen (www.ted.com/talk, 2013)

"Life at 30,000 Feet" TED Talk by Richard Branson (www.ted.com/talk, 2007)

Notes

1 Read the Merriam Webster dictionary's definition of "transcendent" at http://www.merriam-webster.com/dictionary/transcendent.
2 See CEO Michael Rose's comments on the value of art in business in Elysabeth Alfano's 01.23.13 article, "Does business need the arts to be innovative?" online at www.huffingtonpost.com/elysabeth-alfano/business-art-innovation_b_2450438.html.
3 From *Blue Ocean Strategy*, by W. Chan Kim, Harvard Business Review Press, 2005.
4 We draw in this section from *Impatient Optimist*, a collection of Gates quotes edited by Lisa Rogak (B2 Books, 2012); *Bill* Gates, by Jonathan Gatlin (HarperCollins, 1999); and *50 Years of the Playboy Interview* (Playboy Enterprises, 2012). The very interesting *Playboy* interview took place in 1994, when Microsoft was still a virtually unchallenged colossus in the related realms of operating systems and business-oriented applications.
5 From *Impatient Optimist*, by Lisa Rogak (B2 Books, 2012).
6 The recollection is Gates's, and is from the *Playboy* interview.
7 The new foundation grew out of a smaller (but still substantial) initiative founded in 2007, and aimed at improving libraries in the U.S.
8 From an article in the *New York Times*, 12.20.10, by Donald G. McNeil Jr., "Five years in, gauging impact of Gates grants," online at http://www.nytimes.com/2010/12/21/health/21gates.html?_r=0. To its credit, the Gates Foundation has been unusually focused on assessing its own impact in quantifiable ways. The

search for so-called thermostable vaccines continues, with the Gates Foundation making its largest-ever investment in 2015 in a German company – CureVac – that is focused on that challenge. See Matthew Harper's column, "Bill and Melinda Gates Foundation makes its largest ever equity investment in a bio-tech company," in the 03.05.15 *Forbes*, online at http://www.forbes.com/sites/matthewherper/2015/03/05/bill-melinda-gates-foundation-makes-largest-ever-equity-investment-in-a-biotech-company/.

9   See and hear the NPR "All Things Considered" story by Michaeleen Doucleff, 05.08.13, "Why Bill Gates thinks ending polio is worth it," at http://www.npr.org/blogs/health/2013/05/08/182223233/why-bill-gates-thinks-ending-polio-is-worth-it.

10   This statistic is from Jennifer Yang's article, "Bill Gates, the world's cheque-book doctor," in the 04.06.15 edition of the *Star*, online at http://www.thestar.com/news/world/2015/04/06/bill-gates-the-worlds-chequebook-doctor.html.

11   See the TED talk (from March 2015) at https://www.ted.com/talks/bill_gates_the_next_disaster_we_re_not_ready#t-198008.

12   From Walter Isaacson's excellent Jobs biography (Simon & Schuster, 2011), p. 128.

13   This section is derived from the Academy of Achievement's website profile, online at http://www.achievement.org/autodoc/page/win0bio-1.

14   See the soleRebels site at http://www.solerebels.com/pages/solerebels-101.

15   From the above-cited soleRebels site, at http://www.solerebels.com/pages/letter-from-solerebels-founder.

16   Like Jobs, Musk is a fount of creativity – and also like Jobs, comes up short on other dimensions of leader character.

17   In fact, Musk is more often photographed in a T-shirt than in a suit.

18   See the February 2013 talk – actually an interview – at https://www.ted.com/talks/elon_musk_the_mind_behind_tesla_spacex_solarcity#t-16407.

19   See the story on the company's website at http://www.teslamotors.com/about.

20   Again, see the company website: http://www.spacex.com/about.

21   From the Bill & Melinda Gates Foundation website, online at http://www.gatesfoundation.org/Who-We-Are/General-Information/Letter-from-Bill-and-Melinda-Gates.

22   From Helen S. Garson's *Oprah Winfrey: a Biography* (Greenwood, 2004), p. 194.

23   And, of course, excessive optimism can blind people to the problems and dangers inherent in the circumstances in front of them. See a discussion in *The Psychiatric Bulletin*, April 2014, summarized online at http://www.ncbi.nlm.nih.gov/pmc/articles/PMC4115405/.

24   This story is derived from Bunker Roy's July 2011 TED talk, online at http://www.ted.com/talks/bunker_roy?language=en#t-146322.

25   See the Barefoot College's website at http://www.barefootcollege.org/about/.

26   From an article at http://www.macleans.ca/politics/for-the-record-romeo-dallaires-last-speech-in-the-senate/.

27   The Transcendental Club is written up at http://www.age-of-the-sage.org/transcendentalism/transcendental_club.html.

28   This is the closing quatrain of Whitman's most famous poem, "Song of Myself".

14 Judgment

It was beautiful sunny afternoon in Dubrovnik, Croatia, in July 2009.[1] Robert H. Benmosche, the former chairman of MetLife – a global provider of insurance, annuities, and employee benefits – was enjoying a well-deserved retirement on the tranquil shores of the Adriatic Sea. If he turned his eyes away from the ocean to look over his shoulder, he could see his well-tended vineyards beckoning behind him. Life was good.

Then the phone rang. On the line was a member of the executive search committee of the board of American International Group (AIG). The gist of the message was brief, and urgent: Would Benmosche consider coming out of retirement to head a company that was on the brink of disaster?

AIG had been headed for decades by the buccaneering Maurice "Hank" Greenberg, who had led the company out of a relatively placid existence as a conventional insurance company – selling mundane products like property, casualty, and life insurance – into a new incarnation as a purveyor of new and exotic financial products. Greenberg was "famously brutal" with competitors, employees, and customers, and even publicly humiliated members of his own board, referring to them as "stupid."[2] Greenberg had been run out of the company in 2005, thanks in large part to an accounting scandal; but he remained the company's largest shareholder.[3]

The kinds of products that AIG now sold tended to be tied to mortgage-backed securities. AIG's contribution to this bubble was to insure these securities, which were held primarily by Wall Street, foreign banks, and domestic pension funds.[4] But by 2008, the house of cards was collapsing: Tranches of dubious mortgages went into default, the securities behind them went belly-up, and the adventurous insurance companies backing those securities were forced to walk up to the cliff edge. AIG – which by then had a portfolio of $500 billion of instruments related to these securities – was at the front of the line.

But by most reckonings, AIG was one of those "too big to fail" enterprises: a pillar that, if yanked out from under the economy, might bring the global financial system to its knees. Bowing to the inevitable, President George W. Bush and the U.S. Congress approved a staggering $182 billion bailout for AIG, in return for a 92 percent stake in the company. In effect, the insurance giant had been nationalized: perhaps the worst outcome for a formerly swashbuckling company.

Nevertheless, AIG seemed to combine colossal bad judgment with a major tin ear. Just as the bailout was going through, the company's board awarded its executives $165 million in bonuses – which caused enough anger in Congress to nearly derail the bailout.

Benmosche – a formidable presence at 6 feet, 4 inches tall, and known for his insight, spontaneity, and blunt style of speech – must have had mixed emotions about the job offer. He wasn't a young man, he certainly didn't need the money, and his Croatian retirement was in many ways idyllic. Even so, he understood the stakes. For the sake of the international economic system, it was critically important to nurse AIG – a huge, globally entrenched business – back to financial health. It had to be done now, and it had to be done *right*. If the bailout failed, it would be far harder to salvage AIG in the future. Moreover, the company needed some stability, having already had four CEOs in the space of five years.

Ultimately, Benmosche agreed to take the job, but only on his own terms. He wanted the use of a private plane, which he felt was needed to facilitate what he knew would be an intense travel schedule in the coming months and years. He wanted to hold on to his valuable block of MetLife shares: arguably, a potential conflict of interest, since MetLife and AIG were competitors. He let it be known that if he encountered any obstacles from government officials, he would quit, and state publicly where those obstacles had arisen. The AIG board had little bargaining power; Benmosche repeatedly made it clear that he didn't need the job. He also made it clear – if it hadn't been clear already – that he was no diplomat. He was a realist, he knew (or would find out) where the bodies were buried, and he expected all the players involved to act in their own self-interest.

Once in harness, Benmosche's first line of defense was to go on offense, rallying his demoralized employees to once again take pride in their company. This was a risky tactic – most likely, Washington expected the new CEO of the humiliated company to be humble – but Benmosche knew that as long as people had their tails between their legs, AIG could not rebound. Having made sure that he had a board chair who could be the resident diplomat – Harvey Golub, the former CEO of American Express – Benmosche was able to defend his company and his workforce aggressively.

Even as he was rebuilding morale, he was cutting costs dramatically. The payroll shrank from 97,000 to 57,000 – almost in half. At Benmosche's urging, his managers backed off the credit-default swaps that had caused the train wreck, and began designing new products that the company could sell safely, and at a profit.

At the same time, AIG was under enormous pressure to liquidate holdings – the biggest and most valuable of which was the Asia Life business, which the board ultimately spun off in a $35 billion initial public offering.

Board chairman Golub was an advocate of hurrying divestitures, and thereby showing progress. Benmosche disagreed with this strategy. He decided that an auction environment would reduce the liquidation values, and that the company had to demonstrate that it was in control and in no hurry. This visible point of conflict was a clear line in the sand: Someone had to go. Just a year into his chairmanship, Golub resigned, sending a clear signal to the mergers and acquisitions markets – as well as to the government – that Benmosche was in control, and his board was fully behind him.

The bottom line? By 2012, Benmosche had not only repaid the entire $182 billion in bailout money, but had also given the U.S. taxpayers a $22 billion profit on their loan to AIG. Benmosche stepped down in September 2014, and succumbed to cancer four months later.

We open this chapter on judgment with a deliberate contrast between two wildly different individuals – Greenberg and Benmosche – who both led the same company. Of course, in some ways, they were similar. Both were, arguably, business geniuses. Both were blunt and – when circumstances demanded – intimidating. Neither indulged in the kinds of personal extravagance that helped bring down so many business leaders in that era.

But in the realm of judgment, we argue, Greenberg and Benmosche couldn't have been more different. The always-driven Greenberg pushed his company toward the cliff edge. In sharp contrast, Benmosche showed situational awareness and insight. He had strong powers of analysis, and was comfortable with cognitively complex issues. Like Greenberg, he was decisive – but unlike his predecessor once removed, Benmosche exercised effective judgment and leadership, near the very heart of the catastrophe that threatened the global financial system.

Figure 14.1 shows the centrality of judgment to leader character: It's at the very heart of the constellation of the character dimensions. When you have good judgment, you make sound decisions in a timely manner, based on relevant information and a critical analysis of the facts. You appreciate the broader context when reaching decisions. You show flexibility when confronted with new information or situations, and you have an implicit sense of the best way to proceed. You can see into the very depth of challenging issues, and you can reason effectively in uncertain or ambiguous situations.

Noel Tichy and the late Warren Bennis wrote that "Any leader's most important role in any organization is making good judgments – well informed, wise decisions that produce desired outcomes. When a leader shows consistently good judgment, little else matters. When he or she shows poor judgment, nothing else matters."[5]

Judgment is critical to leadership success. As we argued in Chapter 1, judgment serves a special role in activating the other ten dimensions of leadership character, as circumstances demand.

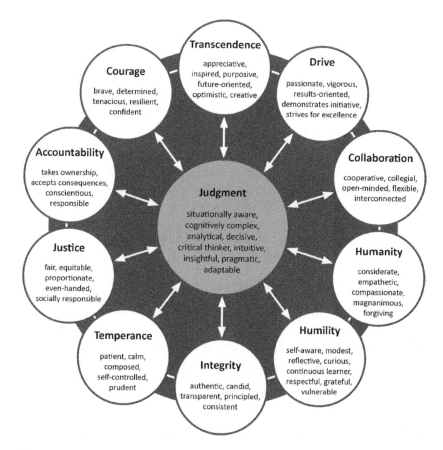

Figure 14.1 Character Dimensions and Associated Elements

Obviously, judgment – with twice as many elements as some of the other dimensions of leader character – is a complicated dimension. Many of these elements involve important cognitive functions that are often over-looked. Whereas the knowledge base associated with competencies such as marketing, accounting, finance, operations, and strategy are obviously important in business success, without strength in the elements of judgment – and the other character dimensions on which it relies – individual and organizational performance can be severely compromised.

Character Elements: What Goes into "Judgment"?

Looking at Figure 14.1, you can see that there are nine character elements that illustrate, and combine to foster, the leadership dimension of judgment. When you are judicious, you are:

Situationally aware: You demonstrate an appreciation for unique circumstances that may dictate unique approaches.

Elyse Allan is the president and CEO of General Electric Canada and vice president of GE. She has been with the company for more than 30 years – working in both the U.S. and Canadian operations – and therefore has an informed appreciation of the challenge of understanding when a situation that looks familiar may actually be new, and demand new responses. As she puts it:

> You might be a very good leader in one situation, but, as the dynamics change – situation, team, or challenge – there are aspects of your leadership approach that you have to change, or you may not be the best leader. You have to learn how to be the most effective leader in different environments ... I think it is a real learning process to develop flexibility. You have to be sensitive to this because you may come in with an approach based on your previous experiences and feel you are prepared ... but your effectiveness can derail easily when you are not assessing the situation, your impact, and interaction with the team.[6]

People with situational awareness know what's going on around them because they actively observe or scan their surroundings. Conversely, the lack of situational awareness explains why we end up needing so many different kinds of leaders for different kinds of situations. Even if a given leader has the capacity to be flexible, if he or she lacks basic situational awareness, a needed shift in approach may not be forthcoming. In this regard, business could take a page from both the military and the law enforcement community, which regularly provide situational awareness training to their personnel.

Cognitively complex: You analyze, make clear sense, and draw sound conclusions in uncertain, complex, and ambiguous circumstances.

"It is unrealistic to expect, in today's world, that you're going to get a job description that delineates everything that will be expected of you," says GE's Allan. "We need to be ensuring that the leaders we're bringing into our organizations have a comfort with ambiguity, complexity, uncertainty, and volatility." Interestingly, in this context, Allan is a strong advocate for the traditional liberal arts education, which she believes helps people "think across disciplines and manage complexity."

Leaders must be able to navigate challenging situations marked by rapid change, or what is sometimes referred to as "VUCA": volatility, uncertainty, complexity, and ambiguity.[7] For example, Michael McCain, discussed in Chapter 11, had to make far-reaching and multi-million dollar decisions based on limited information – uncertainty and ambiguity – more or less in real time, while he and his colleagues worked through their way through a rapidly intensifying food-poisoning crisis.

Analytical: You skillfully analyze situations, and employ logical reasoning.

When Dan Akerson became the CEO of General Motors in 2010, the company was in the midst of one of the most wrenching interludes in its history. It was committed to making an initial public offering to liquidate part of the U.S. government's 61 percent stake in the company – one of the many strange outgrowths of the economic meltdown of 2008. At that point, Akerson was only a year into his job, and he knew that a lot was riding on his ability to figure things out and present them effectively. In his words:

> I was essentially given about 90 days to prepare. On a variety of matters, ranging from marketing to engineering to product development, I had to achieve a level of competency. I was offered executive summaries, but chose to selectively delve into intimate details. It was necessary that I demonstrate a high degree of competency so that future owners were assured that the new management was up to the task.[8]

Akerson underemphasizes a key point: Into which "intimate details," among the mountains of data available to him, should he delve? His powers of judgment on this point – and subsequently, his powers of analysis – helped ensure a successful IPO outcome. Akerson's success is even more remarkable given the fact that he wasn't an "automotive guy," having come up through the ranks in the technology and telecommunications industry. But that training served him well when, at GM, he had to focus intensely on acquiring industry-specific knowledge.

Decisive: You make astute, level-headed decisions in a timely way, and you show clear-sighted discernment of what is required in a given situation.

Cassie Campbell-Pascall is a hero to millions of Canadian ice hockey fans. She was the only captain ever to lead two Canadian teams – male or female – to Olympic gold medals, and has since become a reporter, author, and rinkside "color commentator."

She was (and is) known for her decisiveness, and her willingness to make tough decisions. At one critical juncture, for example, she had to "call out" a teammate – a veteran, and one of the best hockey players in the world – for her consistently mediocre performances against the United States. She challenged the underperformer publicly, in front of the entire team: a move that she wasn't sure of, but decided was the right call, on balance. As she recalls:

> Being a leader sometimes involves communicating tough things and making hard decisions. I believe that, by saying nothing, you can actually make things worse. At least you show you care when communicating a tough message. I think everyone realized I cared.[9]

Not that it went smoothly: Her offended teammate was furious at her for the better part of a month. But then that one-time underperformer played some of the best hockey of her career – and today is one of Campbell's close friends.

President Barack Obama won plaudits for his decisiveness in giving the order to raid Obama bin Laden's compound in Pakistan. The current CEO of GM, Mary Barra, similarly earned praise for publicly and decisively addressing the ignition switch defect that had led to the deaths of multiple drivers. Organizations benefit enormously when their leaders lead decisively.

Skilled at critical thinking: You apply sound analysis and logical reasoning to evaluate ideas, decisions, and outcomes.

It's always risky to begin a sentence with the phrase, "Never before in human history has X been so important." But in light of the ever-increasing complexity of the human condition, the problems posed by a growing and increasingly mobile population, the ecological strain on our host planet, and so on, never before have critical thinkers – in business, and in other fields of endeavor – been such an important resource.

In 1973, two urban planners at Berkeley – Horst Rittel and Melvin Webber – published an article in which they talked about "wicked problems," which they contrasted with "tame problems."[10] Tame problems more or less sit still, and therefore lend themselves to linear sorts of definitions and solutions. Wicked problems aren't wicked in any sort of moral sense; instead, they are wicked in a sort of devilishly complex, unruly sense. They are characterized by (1) submerged facets that increase the chances of unintended consequences, in any attempt to address them, and (2) an unpleasant tendency to morph. They start as one kind of problem, and – even before their first manifestation has been addressed – turn into another kind of problem.

Because business leaders sometimes face their own version of wicked problems, they have to be adept at defining the critical path of problem solving: what's the first step we have to take, what's the second, and so on. And they have to be ready to instantly revise that path as new data become available.

One of the great untold business stories involving a wicked problem and a critical path in the U.S. came in the mid 1970s, when U.S. automakers had to start complying with the increasingly tough strictures of the Clean Air Act of 1970. Three things had to happen almost at once: Cars had to shift from leaded to unleaded gas (to get the lead out of the air), time-tested carburetors had to be replaced with still-experimental fuel injectors (to allow for a more complete and therefore cleaner "burn"), and catalytic converters – a finicky technology mainly used in stationary applications like power plants – had to be introduced into auto emissions systems (to reduce carbon monoxide emissions). And just to complicate things, the automakers, fearing antitrust action on the part of the government, all had to address these three challenges separately.

Critical thinkers at all of the Big Three companies – Chrysler, Ford, and General Motors – found ways to tackle these enormous challenges, and keep selling cars.

Intuitive: You understand things without an apparent need for conscious reasoning.

Note the two hedge words in that summary statement: "apparent" and "conscious." Intuition is often described, colloquially, as a "gut feeling." It's not uncommon to ask a business leader how he or she made a momentous, bet-the-company decision and get back an answer like, "I went with my gut," or, "It just felt right."[11]

But in most such cases, concealed behind those answers are years and years of training, experience, and preparation. The better prepared you are to lean on your intuition, the better your outcome is likely to be. In an 1856 speech, Louis Pasteur observed that "in the fields of observation, chance only favors the mind which is prepared."[12] He was referring to scientific discovery, but the parallels to business are obvious: When you operate in the realm of the half-known, you have to come to the table prepared, and – at the critical moment – you have to be prepared to follow your instincts. Master your domain, understand yourself, and *act*.

Insightful: You grasp the essence of situations, and see into the heart of challenging issues.

J. Erwin Miller, the longtime leader and guiding spirit of the Cummins Engine Company – a leading manufacturer of diesel engines for both vehicles and stationary applications – had a knack for analyzing and recasting difficult situations. By the late 1970s, the diesel-engine industry was coming under increased pressure to reduce the amount of particulates coming out of the stacks of diesel-powered trucks. With one exception, the industry dug in its heels – denying that there was a problem, denying that anything could be done about it, and denying that the industry should have to pick up the tab.

The exception was Cummins's Miller, who publicly stated that his industry – like any other – should be prepared to internalize all the societal and environmental costs of its products. It was a radical proposition, at the time; today, it's more or less a given. Seeing the heart of the problem, and especially looking into the future, is an invaluable component of leadership. David Clark, former CEO of Campbell Canada, often talks about the importance of being able to discern the difference between ice cubes and icebergs. On the surface, he says, it all looks the same. Insight is that critical cognitive function that relies on the other elements of judgment, but constantly seeks to drive for the profound meaning that resides in the data.

Pragmatic: You understand, develop, and implement workable solutions under varied circumstances.

We cited the example of Robert Benmosche, above. His phased response to AIG's dire condition, when he arrived in New York in August 2009, is one good illustration. First, he hammered out an explicit relationship between himself and his new employer. Then he took on the almost impossible task of getting AIG's employees to believe in themselves and their company again, and to believe that the enterprise would survive. He simultaneously began cutting costs and – drawing on the company's enormous database and its analytical skills – began coming up with new core products that were both profitable and sustainable.

Dan Akerson faced a similar challenge: the reclamation of the good name and reputation of General Motors. He had to restore a sense of normalcy in an uncertain environment, and convince employees that the company had a future.

Adaptable: You modify plans, decisions, and actions to adjust to new conditions. This has both personal and business implications.

Charles Brindamour, introduced in Chapter 7, is the CEO of Intact Financial Corporation. Since joining the firm in 1992, he has worked his way up through a number of executive positions both in Europe and Canada, ultimately being named CEO in 2008. Reflecting on the challenges inherent in this record of personal accomplishment, he points first to the need for adaptability:

> It's the adaptation, from step to step, to the fact that, all of a sudden, as you move up, the people reporting to you have different sets of expectations and things that drive them. To adapt, it's important to properly understand what drives the new level of the organization for which you're responsible.[13]

No leadership approach can be universally applied to all situations. Good leadership is about recognizing the specific situation you face, and then matching that situation with the appropriate leadership approach. This means that leaders have to be adaptable – they have to build and maintain a toolkit of solutions – to be effective.

To sum up: the nine elements of judgment collectively enable quality of thinking, both analytically and intuitively, to deliver insight around the issues that surface in a specific context so that you can operate in a pragmatic fashion. As you have seen, there is a long list of elements supporting judgment. While each can be developed independently, they also work together in important ways. For example, one can be analytical but not decisive – in other words, over-analysis can lead to paralysis. Furthermore, being decisive without being insightful is a formula for disaster. Insight is reliant upon being a critical thinker and cognitively complex.

And finally, intuition: Intuition may be just one of several elements, but it is critical when it comes to judgment. As Einstein allegedly observed,

"The intuitive mind is a sacred gift and the rational mind is a faithful servant. We have created a society that honors the servant and has forgotten the gift."[14] There has been much written about left- and right-brain thinking, but simply put, the elements associated with judgment can be in tension. Ensuring that intuition is nurtured is critical.

Judgment Complementing Other Dimensions

Judgment plays a special role in that it is the central thought process that governs reliance on the other character dimensions and, in particular, takes into account the unique circumstances of the situation to guide decisions. Aristotle called it "practical wisdom." Judgment provides the underlying thought processes that allow you to reconcile and resolve the possibilities that emerge from the various dimensions.

For example, the ideals and aspiration that arise from the dimension of transcendence need to be reconciled with the elements of the other dimensions, such as the fairness and equity in justice. The aggressive pace arising from drive often needs to be reconciled with the regulation of temperance.

Throughout the preceding chapters, we have described how the dimensions need to work together to support one another. It is judgment that provides the key mechanism for doing that. As noted in Chapter 1, it acts like the air traffic controller that enables you to dial up and dial down as needed.

Judgment in the Absence of Other Dimensions

Certainly, judgment on its own provides critical thinking, but without the insight that arises from the other ten character dimensions, it may be misdirected. For example, without humility, judgment can become arrogant, particularly if you tend to privilege the intellectual over dimensions such as humanity and collaboration. Similarly, without accountability or justice, you can become detached from the issues you are analyzing.

Judgment is a Forever Process

Judgment is a process that never rests. It starts, proceeds, reaches an outcome – and then starts again.

The cycle of judgment comprises analyzing, deciding, sharing, and implementing.[15] GM's Dan Akerson, for example, pushed hard on the analysis that would feed his judgment (and help float his all-important IPO!). Cassie Campbell-Pascall was a no-nonsense decider, and a take-no-prisoners sharer of her decisions; neither trait was comfortable to those around her, but most people wound up admiring her judgment and courage.

At AIG, Bob Benmosche made a series of tough calls – for example, cutting the workforce almost in half – while constantly sharing his thinking with his beleaguered employees. In his judgment, his team had to believe in itself first, before any other good things could happen; so he made that happen. Irwin Miller publicly broke ranks with his industry, recast the argument in a way that was advantageous to society (and not incidentally, to Cummins), and ultimately saw his judgment prevail.

And finally, GE's Elyse Allan and Intact Financial Corporation's Charles Brindamour remind us that all victories of judgment are temporary, and are likely to present themselves again tomorrow – in the worst case, as *wicked problems.*

Questions to Contemplate

1. Think of one or more judgment calls that you or someone you know had to make. What factors entered into these decisions? What made them right or wrong?
2. What experiences in business or elsewhere were formative in the development of your judgment? Why were they powerful in doing this?
3. What experiences could you design to offer the people whom you lead that would develop or hone their judgment?

Books and Articles to Read

"Daniel Kahneman: The Thought Leader Interview" Michael Schrage (*strategy+business*, 33, Winter 2003)

Judgment: How Winning Leaders Make Great Calls Noel M. Tichy and Warren G. Bennis (Portfolio Trade, 2009)

Judgment Calls: Twelve Stories of Big Decisions and the Teams that Got Them Right Thomas H. Davenport and Brook Manville (Harvard Business Review Press, 2012)

Thinking, Fast and Slow Daniel Kahneman (Anchor Canada, 2013)

"Character, Policy and the Selection of Leaders" George Friedman (*Geopolitical Weekly*, September 4, 2012)

The Emotional Life of Your Brain Richard J. Davidson and Sharon Begley (Plume, 2012)

Practical Wisdom in Management: Business Across Spiritual Traditions Theodore Roosevelt Malloch (Stylus Publishing, 2014)

"The Wise Leader" Ikujiro Nonaka and Hirotaka Takeuchi (*Harvard Business Review*, May 2011)

Videos to Watch

"Using Our Practical Wisdom" TED Talk by Barry Schwartz (www.ted.com/talk, 2010)

"Our Loss of Wisdom" TED Talk by Barry Schwartz (www.ted.com/talk, 2009)

Podcasts to Listen to

Risk, Part 1 & 2: CBC Ideas Radio Show with Kathleen Flaherty and guests (September 11, 2012) www.cbc.ca/player/Radio/Ideas/ID/2323081844/
   Getting Sidetracked: CBC Spark Radio Show with Nora Young (March, 2013) http://www.cbc.ca/books/2013/03/spark-sidetracked.html

Notes

1 This opening scene comes from Benmosche's obituary, "Robert Benmosche, rescuer of A.I.G. after bailout, dies at 70," by Jonathan Kandell, in the 02.27.15 *New York Times*, online at http://www.nytimes.com/2015/02/28/business/dealbook/robert-benmosche-ex-metlife-chief-who-rescued-aig-dies-at-70.html?_r=0. We are also indebted to Steve Mader – Vice Chairman and Managing Director, Board Services Practice, in Korn Ferry's Boston office – for his insights into the Benmosche saga.

2 In 2005, *Fortune* published a scathing Greenberg profile, "All I want in life is an unfair advantage," by Devin Leonard, 08.08.05, online at http://archive.fortune.com/magazines/fortune/fortune_archive/2005/08/08/8267642/index.htm.

3 See the strange article in the 11.09.14 *LA Times*, "Maurice Greenberg puts U.S. handling of AIG bailout on trial," by Dean Starkman, on Greenberg's 2014 lawsuit, which claimed he and other AIG shareholders were owed an additional $40 billion in taxpayer money; online at http://www.latimes.com/business/la-fi-aig-trial-20141109-story.html#page=1. In 2005, Greenberg's holdings were worth an estimated $2.8 billion.

4 It's worth noting, once again, that AIG's core insurance business had continued to remain viable throughout the crisis. The fact that a small division within the company had grown so explosively, and taken on huge levels of leverage, was what put AIG at risk.

5 From *Judgment*, by Noel M. Tichy and Warren G. Bennis, published by Penguin in 2007.

6 See the Allan profile and interview in Gerard Seijts's *Good Leaders Learn* (Routledge, 2014), p. 49.

7 See, for example, Nathan Bennett's and G. James Lemoines's article on VUCA, "What VUCA really means for you," in the 02.14 *Harvard Business Review*, online at https://hbr.org/2014/01/what-vuca-really-means-for-you.

8 See the Akerson profile and interview in Gerard Seijts's *Good Leaders Learn* (Routledge, 2014), p. 57.

9 See the Campbell-Pascall profile and interview in Gerard Seijts's *Good Leaders Learn* (Routledge, 2014), p. 66.

10 See, for example, a related Swedish Morphological Society article, "Wicked Problems," by Tom Ritchey, 2005, online at http://www.swemorph.com/wp.html.

11 See, for example, Modesto A. Maidique's article, "Intuition isn't just about trusting your gut," in the 04.13.11 *Harvard Business Review*, online at https://hbr.org/2011/04/intuition-good-bad-or-indiffer/.

12 While working with local brewers, Pasteur laid the foundations for both modern chemistry and microbiology. See a related article by Brendon Barnett, "Louis

Pasteur: Chance favors the prepared mind," at http://www.pasteurbrewing. com/articles/life-of-pasteur/louis-pasteur-chance-favors-prepared-mind/173. html.

13 See the Brindamour profile and interview in Gerard Seijts's *Good Leaders Learn* (Routledge, 2014), p. 228.

14 We feel obliged to add the "allegedly." See the interesting discussion of the cloudy origins of this quote in Ian Chadwick's blog, "Scripturient," at http:// ianchadwick.com/blog/it-wasnt-einstein-who-said-it/. Einstein was not given to calling things "sacred." His closest quote was, "When I examine myself and my methods of thought I come to the conclusion that the gift of fantasy has meant more to me than my talent for absorbing positive knowledge."

15 See Noel Tichy's and Warren Bennis's interesting article, "Making judgment calls," in the October 2007 *Harvard Business Review*, online at https://hbr. org/2007/10/making-judgment-calls.

15 Leader Character Revisited

In 2007, Michael McCain – the CEO of Maple Leaf Foods whom we introduced in Chapter 11, in the context of a food-poisoning crisis – realized that the whole of his business needed a fundamental restructuring if it was to be cost-competitive going forward. This meant closing low-volume, technically obsolete plants; reorganizing distribution networks; closing or selling off some business units that could never be turned into profitable, world-class operations; and making many other tough decisions affecting employees, customers, shareholders, and other stakeholders.

To do this required McCain to draw upon every one of the eleven dimensions of character introduced in our previous chapters: **integrity** to recognize what needed to be done and to report candidly on the progress to stakeholders through the long transformation period; **transcendence** to visualize the end goal; **drive** to make it happen despite objections from a major shareholder; **courage** to pull the plug on business units that couldn't be turned around and to invest virtually all of his net worth[1] in the transformation; **humanity** to do this while caring about, and taking steps to assist, the many employees who would be losing their jobs as a result of the transformation; **justice** to recognize their claims on the organization for past service and success; **humility** to seek out the very best business practices for leading a deep and comprehensive transformation; **temperance** to understand and accept that the transformation would take 5–7 years to complete; **accountability** to the shareholders for the results of a long-term investment; **collaboration** with a large and diverse group of people and parties too numerous to list; and finally, **judgment**, to bring all these dimensions together into an effective, efficient, and principled change process.

By 2015, the transformation was 90 percent complete, and Maple Leaf Foods' stock price was beginning to reflect its success. Arguably, without the breadth and depth of character displayed by McCain and his leadership team, it would never have happened.

We have established six core principles about leader character throughout this book:

- Leader character can be defined as an amalgam of traits, values, and virtues aligned around eleven character dimensions. Each of these dimensions is essential to effectively lead at any level, but especially at senior levels in organizations.
- All of these dimensions are important. A leader or an organization can't simply pick and choose which ones they want to embrace, and which they want to ignore.
- Each of the eleven dimensions can become a vice when it is deficient, or when it is present in excess without being "moderated" by one or more of the other dimensions. For example, drive without temperance or justice may lead to reckless behavior that jeopardizes individual and organizational success.
- Judgment is the character dimension that channels and melds the other dimensions into contextually informed behaviors. We need leaders with strong judgment which enables them to activate each dimension of character at the right time and in the right amount, to bring forth the right behaviors in the right situation and at the right time.
- Strength of leadership character is associated with successful performance as a leader; successful organizations reinforce character strengths, and select and develop leaders of strong character.
- Leader character is shaped by the context in which people grow up, are educated, work, live, and play. Strength of character can flow in both directions – in other words, character can also shape context.

We elaborate on these key points below.

Leader Character Defined

To help make the concept of character useful in the practice of leadership, we have tried to define it in language that practicing leaders in the public, private, and not-for-profit sector can relate to. Ideally, they can draw on that language in their own leadership activities, and when trying to enable others in the organization to address character development.

From the many writings about leadership that preceded this one, from the deep and rich literature on character, and from our conversations with hundreds of leaders, we have isolated eleven dimensions that meet this requirement. We listed them in the Maple Leaf Foods example at the outset of this chapter: drive, collaboration, humanity, humility, integrity, temperance, justice, accountability, courage, transcendence, and judgment. Throughout this book, we have suggested that each of these dimensions of leader character consists of a number of behaviors, which we call "elements," that are illustrative of the dimension. In doing this, we are aware that there may be other elements that could be thought of as being part of a dimension. Nevertheless, we believe – based on our research, interviews, and data collection – that we have captured the major ones.

We have suggested that each of these dimensions is an amalgam of several things: innate or acquired traits that predispose us to act in certain ways; values, or cognitive/moral beliefs that affect the way we perceive situations, and how we think we should act in those situations; and virtues, which we define as habitual, learned patterns of behaviors.

To make a complex point more clear: All of the elements are virtues, of which some of these virtues are traits (for example, "conscientious") and some of which are values (for example, "principled"). We recognize that there may be people who would like to see this amalgam untangled, to show clearer relationships among these three constructs – but that is the agenda of another round of research.

We have tested our language of leader character with multiple audiences of executives, managers, directors, academics, and students. While a couple of the labels – notably temperance and transcendence – are slightly more difficult for leaders to fully comprehend and accept, for the most part those leaders understand what we're trying to do. Overall, they feel a sense of relief, even gratitude, that we have been able to describe this thing they all consider important – character – in a comprehensive set of clear, measurable constructs. In other words, the practitioners with whom we engaged in our research were searching for a vocabulary of character – whether or not they described it that way – and this is what we have endeavored to create.

Each of the Character Dimensions is Essential

Each character dimension matters – because of what it contributes to leader behavior, and because of what happens to leader behavior if the dimension is missing.

Take integrity, for example: Integrity in leaders is essential if they are to be trusted by others, or if they are to be believed when they express an opinion that is essential for collaboration. In someone with an extremely strong drive to succeed, a lack of integrity can lead to the pursuit of success at any cost, even the costs associated with engaging in unfair or illegal activities. Without integrity, moreover, accountability will always be suspect, because the leader without integrity tends to over-claim the things that go right, and (due to a lack of candor and transparency) seldom owns up to things that go wrong. As noted in previous chapters, it's often asserted that "you can't have too much integrity." But integrity that is not supported by the dimensions of humanity and humility can simply be dogmatic.

We've chosen integrity to make our point, but we could have focused on any of our eleven dimensions. In sum, the dimensions have unique effects on behavior, and they also complement one another in affecting behavior.

Virtues Can Become Vices

All character dimensions matter. We can't just pick and choose which dimensions we like. It would be a serious mistake for a leader or an organization to pick a few that exemplify "leadership." This is what so often has cost organizations that have run into trouble – overweighting dimensions like accountability, courage, drive, and integrity; and underweighting dimensions such as humanity, humility, justice, and temperance. It is strength in all dimensions that helps to ensure that virtues do not become vices.

Consider a Formula 1 driver operating at top speed, but without the capacity to brake. All is fine on the straightaway, but disaster may be lurking at the next turn. In a business setting, if you are trying to be a more collaborative person, you must sometimes put a rein on your drive, because collaboration needs time to develop. The passionate, vigorous, "just do it" approach favored by hard-driving leaders typically inhibits the contribution of others that is so essential to the process of collaboration and the quality of the results.

Judgment is the Character Dimension that Modulates All Others

Strength of character resides in our capacity to call upon any dimension of character at any time. As we described in the chapter on judgment, it serves to modulate the other dimensions given the context. On a daily basis we encounter situations that require us to lean hard on one or more dimensions of character, and use judgment to help us modulate them. While these situational demands can be moment to moment, they may also be more prolonged. For example, in a business start-up, we may need drive and courage to dominate at the outset; and we may need to rely on transcendence to map our future course.

But, in an increasingly turbulent and rapidly changing world – volatile, uncertain, complex, and ambiguous – we need our leaders to be capable of handling a myriad of challenges, and seizing opportunities when they present themselves. Such "broad-band" leaders must have strength of each character dimension and, coupled with excellent judgment, be able to deploy or restrain character dimensions to suit any particular situation.

Linda Hasenfratz, CEO of Linamar, whom we mentioned in Chapter 11, is an example of such a broad-band leader. She grew the business from a successful small to medium-sized enterprise; then led the organization through the financial crisis and the collapse of General Motors and Chrysler; and began to focus on rebuilding the business and eventually transitioning the business into a global player.

By contrast, "narrow-band" leaders – who have developed strength of character along a limited set of dimensions – find themselves leading poorly when the situation unexpectedly changes. Because they lack depth of character, they can't respond to emerging challenges with the appropriate character-supported behaviors.

Character and Context

Individuals' characters are shaped by their experiences in the various contexts within which they live and work. This includes the reactions of other individuals to – and one's personal outcomes from – character-driven behaviors.

When those behaviors are met with approval and success, character is reinforced. When they are met with derision and rejection, or they beget personal or professional failure, a re-examination of one's character-driven behaviors is likely to ensue. This may lead to modification of behaviors, a change in particular character dimensions, or – conceivably – continued rejection and failure, unless the individual decides to seek out a context that welcomes and rewards the behaviors expressed.

Perhaps the most extreme – even appalling – example of this is Nelson Mandela's 27 years of imprisonment, described in Chapter 6. Over that unimaginably long stretch, in brutal places like the Robben Island prison, Mandela transformed himself from a common agitator to an uncommon statesman. He came to see his jailors as human beings like himself – who, unlike himself, were being corrupted by the system they ran. This example underscores the point that while all dimensions of character matter, our personal expression of them will be entirely different based on our experiences and these experiences will be influenced by the contexts within which we live and work. Mandela's early character was shaped by his experiences as an activist and revolutionary; his late character by his brutal treatment at the hands of the authorities, his imprisonment, and his experiences following his release and subsequent life as a politician, statesman, and living legend.

Throughout this book, we have provided examples of companies that took corporate stances that encouraged the development and display of character-related behaviors. In Chapter 2, for example, we reflected on the experience of Parker Hannifin Corporation, which over the course of its near-century of doing business has evolved a distinctive corporate culture – a culture focused on core values of integrity, honesty, respect, and ethical behavior. For many generations, in other words, Parker Hannifin's leaders believed, and acted on the belief that, their company could be an agent either for "good" or "not good" ("evil" seems too strong a word).

This belief was tested substantially when the company began expanding rapidly overseas, and the values of hometown Cleveland, Ohio, were no longer the dominant context. Today, the company runs 341 manufacturing plants in 49 countries around the world. The dominant ethics of those 49 countries aren't necessarily better or worse than the dominant ethic of Cleveland – but they are certainly different, and regularly pose challenges to the company. Can we have global values in a highly heterogeneous world? If it hopes to be consistent, Parker Hannifin's response has to be "yes."

But dealing with context doesn't necessarily mean sermonizing. For example, since 2011, the company's R&D efforts have been focused exclusively on developing products that promise to help address pressing social and environmental issues. That is a context that builds character.

Unfortunately, we can point to many examples in which context erodes character. Philip Zimbardo, psychologist and a professor emeritus at Stanford University, tackled the question of why good people sometimes do bad things. He distinguished among bad apples, bad barrels, and bad barrel makers – and noted that many good apples have been corrupted by bad barrels and bad barrel makers. He noted this firsthand when, in 1971, he designed a mock prison with students randomly assigned to roles as guards and prisoners. As noted in Chapter 3, he had to shut the experiment down after five days when he discovered that the guards were abusing the prisoners and he, as the "barrel maker," was culpable. Zimbardo asserts that the results of the Stanford Prison experiment – and the role of bad barrel makers – help explain the atrocious human rights abuses that took place at the Abu Ghraib prison in Iraq, which was supervised by the U.S. Armed Forces and the CIA.

In a business context, young people may find themselves working in hyper-competitive industries where they are under intense pressure to succeed. It's a dog-eat-dog, win-at-all-cost existence – with huge rewards for winning, and drastic consequences for losing. In these environments, the role models tend to be those who may have lied, cheated, or misrepresented their way to success. Those who may have shown positive character-related behaviors, by contrast, may be referred to as "losers" or "marshmallows," or may be denigrated in other ways.

Are we surprised, therefore, when these forces – corrupt forces, that work to encourage people to reject integrity, to forsake the courage to speak up against what they can clearly see is unethical and perhaps illegal behavior, or to act in ways that betray the confidence and trust placed in them by investors – prove strong enough to turn people away from doing the right thing? And are we surprised when, in a case where someone is compelled to act against his or her character, that person finally capitulates, and changes his or her beliefs to justify the corrupt behaviors?

Numerous scientific studies have demonstrated how relatively easy it is to set up an authoritarian regime of rewards and punishments that can get people to do the "wrong" thing, even though they know it to be wrong. Nick Leeson and the 1995 collapse of Barings Bank provides a prime example. So does the sad story of Lance Armstrong, who not only cheated to win multiple Tours de France, but also compelled his teammates to use performance-enhancing drugs to support him in his pursuits.

Is a corrupt context sufficient to corrupt people's characters? We think so. Character is, after all, an amalgam of traits, values, and virtues and the only ones of these that are relatively immutable are innate traits. But ...

any strong situation can "overrule" or constrain behavior. In a powerfully corrupt context, positive behavioral habits – things like truthfulness, consideration, empathy, compassion, accountability for one's actions, fairness, transparency, and so forth – are shoved aside by others that are much more self-serving.

They may also lead people to dissociate their characters from work – in effect, to leave their "true selves," their character, at home. This allows them to manage the dissonance between what they do at work and what they have been taught, and believe, are the right ways to act. When this happens, great costs can ensue – to individuals, their families or other loved ones, the businesses they work for, and the societies within which they operate. One hard and fast measure of poorly formed characters is the billions of dollars in fines levied on financial institutions that have pleaded guilty to breaking the law. On May 20, 2015, for example, the Federal Reserve imposed fines totaling more than $1.8 billion on six major banking organizations for their unsafe and unsound practices in the foreign exchange markets following the financial meltdown.[2]

To these costs, of course, we have to add the financial and emotional burdens imposed on the victims of these frauds, the distress of the families of the corrupted, the damage to the careers of relatively innocent bystanders, and so on. The costs of contexts without characters can ripple outwards almost endlessly.

Many of these events could be avoided – and the terrible consequences avoided – if there was greater attention paid to developing character in individuals, and to developing a culture of character in organizations. Arden Haynes, a former CEO of Exxon's Canadian subsidiary, Imperial Oil, was once asked by a student as to whether, in his 40-plus year career of climbing the corporate ladder, he had seen things done unethically at Imperial Oil – and if so, whether he had always spoken up about them or changed them himself. After a few moments, his response was:

> I've seen many. Some I have changed immediately because I could; others I realized I could not change then because I lacked the power, influence, or authority to do so. I filed those away in my memory and when, one day, I could do so, I believe that I did. Fortunately, I didn't see anything so heinous that I could neither change nor live with, so I never left the company or made a martyr of myself, which I would have had to do had I lacked the ability to change the situation.[3]

Haynes was a leader whose courage was complemented by other character dimensions. His humanity and sense of justice helped to realize that something was wrong and needed fixing; his temperance stopped him from rushing in and trying to fix something that he could not fix immediately; his humility helped him understand that he had limited power or skills, or simply lacked full awareness of the situation, and that he would need to figure it out better, and perhaps collaborate with others on a solution; his integrity ensured that one day, when possible, he would fix the problem.

As a senior leader, he took accountability for fixing what was wrong, either personally, or – more often – by collaborating with those who could. Overall, his judgment helped him figure out what to do, and when to do it, with the best chance of a successful outcome.

We wrote this book in the belief that character can be practiced, and through that practice, developed. And that's what our final chapter is about.

Notes

1 McCain owned approximately one-third of the company's issued share capital.
2 See the 05.20.15 Fed press release at http://www.federalreserve.gov/newsevents/press/enforcement/20150520a.htm.
3 This quote is a description of what Arden Haynes said in a class at the Ivey Business School taught by Jeffrey Gandz.

16   Developing Character

What remains is for us to make the case for character development.

Simply stated, we believe that case has four parts. First, individuals can work on developing their own character strengths. Second, organizations can contribute to character development of both individuals and the character of the organization itself. Third, these processes must occur if individuals and organizations are to be successful in the contexts within which they operate. And finally, the results from character development will yield critical benefits to the individual and the organization, thereby justifying the effort it takes.

There are some who believe that character cannot be developed – that you either have it or you don't. This is simply wrong. Character can be developed, and there is ample research to prove that point. There is a great deal that people can do to develop their own character strengths; parents, teachers, coaches, and others can develop character in those whose lives they can influence; and organizations can further develop character among their current and future leaders. Yes, it would be a wonderful thing if we could hire into our organizations only people with fully developed character – and sometimes, we manage to do just that. But in most cases, we are imperfect people ourselves, and we hire imperfect people to join us.

Then we undertake to make an imperfect world better. As leaders in organizations, we must define an organizational culture (and supporting values) that is consistent with both the strategy of the enterprise and reflects its character, and we must ensure that organizational systems and processes are in place to promote that desired culture.

And then, hopefully, we reap the rewards of that effort, in the form of a high-performing organization staffed by people of character.

The Individual's Role in Character Development

Warren Bennis, one of the most prominent authorities on leadership, underscores the importance of self-awareness:

> The leader never lies to himself, especially about himself, knows his flaws as well as his assets, and deals with them directly. You are your

own raw material. When you know what you consist of and what you want to make of it, then you can invent yourself.[1]

Bennis's observations could apply equally to leader character development. What is your raw material, and what do you want to make of it?

We suggested in Chapter 3 that character is formed and reformed in the context of the environment – family, work, sports, politics, and so forth – within which people operate. The experiences gained in those settings prompt an ongoing process of recalibration and modification, as individuals analyze their environments; behave in certain ways; experience and reflect on the consequences of those behaviors; make judgments about the appropriateness of those behaviors for satisfying their needs and achieving their goals; and then either decide to continue behaving the same way in similar situations, or to try something new. As humans, we have this potential: to constantly learn, modify, adapt, and experiment as we make our way in life. No, we don't always act on that potential – sometimes we simply fall into habit and transact quite mindlessly – but it is there to be seized upon, if we so choose.

Reflection plays a critical role in the learning process. It involves two distinct kinds of activity. The first is reflection *on* action: the conscious pulling back from hectic activities and multi-tasking that is part of normal, day-to-day life, in order to contemplate those activities and draw lessons from them. Reflection on action allows us to see patterns over time, and perhaps make adjustments in our approach to leading people in organizations. The second is reflection *in* action – the real-time processing of the feedback loops between how we are behaving and how our behaviors are being interpreted by others, how they are responding to them, whether they are getting us to where we want to go, and whether they need modifying.

Both kinds of reflection are critically important. It's always tempting to say that you don't have time for reflection – by which you might mean either exercising judgment in real time (reflection in action) or stepping back to tease out lessons from your life (reflection on action). Seen in this light, reflection is cast as a luxury. In fact, the opposite is true. Leaders don't have the luxury of failing to reflect.

Reflection on action requires addressing four questions:

- *Who am I?* What are my character strengths and deficiencies today?
- *Who am I becoming?* What is my character today, and what is it likely to be tomorrow if I carry on with the way I'm doing things now?
- *What do I want to be?* What is it about my character that I'd like to change, that would bring me satisfaction and success in all facets of my life?
- *What am I going to do to become what I want to be?* What actions will I take, by when, to make my character complete? How will I know that I've got there?

Such reflection requires data. In fact, everyone has lots of data. We get feedback on how we performed or interacted with people after key meetings, in formal and informal appraisals, and from conversations with mentors on the progress we're making in our professions. We get feedback from friends and non-friends, from family, and from colleagues past and present. But this feedback is often fragmented, frequently contradictory, and sometimes given in ways that are not conducive to development. Some of it we expected to hear; at other times, we are surprised by the candor with which people provided the feedback.

Our early quantitative research with executives indicated that they found it difficult to assess what people thought about their leader character; they also found it difficult, as part of ongoing coaching and leadership development, to give people good feedback on their character.

To help with both of these vital processes, we have developed the Leadership Character Insight Assessment (LCIA; see Chapter 2), which is available in two formats: self-assessment and the 360-degree form. This instrument has been very well received by executives, who tell us that it is very useful in promoting the reflection that is central to the developmental process.

A key step in the developmental process is to see oneself as a leader, and acknowledge that whoever you are, you bring a unique perspective and special contribution to the workplace. Failing to see yourself as a leader means that, by default, you are likely to become a bystander.

The second and overlapping step – it should not surprise you – is to become familiar with the principles and precepts in this book. Then use your workplace experiences to test yourself. Along which of the eleven dimensions of leader character do you require additional development? What do your annual or semi-annual evaluations tell you about the strength of your character dimensions?

To the extent that you can control the learning experiences to which your job exposes you, choose them explicitly as opportunities for self-testing, learning, and development. Be conscious of your life experiences providing you with important lessons and challenging your disposition to lead – whether this is a leadership role on a sports team, in a political context, in a volunteer organization, or the inevitable challenges associated with being a parent (or having parents!). What can you learn to move yourself forward?

Think of Frodo in *The Lord of the Rings*, or Luke Skywalker in *Star Wars*: They start as little people with modest ambition, and – step by painstaking step – wind up leading. Look for challenges. If you don't feel that your character is challenged on a regular basis, you are likely not to be asking enough of it. Leaders learn by constantly stretching, reaching out for new performance levels, and discovering creative ways to contribute more to their organizations. They don't rest on their laurels, hunker down in their comfort zones, and become complacent. Stretching is a planned, concerted effort to master those dimensions of leadership in a way that makes a person a better leader. So *take action*.

The Organization's Senior Leaders and Character

The senior leaders in an organization play a number of key roles in promoting the development of leader character. For example: They model the character they want to see throughout the organization. They shape the formal and informal corporate cultures they believe will lead to the organization's success. They coach and mentor people so that they can succeed in those cultures. They hire and promote those who seem to demonstrate the appropriate behaviors, and sometimes fire those who disappoint along that critical dimension. Finally, they provide the resources and personal engagement in character-based formal leadership-development processes and programs.

Let's look at each of these processes.

Modeling Behaviors

First and foremost, the organization's leaders have to model the behaviors they want to promote. Leaders who speak and act with humanity beget others who act in similar ways. Conversely, swaggerers beget swaggerers; buccaneers beget buccaneers; bullies beget bullies; and so on. Such dysfunctional behaviors are likely to create an exodus of people who won't stand for it, meaning that over time, you will lose your best people.

Any character-associated behaviors expressed or enacted by senior leaders, whether good or bad, are perceived by others – especially those at early stages of their leadership development – as the behaviors that are valued in the organization. Not surprisingly, those impressionable younger people tend to imitate those behaviors.

Don McAskill, former chairman at Warner-Lambert, had a practice of always asking the person who completed an important assignment to make the presentation of the work to the senior-executive team, even though he or she might be quite junior in the organization. Clearly, McAskill was modeling accountability and respect – and that example was never forgotten by those who had the opportunity to work with him.

This also speaks to the importance of self-awareness. As George Cope, president and CEO of Bell Canada enterprises, observes:

> It's important for leaders to reflect often on their behaviour. Your behaviour becomes the permission for other behaviours in the company. I firmly believe that if you start to cross the line in any negative way, everyone else is going to cross the line.[2]

What happens when appropriate, character-driven behavior is *not* demonstrated from the top of the organization? In many cases, it poses a real dilemma for individuals who want to see good behaviors modeled.

They have to be prepared to put themselves on the line by disagreeing with some aspect of leadership philosophy or practice. Sometimes this means that they have to challenge their senior leaders' words or actions.

This is generally a risky proposition, at best. But it's sometimes necessary to take that kind of risk – that is, to act on deeply held values or beliefs. Of course, people need to pick their moments. They need to learn when to say things, how to frame the problem, what tone to strike; and so forth. But when not acting is not an alternative, integrity must be called upon, and the risk must be taken.

Shaping Culture

Corporate cultures – those shared beliefs, values, and behaviors that have so much impact on how we think and act in organizations – present an interesting paradox: They are both strong and fragile.

They are strong in the sense that they influence whom organizations hire and fire, the expectations people have about what will be rewarded and punished, and how people act when no one is watching them. They are fragile in the sense that one action by a senior leader that is not challenged and reversed can undermine people's perceptions of what the real versus espoused corporate culture is.

For example, in one situation, the CEO of a large bank promoted a regional senior vice president to executive vice president status. The newly minted EVP was a man who was widely known as a bully – with little respect for others, and ruthless in his business dealings inside the bank and with outsiders, whether suppliers, partners, or others. This trait had shown up several times on the SVP's 360-degree assessment.

When asked why he had made the promotion decision, the CEO referred to the great business results achieved by the former SVP. The CEO felt that these results demanded the recognition of promotion. When questioned further, it was clear that the CEO had never even thought about what the promotion choice would say about the character-related values that he himself had spent years establishing within the organization, prominent among which was consideration and respect for every individual.

Nor had he thought enough about whether the results he was celebrating by means of the promotion, were sustainable. As we have described, there are many results that appear outstanding in the short run but which actually undermine the business in the long run. By making the ill-advised promotion, the CEO had undercut much of the culture that he had spent the previous ten years trying to build – and he had implicitly embraced an unsustainable business model going forward.

No, a great culture and great results are not at odds. Neither are they separable. Each can, and should, sustain the other.

Personal Coaching and Engagement

Beyond modeling, the organization's leaders have to put their own time –
as well as the organization's money – into leader character development.
They can do this by personally coaching individuals when they encounter
those "teachable moments" that would otherwise slip by; ensuring that
resources are made available for character-based leadership-development
programs; developing more formal, character-infused statements of
corporate culture; and taking every opportunity to refer to character when
they make crucial decisions.

For example, Antoni Cimolino – artistic director of the Stratford
Shakespeare Festival, whom we introduced in Chapter 6 – has spoken
about the responsibilities inherent in helping young people become better
leaders:

> You can't just give someone an opportunity and walk away. There is
> an ongoing responsibility to be there as an ear and source of advice.
> There is also a responsibility to be very frank and honest. You have put
> those young people in positions where they could sail and fly, or they
> could have a very scarring experience that could set them back sev-
> eral years in their development. It's very important for leaders to take
> responsibility for the opportunities they've provided to young people,
> and to ensure those people are successful.[3]

Of course, these same responsibilities – which in one light might appear to
be a burden – can be among the great joys of leadership. Personal coaching
and engagement are in many ways their own best reward.

Hiring and Promoting for Character

The hiring process is rife with both challenges and opportunities. For
example, we never know what we don't know – a particular challenge in
the realm of character, which is really only revealed by how people behave
in situations. We don't know whether someone has courage until they've
faced a major challenge and done the right thing under those trying
conditions. Similarly, we don't know if people have humility unless they've
experienced failure, acknowledged it, and learned from it.

At the same time, every job opening is an opportunity to reinforce or
upgrade organizational culture and character. In our experience, however, this is often a lost opportunity. While it is standard procedure for
senior executives and corporate directors to establish selection criteria
for competencies, it's relatively rare for them to discuss the character
dimensions they expect in successful candidates. Nor is it common to
address character dimensions when reviewing executive or managerial
performance.

Why? Frankly, because it's hard. Most of us lack the vocabulary to have these discussions behind closed doors with people we know and trust, let alone in the context of a job interview. It's a very human trait: When we are uncertain of our ground, we look for ways to avoid conflict – and one way we do this is to not ask the tough questions.

Regrettably, systematic and thorough character assessment is seldom done well. Often it is driven by an "absence of negatives," rather than a focus on positive character dimensions. To say, "I've heard nothing bad about X or Y" certainly doesn't mean that an individual has demonstrated courage, collaboration, humility, or other valued character dimensions. But to develop a deeper appreciation of, say, a person's capacity for collaboration requires an extensive examination of a person's work history over time – for example, through the highs and lows of a business cycle.

Obviously, this is extremely difficult to accomplish in a job-application context. It is made all the more difficult when the candidate has a sterling reputation, has achieved positions of leadership prominence, and may even be a personal acquaintance or friend. It gets still harder when the candidate appears to have the competencies that you urgently need. In such situations, we tend to "go easy" on the candidate, and squint at blemishes that might otherwise slow us down.

But difficulty is not a good enough reason to drop this ball. Both in promotion and recruitment situations, we need to look to character to attempt to predict how someone will behave in future circumstances. Reference checks can be hit or miss, in this litigious era; but that's no excuse for not pursuing every good lead – and asking the probing questions. In the interview setting, we need to pose the well-constructed and tough questions – about how candidates have behaved in tough situations in the past, or how they think they would behave in specific situations in the future – that get us closer to unearthing leader character. This kind of behavioral interviewing is not a new idea, of course; but it takes on new importance in an organization whose leaders are focused on building leader character.

Leadership-Development Programs

People learn best when they can immediately relate what they are being asked to learn to what is important in their own context. To learn effectively, you have to be able to "make meaning" of whatever it is you're learning in the context in which you work. This argues for an organization's leaders thinking carefully about the kinds of experiential learning that will foster leader character development. What is the sequence of experiences that will test various elements of leader character, and help the emerging leader understand what he or she has to work on?

Not long ago, we visited the headquarters of a Fortune 500 manufacturing company in the U.S. Midwest. After we gave appropriate assurances of non-disclosure, we were ushered into a large, windowless room, on three walls of which was a Mercator projection of the globe. But it was a map like no other. Everywhere, little hooks stuck out, most of which had two colored tags hanging from them. Each hook was an executive position in the company. One tag indicated the type of development opportunity represented by this particular job; the other tag represented the incumbent in that job. On a regular basis – we were told – the company's leaders assembled in this room, and over the course of many hours, moved tags around to fill new jobs that had been created, or existing ones that had become vacant.

It was an impressive commitment of senior-executive hours to what might otherwise seem like a function of the Human Resource department. "So is your primary goal to meet the company's needs," we asked, "or is it to meet the needs of the individuals involved?" "Yes," came back their answer. "It's the same thing."

Great companies put extraordinary emphasis on leadership development – standing back from time to time and reviewing the development of promising individuals within the company, identifying those who need certain experiences that they are not getting in current roles, and moving them accordingly. While many delegate this activity to their human resources function, the best organizations – like the Midwestern manufacturer cited above – fully engage their senior general and functional executives in these discussions. For example, Jeffrey Immelt, the CEO of General Electric, identifies their process – invented more than a half-century ago, and dubbed "Session C" – as being a central pillar of the company's architecture, and critical to providing the pipeline of talent that the company needs.

Unfortunately, these two companies may be the exception to the rule. The management consulting firm McKinsey estimated that in the U.S. alone, in 2014, companies spent more than \$14 billion on leadership-development programs, many of which were either a complete waste of time or only marginally useful. They identified the main problems as overlooking context, decoupling reflection from real work, and failing to measure results. But they also described a fourth reason – underestimating mindsets, which they defined as "reluctance to address the root cause of why leaders act the way they do."[4]

We argue that these underlying mindsets are really the dimensions of character that we have described in this book. Failure to address character clearly, systematically, and aggressively leaves many leadership-development programs merely scratching the surface of possibilities. While they are often good at addressing leadership competencies, leadership character often gets ignored. It would be a far better approach to tailor leadership-development programs to the needs of the organization and its people, so that they address both the competencies that leaders have to call upon and the character dimensions that they need to develop.

Blue Skies and Black Swans

The responsibility for developing leader character resides in two places: with the individual, and also with the organization.

When the individual cultivates the eleven dimensions of leader character in reasonably balanced amounts, he or she prepares to lead. But that's not enough. The responsibility for developing leader character extends to the people who set the tone for the organization – that is, its senior leaders.

It is a virtuous circle. Individuals lead by example. The organization follows that example through both behaviors and designing systems and processes, and – by so doing – reinforces that example in the minds of future generations of leaders. In a virtuous circle, the sky is blue and limitless.

We opened this book with the story of a disaster: the global financial crisis that, we argued, was the direct result of a failure of leader character. That crisis is now well behind us – although a decade later, we still live with its outfalls. Slow economic growth, high unemployment in many countries, forced austerity measures in others, severely reduced retirement savings – the list goes on and on. Unfortunately, the damage wreaked by poor leader character tends to persist, and the base of that persistent misery is broad.

Writing about unpredictable crises – which he called "Black Swan" events – Nassim Taleb points out that the only reasonable defense that organizations have is "robustness" – that is, reserves of assets and people that can be deployed to deal with what could not have been predicted.[5]

We believe that depth of leader character – in both leaders and the organizations they direct – provides exactly that kind of robustness, and makes it possible for organizations to explore opportunities and respond to crises.

Developing leader character is a lifelong journey in which there is no limit to the possibilities, and no end. Those possibilities exist in every moment of every day. Each step taken toward strengthening character reveals more of the depth of that challenge, and that opportunity.

Notes

1 Bennis, Warren, *On Becoming a Leader* (New York, NY: Random House Business Books, 1989).
2 This quote is taken from *Good Leaders Learn: Lessons from Lifetimes of Leadership* (Routledge, 2014) by Gerard Seijts.
3 Ibid.
4 This estimate is in a *McKinsey Quarterly* article from January 2014, "Why leadership-development programs fail," by Pierre Gurdjian, Thomas Halbelsen, and Kevin Lane, online at http://www.mckinsey.com/insights/leading_in_the_21st_century/why_leadership-development_programs_fail.
5 Taleb, Nassim, *The Black Swan: The Impact of the Highly Improbable* (second edition) (New York, NY: The Random House Publishing Group, 2010).

Index

Made in the USA
Las Vegas, NV
31 August 2022